编审委员会

上海市外贸经济教育高地建设项目

复旦卓越

21世纪国际经济与贸易专业教材新系

国际经济学（双语）

International Economics

黄　敏　主　编■

董　理　吕　健　副主编■

复旦大學 出版社

内容提要

    本书是一本长期从事国际经济学双语教学的教师，按照目前我国经济学领域双语教学的实际情况编写的内容精练、言语通俗、理论与实践相结合的教材。

    作为经济学的基础课程教材，全书分为十一章，包括古典贸易理论、新古典贸易理论、现代贸易理论、关税与非关税壁垒、区域贸易安排、国际收支与汇率、汇率决定理论、国际收支调节、开放经济中的宏观经济政策、宏观经济政策的国际传导与协调、国际要素流动与跨国公司。本书在编写过程中充分考虑易用性，在每章篇首列出本章将出现的专业词汇，并给出中文释义，方便读者学习；在一些逻辑性较强、内容较难的章节，给出逻辑推演图或说明，帮助读者理解。

    本书适合高校财经类专业师生作为教材使用，也可作为实务工作者的参考读物。

总　　序

　　现代经济发展的实践表明,国际贸易是经济增长的强大推动力。第二次世界大战后,国际贸易的迅速发展在全球范围内引起了国际分工体系的革命性变革和福利分配格局的重组,极大地促进了经济增长。中国实行改革开放和加入世界贸易组织,加速了对外开放的步伐,外贸业务增长迅速,对外贸易对经济增长的贡献度不断提高,市场对外贸人才的需求急剧增加。

　　为了适应国际经济理论的不断创新与拓展以及外贸业务发展的需要,加快培养出更多掌握经济学理论知识、具有良好的外语基础、熟悉WTO 的游戏规则、了解国际惯例、熟悉国际市场运作规则、具有浓厚的国际意识、掌握具体操作能力的国际经济与贸易专业应用型人才,必须从国际经济与贸易专业的课程体系、课程内容、教学方法、教材编写等方面进行探索和创新。

　　"复旦卓越·21 世纪国际经济与贸易专业教材新系"教材编委会精心策划,在总结过去教材建设经验的基础上,结合应用型本科教育的特点,借鉴国内外经验做法,经过反复研究论证和撰写,推出了"复旦卓越·21 世纪国际经济与贸易专业教材新系"。这套系列教材包括《国际结算》、《国际经济学》、《外贸实务》、《国际运输与保险》、《WTO 规则与运作》、《外贸函电》、《单证实务》、《国际服务贸易》、《报关实务》、《进出口商品检验》、《国际商务谈判》、《国际贸易专业英语》等十几种。

　　这套系列教材同时作为上海市十大教育高地之一———外贸经济本科教育高地的标志性教材和国际经济与贸易专业人才培养的重要成果,具有"新、特、实、强"等特点。设计思路新颖,强调学以致用,突出"以学生为中心"的思想;力求创新写作体例和研究分析方法;观点内容着力体现前瞻性、前沿性、动态性,并做到深度和广度适宜。课程体系体现涉外经济类专业特点,采用中文和英文双语相结合的办法,凸显双语教学特色;注重实践性、实用性、可操作性,便于实践教学。编写教师的阵容庞大,起点高,教学经验丰富,研究能力强。

我们希望,通过这套系列教材积极探索出一条国际经济与贸易专业教学改革的新路子,为国际经济与贸易学科在中国的发展做出贡献。由于我们的理论水平和对外贸易实务操作技能有限,这套教材会存在许多不足之处。希望通过这套教材的出版,与国际贸易学界、政界以及从事实务工作的同仁共同研究和探讨,进一步提高教材的编写水平,提高教学和科研质量。

丛书编审委员会
2008 年 2 月

前　言

近年来,随着我国高等教育国际化的不断推进,双语教学在各高校得到大力推广。作为经济学科的核心课程,越来越多的高校都对《国际经济学》采取双语教学。在双语教学中,大家的一个共同感受就是合适的教材难寻。目前国内双语教材的出版主要有两种形式:一是将国外的英文原版教材加以影印,二是对国外的英文教材加以删减改编。

但总的来说,国外教材使用起来并不便当,主要表现在:一是篇幅过长,对书中出现的所有知识点都从 ABC 开始介绍,大量的案例也挤占了宝贵的篇幅资源。而在国内,学生学习《国际经济学》之前都已经过《西方经济学》的熏陶,完全可以略去这部分内容或从简介绍。另外,现在网络资源如此发达,师生搜寻新鲜案例非常便捷,课程网站的广泛建设也为案例提供了丰富而及时的补充。二是难易程度与国内教学需要不匹配。供本科使用的国外教材大多属初级程度,而国内汉语教材则属初级偏上中级程度。这就造成了为双语教学而牺牲课程难度要求的局面,使学生获得的课程专业知识打了折扣。三是国外教材内容战线拉得过长,不适合国内的教学安排。国内双语专业课程大多安排在一学期完成,每周三课时,这就需要教材内容要精,使学生在有限的学时中获得最大的收获。

正是基于这样的思考,促使我们尝试自己编写双语教材。这本《国际经济学》双语教材有这样三个特点:一是融中外教材之长,定位中高年级本科生。在教材难度要求和通俗易读间进行了较好的把握,既保证易于理解又使教材保持一定的深度。二是偏重理论分析推演,简化知识现象介绍。《国际经济学》的精髓在于它对理论的演绎、对思维的训练,而不应只是对结论的归纳、对现象的介绍。这在什么知识都可轻松百度、谷歌一下的当今显得尤为重要。掌握了理论的演绎过程,才能了解它的适用范围和局限,才不至于在眼花缭乱的理论丛林中无所适从或滥用误用。而经济思维的训练将会使人一生受益。三是读者友好。本书在编写过程中充分考虑易用性,在每章篇首列出本章将出现的专业词汇,给出中文释义,方便读者学习。在一些逻辑性较强、内容较难的章节,给出了逻辑推演图或说明,帮助读者理解。

本书在章节安排上,遵从所介绍理论的内在逻辑。第一至第五章为国际贸易部分,具体为古典贸易理论、新古典贸易理论、现代贸易理论、关税与非关税壁垒、区域贸易安排。逻辑顺序为推崇自由贸易的贸易理论、现实中的贸易保护、人们所做的折中努力。第六至第十章为国际金融部分,具体为国际收支与汇率、汇率决定理论、国际收支调节、开放经济中的宏观经济政策、宏观经济政策的国际传导与协调。在第六章中对后面涉及的国际金融知识进行介绍,然后按汇率理论、国际收支理论、宏观政策效果、国际传导协调与合作进行推进。第十一章为国际要素流动与跨国公司,介绍涉及国际贸易的劳动要素流动、涉及国际金融的资本要素流动及其集中体现——跨国公司。

　　本书的编者均为长期从事《国际经济学》双语教学的教师,具体为:董理(第一、四章)、周扬波(第二章)、陶凌云(第三章)、吕健(第五、十一章)、王艳娟(第六章)、黄敏(第七、九、十章)、刘霞(第八章)。全书编写提纲由黄敏拟定,初稿写成后由董理对国际贸易部分进行了统稿,吕健对其余部分进行了统稿,最后由黄敏总撰、定稿。

　　在本书编写过程中,我们借鉴了国内外的优秀教材和著作;另外,复旦大学出版社给予了大力支持,在此一并表示感谢。限于编者水平,书中纰漏之处敬请专家和读者批评指正。

编　者

2010 年 12 月于上海

Table of Contents

Chapter 1

Classical Theories of International Trade

Key Concepts and Terms

Mercantilism	重商主义
Tariff	关税
Quota	配额
Absolute Advantage	绝对优势
Comparative Advantage	相对优势
Labor Theory of Value	劳动价值论
Specialization	专业化
Complete Specialization	完全专业化
Partial Specialization	部分专业化
Opportunity Cost	机会成本
Constant Opportunity Cost	不变机会成本
Increasing Opportunity Cost	递增机会成本
Marginal Rate of Transformation（MRT）	边际转换率
Production Possibilities Frontier（PPF）	生产可能性边界
Reciprocal Demand	相互需求
Trade Triangle	贸易三角形
Offer Curve	提供曲线
Terms of Trade	贸易条件
Income Terms of Trade	收入贸易条件
Single Factoral Terms of Trade	单要素贸易条件
Double Factoral Terms of Trade	双要素贸易条件

Why does international trade occur and what are its effects on economy? To find the answers to these doubts rooted in everybody's mind, economists have evolved a vast range of theories. Among them, classical theories based on the labor theory of value provide basic explanations.

1.1 Mercantilism

Mercantilism refers to the collections of economic thoughts that came into existence in Europe during the period from 1500 to 1750. It can not be classified as a formal school of thought, but rather as a collection of similar attitudes toward domestic economic activities and the role of international trade that tended to dominate economic thinking and policies during this period.

According to the mercantilists, the central question was how a country could regulate its domestic and international affairs so as to promote its own interests. The solution lay in a strong foreign trade sector. If a country could achieve a favorable trade balance, it would receive payments from the rest of the world in the form of gold and silver. Such revenues would contribute to an increase in spending and thus a rise in domestic output and employment. To promote a favorable trade balance, the mercantilists advocated government regulation of trade. Tariffs, quotas, and other commercial policies were proposed by the mercantilists to decrease imports in order to protect the country's trade position.

By the eighteenth century, the economic policies of the mercantilists were under strong attack. It was believed that a favorable trade balance was possible only in the short run, for over time it would automatically be eliminated. Mercantilist policies would provide at best only short-term economic advantages.

The mercantilists were also attacked for their static view of the world economy. To the mercantilist, the world's economic pie was of a constant size. This meant that one country's gains from trade came at the expense of its trading partners; not all countries could simultaneously enjoy the benefits of international trade. This view was challenged with the publication in 1776 of Adam Smith's *Wealth of Nations*. According to Smith, the world's economic pie is not of a fixed size. International trade permits countries to take advantage of specialization and the division of labor, which increases the general level of productivity within a country and thus increases the world output. Smith's dynamic view of trade suggested that both trading partners could simultaneously enjoy higher level of production and consumption with free trade.

1.2   Trade Based on Absolute Advantage: Adam Smith

Adam Smith was a leading advocator of free trade on the grounds that it promoted the international division of labor. With free trade, countries could concentrate their production on the goods they could produce most cheaply and enjoy all the consequent benefits from the labor division.

The theory of absolute advantage accepts the idea that cost differences govern the international movement of goods and seeks to explain why costs differ among countries. It maintains that productivities of factor inputs represent the major determinant of production cost. Such productivities are based on natural and acquired advantages. Natural advantages include factors relating to climate, soil, and mineral wealth, whereas acquired advantages include special skills and techniques. Given a natural or acquired advantage in the production of a good, a country would produce that good at lower cost, becoming more competitive than its trading partner. The theory thus views the determination of competitiveness from the supply side of the market.

Here, the concept of cost is founded upon the labor theory of value, which assumes that within each country, (1) labor is the only factor of production and is homogeneous (of one quality) and (2) the cost or price of a good depends exclusively upon the amount of labor required to produce it. For example, if China uses less labor to manufacture a yard of cloth than the United States, Chinese production cost will be lower.

The theory of absolute advantage claims that in a 2-country, 2-product world, international specialization and trade will be beneficial when one country has an absolute cost advantage (that is, uses less labor to produce a unit of output) in one good and the other country has an absolute cost advantage in the other good. For the world to benefit from specialization, each country must have a good that it is absolutely more efficient in producing than its trading partner. A country will import those goods in which it has an absolute cost disadvantage and will export those goods in which it has an absolute cost advantage.

An arithmetic example helps illustrate the principle of absolute advantage. Referring to Table 1-1, suppose a worker in the United Kingdom can produce 5 sets of iPad or 20 yards of cloth in an hour, while a U.S. worker can produce 15 sets of iPad or 10 yards of cloth in an hour. Clearly, the United States has an absolute advantage in iPad production; its iPad workers' productivity (output per worker hour) is higher than that of the United Kingdom, which leads to lower costs (less labor required to produce a set of iPad). In like manner, the United Kingdom has an absolute advantage in cloth production.

Table 1-1　A Case of Absolute Advantage

Country	Output per Labor Hour	
	iPad	Cloth
U.K.	5 sets	20 yards
U.S.	15 sets	10 yards

According to the theory of absolute advantage, each country benefits by specializing in and exporting the good that it produces at a lower cost than the other country, while importing the good that it produces at a higher cost. Because the world uses its resources more efficiently as the result of specializing, there occurs an increase in the world output which in turn is distributed to the two countries through the trade.

1.3　Trade Based on Comparative Advantage: David Ricardo

According to the theory of absolute advantage, mutually beneficial trade requires each country to be the least-cost producer of at least one good that it can export to its trading partner. But what if a country is more efficient than its trading partner in the production of all goods? To answer this question, David Ricardo (1772-1823) developed a principle to show that mutually beneficial trade can occur even when one country is absolutely more efficient in the production of all goods.

The theory of comparative advantage also emphasizes the supply side of the market. It believes the immediate basis for trade stems from comparative (relative) cost differences between countries. Indeed, countries often develop comparative advantages, as shown in Table 1-2.

According to the theory of comparative advantage, even if a country has an absolute cost disadvantage in the production of both goods, a basis for mutually beneficial trade may still exist. The more efficient country should specialize in and export that good in which it is relatively more efficient (where its absolute advantage is bigger). The less efficient country should specialize in and export the good in which it is relatively less inefficient (where its absolute disadvantage is smaller).

1.3.1　An Example of Comparative Advantage

To demonstrate the principle of comparative advantage, let us formulate a simplified model. We assume: (1) there are only two countries with fixed level of technology in the world; (2) each country owns only one input — labor - , which is fixed endowed and homogenous and can move across industries but cannot flow across countries; (3) each country produces two commodities; (4) perfect competition and free trade prevail in markets.

To see how comparative advantage works, refer to Table 1-2, where the data shows one U.S. worker can produce either 5 sets of iPad or 15 yards of cloth per hour (first row), and one Chinese worker can produce 1 set of iPad or 5 yards of cloth per hour (second row). Compare the two countries in Table 1-2, notice that the U.S. has an absolute advantage in the production of both iPad and cloth. If you were using the concept of absolute advantage alone as the basis for trade, no trade would occur between the U. S. and China. However, the theory of comparative advantage shows that mutually beneficial trade can still occur between the two countries.

Table 1-2　A Case of Comparative Advantage

Country	Output per Labor Hour		
	iPad	Cloth	Relative Cost
U.S.	5 sets	15 yards	1 iPad = 3 yards of cloth
China	1 set	5 yards	1 iPad = 5 yards of cloth

As Table 1-2 indicates, U. S. labor has a 5-to-1 absolute advantage in the production of iPad. In other words, U.S. workers can produce five iPads with the input with which Chinese worker can produce one iPad. U.S. labor also has a 15-to-5 or 3-to-1 absolute advantage in the production of cloth. China has an absolute disadvantage in the production of iPad and cloth. That is, U.S. workers can produce both more iPads and more yards of cloth than workers in China.

In this example, the U.S. has a greater absolute advantage in producing iPad than in producing cloth. However, China's absolute disadvantage is smaller in producing cloth than in producing iPad. Using Ricardo's logic, the U.S. has a comparative advantage in iPad because its degree of absolute advantage is larger and a comparative disadvantage in cloth because its absolute advantage in cloth is smaller. Similarly, China has a comparative advantage in cloth and a comparative disadvantage in iPad. Comparative advantage, as opposed to absolute advantage, is a relative relationship.

1.3.2 Gains from Specialization and Trade with Comparative Advantage

Now, assume trade opens up between the U.S. and China. The U.S. could benefit from importing cloth from and exporting iPads to China. China could benefit from importing iPads from and exporting cloth to the U.S. For each worker that the U.S. transfers from cloth production to iPad production, the U.S. output of iPads increases by 5 and U.S. cloth production falls by 15 yards. As China transfers 3 workers from iPad production to cloth production, its cloth production increases by 15 yards and its iPad production falls by 3. In this case, there is a net increase in the world output, because cloth production remains constant and iPad production increases by 2. The result is shown in Table 1-3.

Table 1-3 The Change in the World Output Resulting from Specialization

Country	Change in the Production of	
	iPad	Cloth
U.S.	+5 sets	−15 yards
China	−3 sets	+15 yards
Change in the World Output	+2 sets	0

Again, the gain from production and trade is the increase in the world output that results from each country specializing in its production according to its comparative advantage. This increase in output would be allocated between the two countries through the process of international trade. How this increase in output is exactly distributed between them is the question we will answer later.

1.3.3   Comparative Advantage in Money Terms

Comparative advantage can be shown in terms of money prices. Refer to the comparative advantage example of Table 1-2. It assumes that labor is the only input and is homogeneous. Recall that (1) the United States has an absolute advantage in the production of both iPad and cloth; and (2) the United States has a comparative advantage in iPad production, while China has a comparative advantage in cloth production. See Table 1-4. Even though China is absolutely less efficient in producing both goods, it will export cloth (the product of its comparative advantage) when its money wages are so much lower than those of the United States that it is cheaper to make cloth in China. Let us see how this works.

Table 1-4   Comparative Advantage in Money Prices

Country	Labor Input	Hourly Wage Rate	iPad (sets)		Cloth (yards)	
			Quantity	Price	Quantity	Price
U.S.	1	$20	5	$4	15	$1.33
China	1	$5	1	$5	5	$1

Suppose the wage rate is $20 per hour in the United States, as indicated in Table 1-4. If U.S. workers can produce 15 yards of cloth in an hour, the average cost of producing a yard of cloth is $1.33 ($20/15 yards = $1.33 per yard). Similarly, the average cost of producing a set of iPad in the United States is $4. Because markets are assumed to be perfectly competitive, in the long run a product's price equals its average cost of production. The prices of iPad and cloth produced in the United States are shown in Table 1-4.

Suppose now that the wage rate is $5 per hour in China. Thus, the average cost (price) of producing a yard of cloth in China is $1 ($5/5 yards = $1 per yard), and the average cost (price) of producing a set of iPad is $5. These prices are also shown in Table 1-4.

Compare the costs of producing these products in the United States with those in China, and we can find that China has lower costs in cloth production but higher costs in iPad production. China thus has a comparative advantage in cloth.

We conclude that even though China is not as efficient as the United States in the production of cloth, its lower wage rate in terms of dollars compensates for its inefficiency. At this wage rate, China's average cost in dollars of producing cloth is less than the U.S. average cost. With perfectly competitive markets, China's selling price of cloth is lower than its U.S. selling price, and China exports cloth to the United States.

1.4   Comparative Advantage and Opportunity Cost

Our explanation of comparative advantage between the U.S. and China in the previous section is based on the assumption that labor is homogeneous and is the only factor used to produce cloth and iPads. Without this assumption, comparing the productivity of U.S. workers with that of China's workers would not be possible. Because labor is actually not homogeneous between countries and is just one of several factors of production, we must develop a more general theory beyond the labor theory of value.

Opportunity Cost

The concept of opportunity cost enables us to develop a general theory of comparative advantage that takes into account all factors of production. In this context, opportunity cost is the quantity of one good that must be given up to release enough resources to produce one more unit of another good. Return to Table 1-2 and consider what would happen if the U.S. transfers one worker from iPad production to cloth production. In this case, the U.S. would add 15 yards of cloth but would have to abandon 5 iPads. The opportunity cost of producing 1 yard of cloth is 1/3 iPad. In the U.S., the quantity of one good that it must abandon to produce each additional unit of another good, i. e. the marginal rate of transformation (MRT), is 1 iPad for 3 yards of cloth or 1 yard of cloth for 1/3 iPad.

As for China, the opportunity cost of 1 iPad is 5 yards of cloth, or 1 yard of cloth costs 1/5 iPad. This means that in China the marginal rate of transformation for the two goods is 1 iPad for 5 yards of cloth. Notice that the marginal rate of transformation of the U.S. is different from that of China. The U.S. can exchange 1 iPad for 3 yards of cloth while China can exchange 1 iPad for 5 yards of cloth.

Comparing the different marginal rates of transformation of both countries, the U.S. opportunity cost is lower for iPad. The U.S. gives up 3 yards of cloth to produce 1 iPad while China has to give up 5 yards of cloth to produce 1 iPad. China's opportunity cost is lower for cloth. China gives up only 1/5 iPad to produce 1 yard of cloth while the U.S. has to give up 1/3 iPad to produce 1 yard of cloth.

Although the U.S. has an absolute advantage in the production of both iPads and cloth, it has a comparative advantage in the production of iPad. While China has an absolute disadvantage in the production of both iPad and cloth, it has a comparative advantage in the production of cloth. Because the opportunity cost of the same good differs with countries, both countries can benefit from trade. Traders can buy cloth in China and ship it to the U.S. to sell for profits. In the same way, traders can buy iPads in the U.S. and ship them to China to sell for profits there.

1.4.1   Gains from Specialization and Trade with Opportunity Costs

In Table 1-2, notice that there are limits to mutually beneficial transaction. No one in the U.S. would pay more than 1/3 iPad for a yard of cloth. Why would anyone pay more for an imported good if the domestic price is lower? Similarly, no one in China would pay more than 5 yards of cloth to obtain an iPad. For profitable transaction to take place, the price of iPad relative to the price of cloth would have to be between 1 iPad for 3 yards of cloth and 1 iPad for 5 yards of cloth.

Given the limits of 1 iPad for 3 yards of cloth and 1 iPad for 5 yards of cloth, we assume that the exchange ratio for trade between the two countries is 1 iPad for 4 yards of cloth. With this exchange ratio, we can examine Table 1-5 to determine the gains from trade. The first row of the table shows each country's maximum production of the two goods when all resources of a country are used to produce the good in which it has a comparative advantage. For example, the U.S. is capable of producing 100 iPads if all of its resources are devoted to the production of iPad. Similarly, China could produce 300 yards of cloth if all of its resources are devoted to the production of cloth.

Table 1-5   Production and Consumption with and without Trade

Based on an exchange ratio of 1 iPad = 4 yards of cloth

Item	Country	
	U.S.	China
Production at Full Employment	100 iPads 0 yard of cloth	0 iPad 300 yards of cloth
Consumption with Trade	50 iPads 200 yards of cloth	50 iPads 100 yards of cloth
Domestic Production and Consumption without Trade	50 iPads 150 yards of cloth	40 iPads 100 yards of cloth
Gains from Specialization and Trade	50 yards of cloth	10 iPads

Assume that the U.S. consumes 50 iPads and exports 50 iPads to China. At the exchange ratio of 1 iPad for 4 yards of cloth, the U.S. would import 200 yards of cloth from China. Looking at this exchange from the other perspective, China would export the 200 yards of cloth and importing the 50 iPads. These exchanges are identified as consumption with trade in the second row of Table 1-5.

The gains from specialization and trade are what each country can consume with trade beyond what it can consume under conditions of autarky, or without trade. If both countries decide not to trade with each other, how much of each good could they consume? The U.S. could produce and consume 50 iPads and use its remaining resources to produce and consume cloth. Given the U.S. opportunity cost, 1 iPad for 3 yards of cloth, it could have produced and consumed only 150 yards of cloth. That means without trade, the U.S. has 50 yards less of cloth to consume. By trading at the international exchange ratio of 1 iPad for 4 yards of cloth, the U.S. is able to consume more cloth through trade.

The situation is the same for China. China could have produced and consumed only 100 yards of cloth and devoted its remaining resources to the domestic production of iPad. Given its opportunity cost of 1 iPad for 5 yards of cloth, China could have produced and consumed only 40 iPads. Without trade,

China has 10 fewer iPads to consume. As the example shows, both countries are better off when they specialize and trade.

1.4.2　Production Possibilities Frontier and Constant Opportunity Costs

The theory of comparative advantage explains how specialization and trade leads to gains from trade for both countries. Using information contained in Table 1-4, we can employ graphical analysis to provide a visual understanding of the theory of comparative advantage.

The Production Possibilities Frontier

The focus of graphical analysis is the production possibilities frontier. A production possibilities frontier (PPF) shows the different combinations of two goods that can be produced when all of a country's factors of production are fully employed in their most efficient way. By using "most efficient", we mean that the economy produces a given mix of goods at the least cost given the current level of technology.

Table 1-6 shows hypothetical PPFs for the U.S. and China, assuming each country can produce both cloth and iPads under constant costs. By fully using all of its resources, the U.S. could produce either 100 iPads or 0 yard of cloth or 0 iPad and 300 yards of cloth. Because resources are mobile within a country, any combination between these two extremes could be produced. As Table 1-6 indicates, for each group of 10 iPads that the U.S. does not produce, enough resources are released to produce an additional 30 yards of cloth. This means the opportunity cost of 10 iPads is 30 yards of cloth, or 1 iPad for 3 yards of cloth.

Table 1-6　Production Possibilities Frontiers for the U.S. and China at Full Employment

U.S.		China	
Number of iPad	Yards of Cloth	Number of iPad	Yards of Cloth
100	0	60	0
90	30	50	50
80	60	40	100
70	90	30	150

continued

U.S.		China	
Number of iPad	Yards of Cloth	Number of iPad	Yards of Cloth
60	120	20	200
50	150	10	250
40	180	0	300
30	210		
20	240		
10	270		
0	300		

China can produce either 60 iPads and 0 yard of cloth, or 0 iPad and 300 yards of cloth, or any combination between these two extremes. This means that China can increase its output by 50 yards of cloth for each group of 10 iPads it does not produce. China's opportunity cost is 1 iPad for 5 yards of cloth. The PPFs in Table 1-5 are graphed in Figure 1-1, where each point on a country's PPF represents one combination of cloth and iPads that the country can produce. These frontiers are straight lines because the opportunity cost of each good is constant.

Production and Consumption without Specialization and Trade

Without specialization and trade, the U. S. and China can produce and consume at any point along their respective production possibilities frontiers, as shown in Figure 1-1. Points below the PPF, say, Point B or B', represent possible production combinations that can be produced but are inefficient because there would be some unemployed resources. Points above the PPF, say, Point C or C', represent production combinations that are not possible for a country to produce with available resources and technology. The downward slope of the PPF indicates that to produce more cloth, a country has to give up a certain quantity of iPad, and vice versa. The slope of PPF is referred to as the marginal rate of transformation (MRT), which shows the amount of one product a country must sacrifice to get one additional unit of the other product. Although the opportunity costs are constant in both countries, these costs differ between them.

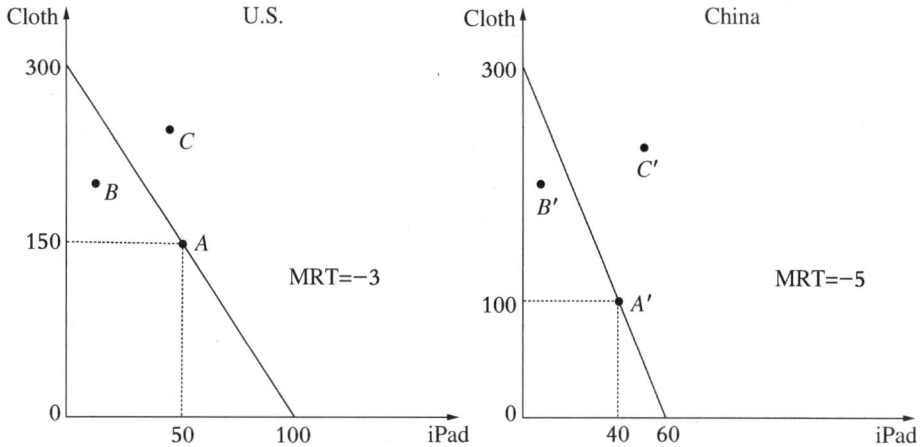

Figure 1-1   Production Possibilities Frontiers under Constant Costs for the U.S. and China

Figure 1-1 shows the slope of the U.S. curve is -3 yards of cloth per iPad. This means that the U.S. must give up 3 yards of cloth to get 1 more iPad. The slope of China's PPF is -5 yards of cloth per iPad, so China must give up 5 yards of cloth to get 1 more iPad.

When the market is perfectly competitive, the price of a product will equal its average cost. Under this condition, the price of 1 iPad in the U.S. will be 3 times that of 1 yard of cloth ($P_i/P_c = 3$). For China, the price of 1 iPad will be 5 times that of 1 yard of cloth ($P_i/P_c = 5$). Notice that the relative price ratios in both countries reflect the opportunity costs of producing each good.

Suppose the U.S. decides to produce and consume at Point A on its frontier, that is, 50 iPads and 150 yards of cloth, and China decides to produce and consume at Point A' on its frontier, that is, 40 iPads and 100 yards of cloth. The total world production and consumption of iPads and cloth is the sum of both countries' outputs $-$ 90 iPads and 250 yards of cloth. Because the opportunity costs are different in each country, mutually beneficial trade is possible.

Production and Consumption with Specialization and Trade

Now, assume that trade opens up between the U.S. and China. The U.S. could benefit from importing cloth from China and exporting cloth to China. China could benefit from importing iPads from the U.S. and exporting cloth to the

U.S. In Figure 1-2, suppose the U.S. and China before specialization and trade produce and consume at Point A and A′, respectively. Given different opportunity costs in each country, the U.S. would specialize in the production of iPad, transferring its production from Point A to Point D on its PPF. China specializes in the production of cloth, moving from Point A′ to Point D′. With each country specializing in the production of the good in which it has a comparative advantage, the world output increases to 100 iPads and 300 yards of cloth. In other words, 10 more iPads and 50 more yards of cloth are produced in the world.

Before trade, the U.S. and China's consumption possibilities are limited to points along their respective PPFs. With specialization and trade, both countries can achieve consumption points beyond their respective frontiers. With trade, the set of consumption points that a country can achieve is determined by the terms of trade — the relative price of trading iPads for cloth, and vice versa. For there to be mutually beneficial trade, the price of iPad and cloth would have to be between 1 iPad for 3 yards of cloth and 1 iPad for 5 yards of cloth.

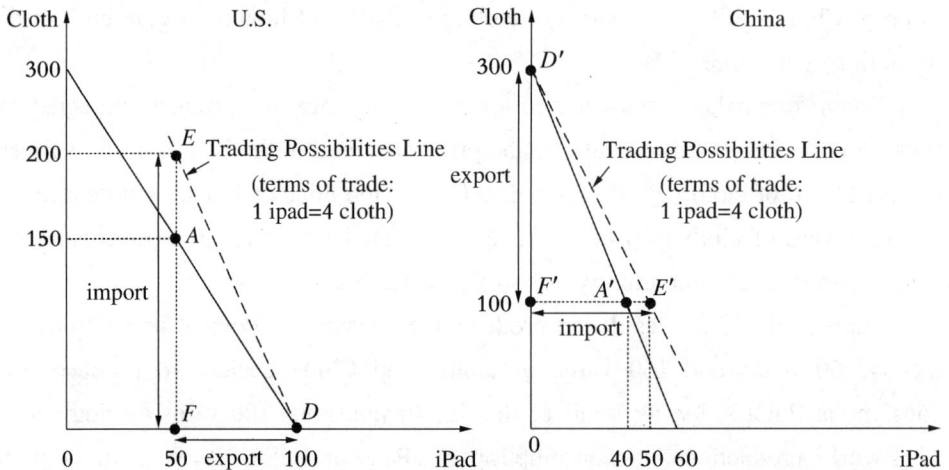

Figure 1-2 Specialization and Trade under Constant Opportunity Costs

Given these limits to trade, assume the terms of trade are 1 iPad for 4 yards of cloth. With this exchange ratio, the possibility of trading on these more favorable terms permits each country to enhance its PPF with a trading possibilities line shown as the dashed lines in Figure 1-2. A trading possibilities line shows the options a country has when it specializes in the production of one good and exports it to obtain the other good.

Suppose the U.S. decides to specialize in ipad and export 50 iPads to China in exchange for 200 yards of cloth. Starting at Point D in Figure 1-2, the U.S. will move along the trading possibilities line to Point E. Compared to no trade, Point E represents a gain in consumption for the U.S.. At Point A, the U.S. produces and consumes 50 iPads and 150 yards of cloth. At Point E, the U.S. consumes 50 iPads and 200 yards of cloth. The gain from trade for the U.S. is 50 yards of cloth.

China, specializing in cloth, exports 200 yards of cloth for 50 iPads. As a result, China moves along its trading possibilities line to Point E'. Compared to its consumption with no trade at Point A', there is also a gain in consumption for China at Point E'. At Point A', China produces and consumes 40 iPads and 100 yards of cloth. At Point E', China consumes 50 iPads and 100 yards of cloth. The consumption gain for China is 10 iPads. As the example shows, both countries are better off by specializing and trade than they would be without trade.

Terms of Trade

In our example, both countries gain from trade at the international exchange ratio, 1 iPad for 4 yards of cloth. A change in this ratio toward 1 iPad for 3 yards of cloth or 1 iPad for 5 yards of cloth would change the distribution of the gains from trade. The closer the ratio moves toward 1 iPad for 3 yards of cloth, the more favorable the exchange is for China because it obtains more iPads for each yard of cloth. Obviously, changes in this direction are less favorable for the U.S. because it will obtain fewer yards of cloth for each iPad. However, the closer the ratio moves toward 1 iPad for 5 yards of cloth, the more favorable the exchange is for the U.S. and the less favorable it is for China. Outside these two limits, one of the two countries will not trade, for it could do better without trade.

Changes in the Gains from Specialization and Trade

How each country fares trading at 1 iPad for 3.5 yards of cloth is illustrated in Table 1-7. In the second row in Table 1-7, we see the U.S. trades 50 iPads with China. At this exchange ratio, the U.S. receives 175 yards of cloth, as compared to 200 yards when the exchange ratio is 1 iPad for 4 yards of cloth. China obtains 50 iPads but gives up fewer yards of cloth to obtain those 50 iPads.

China is better off at the ratio of 1 iPad for 3.5 yards of cloth. The U.S. is worse off compared to the international exchange ratio of 1 iPad for 4 yards of cloth, but the U.S. is still considerably better off trading than attempting to transform iPads into cloth domestically.

Table 1-7　Production and Consumption with and without Trade

Based on an exchange ratio of 1 iPad = 3.5 yards of cloth

Item	Country	
	U.S.	China
Production at Full Employment	100 iPads 0 yard of cloth	0 iPad 300 yards of cloth
Consumption with Trade	50 iPads 175 yards of cloth	50 iPads 125 yards of cloth
Domestic Production and Consumption without Trade	50 iPads 150 yards of cloth	40 iPads 100 yards of cloth
Gains from Specialization and Trade	0 iPad 25 yards of cloth	10 iPads 25 yards of cloth

The results shown in Table 1-7 are illustrated with PPFs in Figure 1-3. As the international exchange ratio (terms of trade) changes from 1 iPad for 4 yards of cloth to 1 iPad for 3.5 yards of cloth, the trading possibilities line moves for each country. For the U.S., the trading possibilities line rotates inward, indicating a less favorable trading condition. For China, its trading possibilities curve rotates outward, indicating a more favorable trading condition. As the figure shows, without specialization and trade, the U.S. produces and consumes at Point A and China produces and consumes at Point A'. With trade at an international exchange ratio of 1 iPad for 4 yards of cloth, the U.S. produces at Point D and consumes at Point E. China produces at Point D' and consumes at Point E'. With the new international exchange ratio of 1 iPad for 3.5 yards of cloth, the U.S. produces at Point D but now consumes at Point G. The U.S. is worse off compared to the previous trading position but is still better off than not trading with China. For China, the new international exchange ratio allows it to produce at Point D' but now it consumes at Point G'. In China's case, it is better off compared to the previous trading position as it obtains more of the gains from trade.

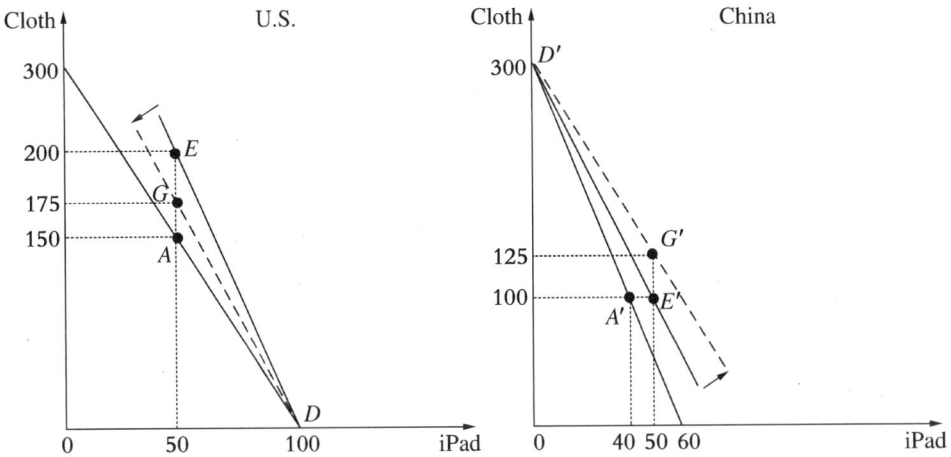

Figure 1-3   Changes in the Terms of Trade for the U.S. and China

Distribution of the Gains from Trade

The difference between the opportunity costs of producing the product domestically versus the cost of purchasing the product from another country determines the gains a country receives from trade. The terms of trade measures the relationship between the price a country receives for its exports versus the price a country pays for its imports. In our example, the terms of trade for the U.S. would be the price of iPad divided by the price of cloth. The higher this price ratio is, the more favorable the terms of trade are for the U.S. If the terms of trade change from 1 iPad for 4 yards of cloth to 1 iPad for 4.5 yards of cloth, then the U.S. would be better off because a smaller quantity of U.S. exports are required to obtain a given quantity of imports. In this case, the U.S. is paying less for each unit of cloth. For China, it is the reverse. China's terms of trade would be the price of cloth divided by the price of iPad.

Changes in a country's terms of trade over time indicate whether a country can obtain more or less quantity of imports per unit of exports. However, an improvement in a country's terms of trade does not necessarily reflect an improvement in a country's overall welfare. Likewise, deterioration in a country's terms of trade does not necessarily reflect an analogous deterioration in a country's overall welfare.

A change in a country's terms of trade may reflect a change in either international or domestic economic conditions. Assume a country's terms of trade change as a result of a change in international conditions. For example, suppose there is an increase in the demand for U.S. exports. As a result, the price of U.S. exports increases and the U.S. terms of trade improve. We can conclude that an improvement in the terms of trade resulting from a change in international conditions enhances U.S. welfare and that deterioration in the terms of trade is equivalent to a reduction in U.S. welfare.

When the terms of trade change as a result of a change in domestic economic conditions, the effect on a country's welfare is uncertain. For example, suppose that the U.S. has a tremendous increase in technology and now can produce a large number of iPads inexpensively. The increase in the supply of iPads will cause the world price of iPad to decline, which in turn will cause deterioration in the U.S. terms of trade. The reduction in the U.S. terms of trade decreases its welfare, but the additional iPads the U.S. produces increase its. welfare. The net effect on total welfare depends on which is larger — the decrease due to the change in terms of trade or the increase due to increased production. Although the changes in terms of trade do not accurately measure changes in a country's welfare in all cases, businesses and governments often use it as a rough indicator to show how a country is performing in the world economy.

Complete Specialization

In our example, when we allow for international trade, each country then specializes completely in the production of the good in which it has a comparative advantage and imports the other good. The opening of trade ends up wiping out the industry with a comparative disadvantage in each country. The cloth industry ceases existing in the U.S. and iPad industry disappears in China.

Complete specialization occurs because as production expands in the industry with a comparative advantage, the domestic cost of producing the product does not rise. Constant costs are assumed to prevail over the entire range of production. In this case, the firm's cost curves and the product's supply curves are horizontal. Constant costs are illustrated in Figure 1-4. Constant costs imply that the resources used to produce both iPads and cloth are completely flexible in the production of both goods. When constant costs prevail, a country does not lose its comparative

advantage as it produces more of the good. As a result, the country completely
specializes in the production of the good in which it has a comparative advantage.

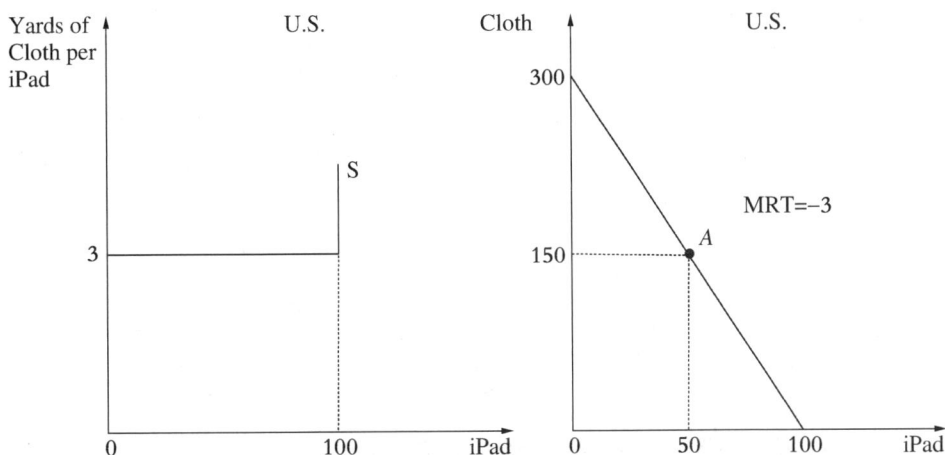

Yards of Cloth per iPad | U.S. | Cloth | U.S.

Figure 1-4   Supply Curves of a Good and the Production Possibilities Frontier

1.4.3   Trade under Increasing Opportunity Costs

Increasing Costs and the Production Possibilities Frontier

In the real world, the assumption of constant cost may not be practical.
Rather, a country may be subject to increasing opportunity costs as more of a good
is produced. With increasing opportunity costs, as the production of one good,
say iPad, increases, the economy must give up ever increasing quantities of the
other good, say, cloth. Increasing costs are illustrated in Figure 1-5 which shows
an upward-sloping supply curve. This implies that the PPF for a country is
concave to the origin.

Referring to Figure 1-5, suppose a country is currently producing at Point A,
i. e. 300 yards of cloth and 0 iPad. As the economy moves from Point A toward
Point H, producing more and more iPads, the output of cloth falls by increasing
quantities. To produce the first 20 iPads, only 20 yards of cloth are given up. To
produce the second 20 iPads, an additional 40 yards of cloth are sacrificed. To
produce the third 20 iPads, an additional 60 yards of cloth are given up. Notice
that each successive iPad produced requires an ever larger amount of foregone
output of cloth. The same increasing cost phenomenon occurs for the production of

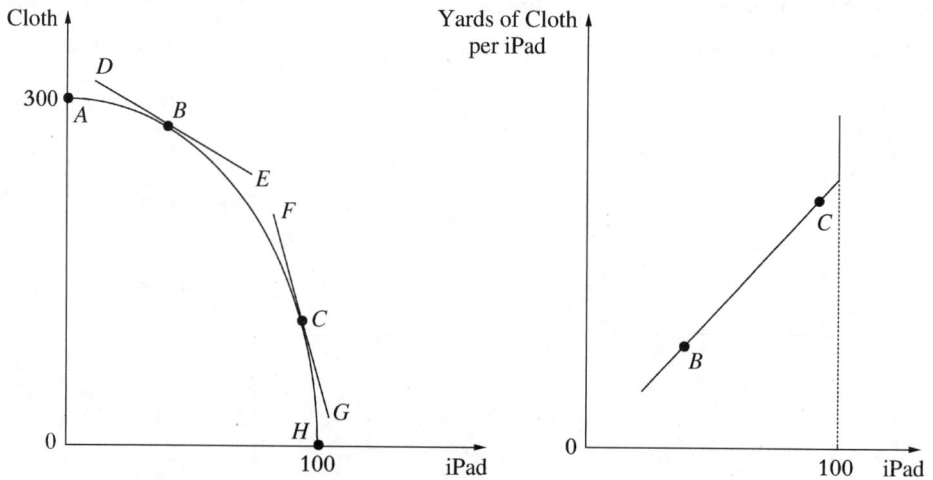

Figure 1-5　Production Possibilities Frontier and Supply Curve
under Increasing Cost Conditions

each additional yard of cloth. Moving along the PPF in the other direction, from Point H towards Point A, the production of cloth also has increasing opportunity costs.

Just as in the constant cost case, the marginal rate of transformation is equal to the slope of the PPF. However, with increasing costs, the slope of the PPF changes at every point along the curve. The slope of the PPF at any point is represented graphically by the slope of a tangent to that point. For example, in Figure1-5, the slope of its PPF at Point B is equal to the slope of its tangent DE. Similarly, the slope of the tangent FG represents the slope of the PPF at Point C. Notice that the tangent FG is steeper than the tangent DE, implying increasing costs.

There are two reasons why a country has increasing opportunity costs. First, the factors of production used to produce the products are specialized in the production of a particular product, say, iPad. An example of product-specific resources would include highly skilled labor for the production of iPad that is not skilled in the production of cloth. Therefore, as the country moves from Point A toward Point H in Figure 1-5, the first resource used to produce iPads are better equipped to manufacture iPads than cloth, and the cost of an iPad is relatively low. As the country continues to move toward Point H, additional resources are used to produce iPads, although some of these resources are better suited to produce cloth than iPads. The opportunity costs of iPad increase because each additional iPad produced requires larger reductions in cloth production.

The other reason for increasing opportunity costs is the unrealistic premise that all resources are identical in the sense that all workers and capital have the same productivity in the production of both iPad and cloth. However, if the iPad and cloth industries use resources in different relative proportions, increasing opportunity costs will occur. For instance, the cloth industry may require larger amount of labor, whereas the iPad industry may require larger amount of capital. As resources move between the two industries, the different production mixes cause costs to rise. If unit cost rises with an increase in production, then as the U. S. expands its production of iPad and contracts its production of cloth, the price of iPad rises and the price of cloth falls. As China contracts its production of iPad and expands its production of cloth, the price of iPad falls and the price of cloth rises.

Production and Consumption without Specialization and Trade

Without specialization and trade, the U. S. and China can produce and consume at any point on their PPFs. The only difference is that the two countries now have increasing opportunity costs. In Figure 1-6, assume that, given tastes and preferences of the consumers in both countries, the U.S. decides to produce at Point A on its frontier and China decides to produce at Point A' on its frontier.

Without trade, the line CD represents the U. S. marginal rate of transformation or opportunity cost which is equal to the slope of the PPF. If the slope is -3, then the opportunity cost of iPad in the U.S. is 1 iPad for 3 yards of cloth. Similarly, without trade, the Line C'D' represents China's marginal rate of transformation. If the slope of Line C'D' is -5, then China's opportunity cost of iPad is 1 iPad for 5 yards of cloth. Comparing the U. S. marginal rate of transformation with that of China, we can find iPad is less costly in the U.S. than in China. In a world of constant opportunity costs, a country should specialize in the production of the product it produces at lower cost than the other country. The same is true in the world of increasing opportunity costs. As before, the U. S. should specialize in the production of iPad and China in cloth.

Production and Consumption with Specialization and Trade

As international trade opens up between the U. S. and China, the U. S. specializes in the production of iPad by transferring resources from its cloth industry to its iPad industry. This means the U.S. would move downward along its PPF from Point *A* toward Point *H*, as illustrated in Figure 1-6. As its specialization increases, the U. S. opportunity cost of iPad in terms of cloth increases. The opposite movement occurs in China as it transfers resources from its iPad industry to its cloth industry. This means China would move up along its PPF from Point *A'* toward Point *H'* and China's opportunity cost of iPad in terms of cloth decreases. International specialization continues until the opportunity cost of iPad and cloth are the same in both countries.

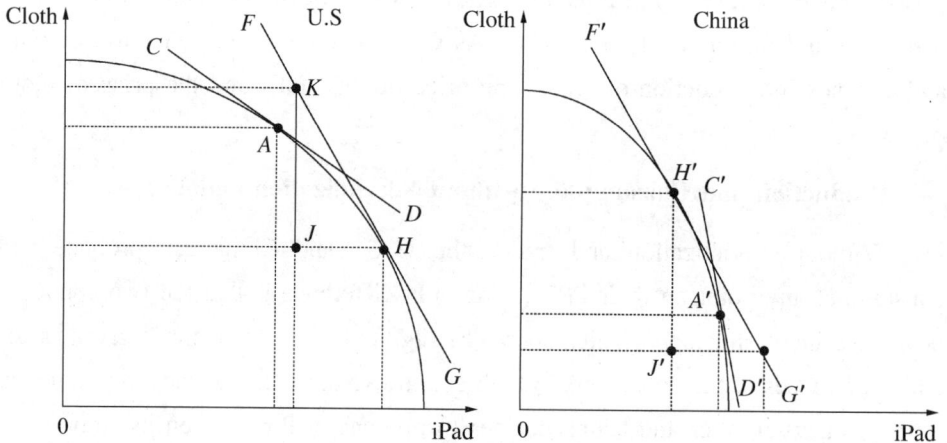

Figure 1-6   Specialization and Trade under Increasing Cost Conditions

Figure 1-6 illustrates the final outcome of international specialization according to comparative advantage based on assumed terms of trade of 1 iPad for 4 yards of cloth. The terms of trade or relative price coincides with the absolute slopes of the U.S. and China's trading possibilities curves, *FG* and *F'G'*. The U.S. shifts its production from *A* to *H* and China shifts its production from *A'* to *H'*. The U. S. consumes at Point *K* on its trading possibilities line *FG*, and achieves this consumption point when it exports *JH* iPads to China in exchange for *JK* yards of China's cloth. China consumes at Point *K'* on its trading possibilities line *F'G'*, and achieves this consumption point when it exports *J'H'* cloth to the

U.S. in exchange for $J'K'$ iPads from the U.S..

Specialization and trade under increasing cost conditions does not significantly change the conclusions we reached concerning the benefits of trade. Specializing in and exporting the good in which the country has a comparative advantage and trading for the other good enables both countries to become better off by consuming beyond their respective PPFs. However, production under increasing cost conditions constitutes a mechanism that forces prices to converge and results in neither country specializing completely in the production of the good in which it has a comparative advantage. In the case of increasing costs, both countries continue to produce both goods after trade and it is called as partial specialization.

1.5   Comparative Advantage with More Than Two Commodities and Countries

We now extend the theory of comparative advantage to the case of more than two commodities and then to the case of more than two countries. In each case, we will see that the theory of comparative advantage is easily generalized.

1.5.1   Comparative Advantage with More Than Two Commodities

Table 1-8 shows the dollar and the pound cost, or price, of five commodities in the United States and the United Kingdom.

Table 1-8   Commodity Prices in the U.S. and U.K.

Commodity	Price in the U.S. ($)	Price in the U.K. (£)
A	2	6
B	4	4
C	6	3
D	8	2
E	10	1

To determine which commodities will be exported and imported by the U.S. and U. K, we must first express all commodity prices in terms of the same currency and then compare prices in both countries. For example, if the exchange rate between the dollar and the pound is £1 = $2, the dollar prices of the commodities in the U.K. would be:

Commodity	A	B	C	D	E
Dollar price in the U. K	12	8	6	4	2

At this exchange rate, the dollar prices of Commodities A and B are lower in the U.S. than in the U.K.; Commodity C is equally priced in the two countries; and the prices of Commodities D and E are lower in the U.K.. As a result, the U.S. will export Commodities A and B to the U.K. and import Commodities D and E from the U.K., leaving Commodity C not traded.

Now assume that the exchange rate between the dollar and the pound becomes £ 1 = \$ 3. The dollar prices of the commodities in the U.K. would be:

Commodity	A	B	C	D	E
Dollar price in the U.K.	18	12	9	6	3

At this exchange rate, the dollar prices of Commodities A, B and C are lower in the U.S. than in the U.K.; while the prices of Commodities D and E are lower in the U.K. Thus, the U.S. will export Commodities A, B and C to the U.K. and import Commodities D and E from the U.K..

Finally, if the exchange rate turns to be £1 = \$1, the dollar prices of the commodities in the U.K. would be:

Commodity	A	B	C	D	E
Dollar price in the U.K.	6	4	3	2	1

In this case, the U.S. would export only Commodity A to the U.K. and import all other commodities, with the exception of Commodity B.

If the exchange rate between dollar and pound is flexible and is determined exclusively by trade forces, then the actual exchange rate will settle at the level at which the value of the U.S. exports to the U.K. exactly equals the value of the U.S. imports from the U.K.. Once this equilibrium exchange rate is established, we will be able to determine exactly which commodities are exported by the U.S. and which are exported by the U.K.. Each country will then have a comparative advantage in the commodities that it exports at the particular equilibrium exchange rate established.

What we can say on the basis of Table 1-7 is that the U.S. comparative advantage is the greatest in Commodity A, and the U.S. must export at least this commodity. For this to be possible, the exchange rate between dollar and pound must be £1 > \$0.33. The U.K. comparative advantage is the highest in Commodity E, so that the U.K. must export at least Commodity E. For this to be possible, the exchange rate between dollar and pound must be £1 < \$10. The discussion can be generalized to cover any number of commodities.

1.5.2   Comparative Advantage with More Than Two Countries

Suppose that, instead of two countries and five commodities, we have two commodities (wheat and cloth) and five countries (A, B, C, D and E). Table 1-9 ranks these countries from the lowest to the highest in terms of their internal P_W/P_C values. With trade, the equilibrium P_W/P_C will be somewhere between 1 and 5, that is $1 < P_W/P_C < 5$.

Table 1-9   Ranking of Countries in Terms of International P_W/P_C

Country	A	B	C	D	E
P_W/P_C	1	2	3	4	5

Given the equilibrium $P_W/P_C = 3$ with trade, Countries A and B will export wheat to Countries D and E in exchange for cloth. Country C will not engage in international trade in this case because its pre-trade P_W/P_C equals the equilibrium P_W/P_C with trade. Given a trade equilibrium $P_W/P_C = 4$, Countries A, B and C will export wheat to Country E in exchange for cloth, and Country D will not engage in the international trade. If the equilibrium turns to be $P_W/P_C = 2$ with trade, Country A will export wheat to all the other countries except Country B, in exchange for cloth.

This discussion can easily be extended to any number of countries and commodities. Thus, the conclusions reached on the basis of our simple model with only two countries and two commodities can be generalized and are applicable to the case of more than two countries and commodities.

1.6   Theory of Reciprocal Demand

Theory of reciprocal demand suggests that the actual price at which trade takes place depends on the trading partners' interacting demands. This theory is a complementary of the comparative advantage theory. It was first formulated by John Stuart Mill, and then put into graphic form by Alfred Marshall and F. Y. Edgeworth.

According to the theory of reciprocal demand, final terms of trade will be closer to the domestic price ratio of the country with stronger demand for the imported good. The reciprocal demand theory thus contends that the equilibrium terms of trade depend on the relative strength of each country's demand for the other country's product.

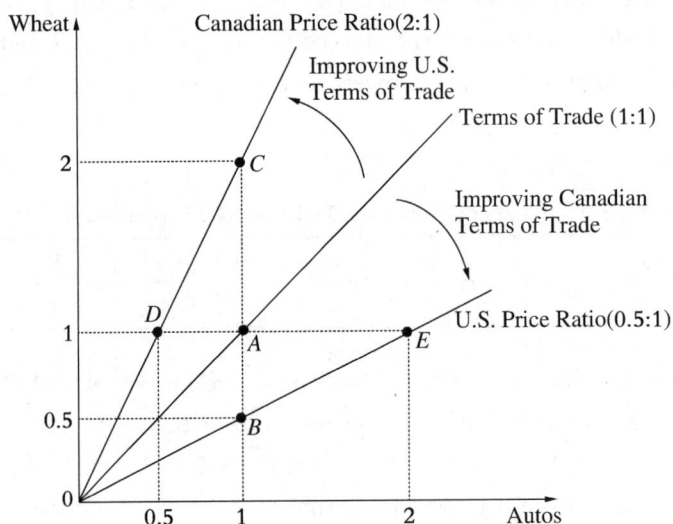

Figure 1-7 Equilibrium Terms-of-Trade Limits

Suppose Canada, which has a comparative advantage in the production of wheat, expresses an enormous demand for autos, both domestically produced and imported. Because the price that Canada is willing to pay for autos rises, the United States will realize most of the gains from trade. Starting at Point A in Figure 1-7, where the gains from trade are evenly divided between the two countries, improved U. S. terms of trade suggest that a given quantity of auto exports could buy larger amount of wheat imports. The United States will achieve a post-trade consumption point farther outside its PPF. At the outer extreme, the Canadian auto demand could be so enormous that the terms of trade would be at its domestic price — ratio. The United States would then be the only country to gain from trade.

Again starting at Point A in Figure 1-7, suppose the United States expresses an enormous demand for wheat, both domestically produced and imported. Because the price the United States is willing to pay for wheat rises, Canada will enjoy most of the gains from trade. Improved Canadian terms of trade suggest that a given quantity of wheat exports could buy increasing quantity of auto imports. At the extreme, the terms of trade could be at the U.S. domestic price ratio, in which case only Canada could gain from trade.

According to Mill's theory, the equilibrium terms of trade depend on both Canadian demand for autos and wheat and the U. S. demand for the same products. The stronger Canadian demand for autos relative to U.S. demand for wheat, the closer the terms of trade will be to Canadian domestic price ratio, and vice versa.

The reciprocal demand theory best applies when both countries are of equal economic size, so that the demand of each country has a noticeable effect on the market price. Given two countries of unequal economic size, it is possible that the relative demand strength of the smaller country will be dwarfed by that of the larger country. In this case, the domestic price ratio of the larger country will prevail. Assuming the absence of monopolistic elements working in the markets, the small nation can export as much of the commodity as it desires, enjoying the largest gains from trade.

Consider trade in crude oil and autos between Venezuela and the United States before the rise of the OPEC, the oil cartel. Venezuela, as a small country, accounted for only a very small share of the U.S. -Venezuela market, whereas the U.S. market share was overwhelmingly large. Because Venezuelan consumers and producers had no influence on market price levels, they were in effect price takers. In trading with the U.S., no matter what the Venezuelan demand was for crude oil and autos, it was not strong enough to affect U.S. price levels. As a result, Venezuela traded according to the U.S. domestic price ratio, buying and selling autos and crude oil at the price levels existing with the U.S..

The above example implies if two countries of approximately the same size and with similar taste patterns participate in international trade, the gains from trade will be shared almost equally between them. However, if one country is significantly larger than the other, the larger country attains fewer gains from trade while the smaller country attains most of the gains from trade. This situation is characterized as the **importance of being unimportant**. What's more, when countries are very dissimilar in size, there is a strong possibility that the larger country will continue to produce its comparative disadvantage good because the smaller country is unable to supply all of the world's demand for this product.

1.7 Offer Curve and Terms of Trade

1.7.1 Offer Curve

The offer curve (or reciprocal demand curve) of a country indicates the quantity of imports and exports the country is willing to buy and sell on the world market at all possible relative prices. In short, the curve shows the country's willingness to trade at various possible terms of trade. The offer curve really is a combination of a demand curve and a supply curve. The two-pronged natures of the curve distinguish it from most graphic devices in economies.

There are several methods of deriving an offer curve, but we will concentrate on the method that builds directly upon PPF-indifference curve diagram. This method is called the trade triangle approach.

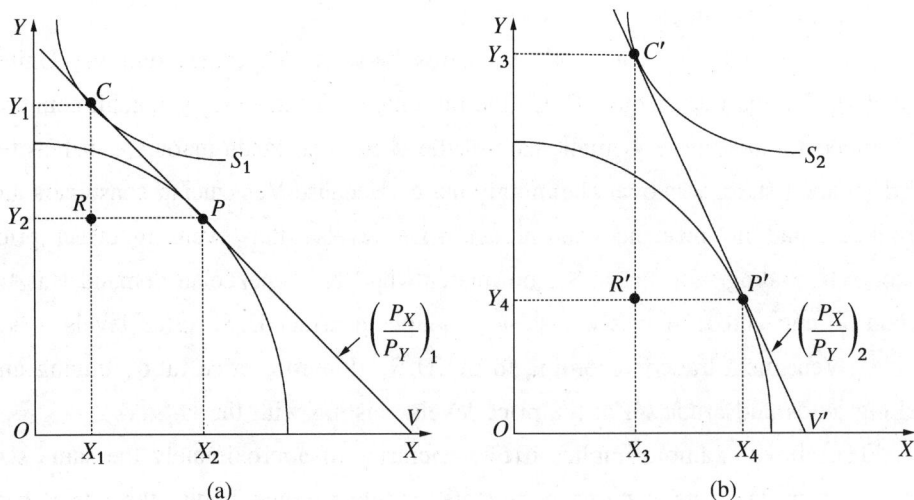

(a)   (b)

Figure 1-8 Trade Triangles at Two Possible Terms of Trade

Consider Figure 1-8(a), which shows the equilibrium trading position for a country at world price $(P_X/P_Y)_1$. Free trade is occurring, and the country is producing OX_2 of Good X and OY_2 of Good Y (at Point P). Consumption is OX_1 of Good X and OY_1 of Good Y (at Point C). With these amounts of production and consumption, X_1X_2 of Good X is exported and Y_1Y_2 of Good Y is imported. This trade pattern is reflected in trade triangle RCP, with Line RP representing the exports and Line RC representing the imports the country is willing to undertake at the terms of trade $(P_X/P_Y)_1$.

Consider Figure 1-8(b). The country now faces a steeper world price line than it did in Figure 1-8 (a), and its production and consumption have correspondingly adjusted. Since $(P_X/P_Y)_2$ in Figure 1-8 (b) is greater than $(P_X/P_Y)_1$ in Figure 1-8(a), producers have responded to the relatively higher price of X and to the relatively lower price of Y by increasing their production of X and decreasing their production of Y. Production now takes place at P', with OX_4 of Good X and OY_4 of Good Y being produced. At the price $(P_X/P_Y)_2$, consumption takes place at Point C' with OX_3 of Good X and OY_3 of Good Y consumed. Exports of this country are now X_3X_4 of Good X, and imports are Y_4Y_3 of Good Y. This volume of trade is represented by the trade triangle $R'C'P'$.

It is clear from Figure 1-8 that different trade volumes exist at the two different sets of relative commodity prices. The offer curve diagram takes the information from Panels (a) and (b) of Figure 1-8 and plots it onto a new curve (see Figure 1-9). This figure does not show production or consumption but represents only the quantities of exports and imports at the two sets of prices. The key geometrical difference between the two figures is that the P_X/P_Y price ratios are upward-sloping in Figure 1-9 rather than downward-sloping. Thus, $(P_X/P_Y)_1$ in Figure 1-9 is the same price ratio as $(P_X/P_Y)_1$ in Figure 1-8(a). Note that the angle OVC in Figure 1-8(a), where the price line hits the X axis, is the same size as the angle formed at the origin in Figure 1-9 between the $(P_X/P_Y)_1$ line and the X axis. At this set of prices, the country exports quantity OX_5 which is equal to X_1X_2 in Figure 1-8(a). Similarly, the country imports quantity OY_5 which is equal to Y_2Y_1 in Figure 1-8 (a). With the exports and imports thus plotted, Point T represents the volume of trade associated with the price ratio $(P_X/P_Y)_1$. Point T is a point that corresponds to the volume of trade indicated by the horizontal and vertical sides of the trade triangle *RCP* in Figure 1-8(a).

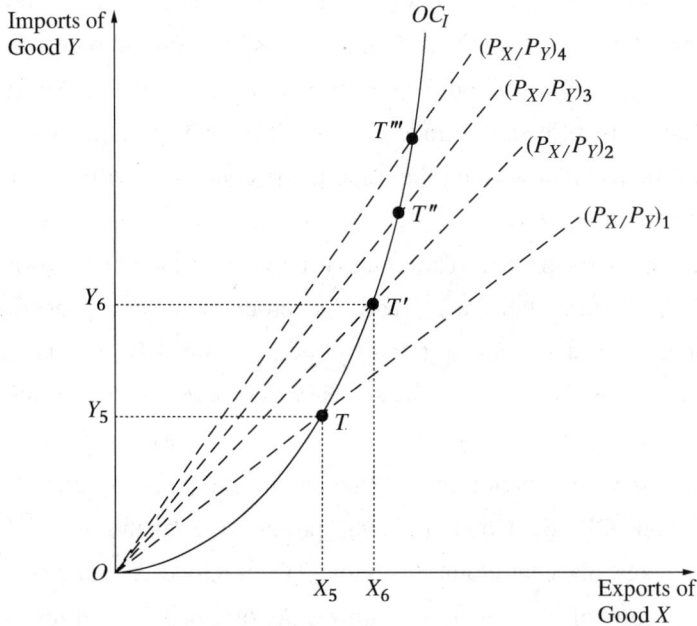

**Figure 1-9   Alternative Terms of Trade and Export-Import
Combinations on the Offer Curve**

The higher relative price ratio $(P_X/P_Y)_2$ in Figure 1-8(b) is represented by a steeper price line in Figure 1-9, as it was in Figure 1-8(b). A higher price of X in the world market means that greater quantities of X are exported. Quantity of exports OX_6 in Figure 1-9 corresponds to quantity of exports X_3X_4 in Figure 1-8(b). At this new, higher relative price of Good X, Good Y is relatively lower priced. Therefore, quantity of imports OY_6 in Figure 1-9, which equals quantity Y_4Y_3 in Figure 1-8(b), is greater than quantity of imports OY_5. The volume of trade at prices $(P_X/P_Y)_2$ is thus represented by Point T'.

We have now obtained two points on this country's offer curve. We can visualize the remainder of the curve by mentally constructing trade triangles in Figure 1-8 for every set of possible prices. The sides of these trade triangles would be plotted in Figure 1-9 and be indicated by illustrative Points T'' and T'''. The construction of the offer curve is completed by connecting all possible points at which a country is willing to trade. We label the resulting curve as OC_I and designate the country as Country I.

The most useful feature of the offer curve diagram is that it can bring two trading countries together in one diagram. To accomplish this, the offer curve of Country I's trading partner, Country II, needs also to be developed. There is nothing new analytically about Country II's offer curve. The trade triangles for that country are plotted in the same manner as those for Country I. The only difference is that Country II exports Good Y and imports Good X. Thus, Country II's offer curve appears as the curve OC_{II} in Figure 1-10. This curve reflects Country II's willingness to trade at alternative relative prices. Of course, a lower P_X/P_Y means that Country II has a greater willingness to trade, because a lower relative price for Good X means a greater incentive for Country II's consumers to import it. Similarly, a lower P_X/P_Y means a relatively higher price of Good Y, leading to a greater willingness by Country II to export it.

1.7.2 Equilibrium Terms of Trade

With the two countries' offer curves brought together in one figure, we can indicate the trading equilibrium and show the equilibrium terms of trade. The horizontal axis indicated exports of Good X for Country I and imports of Good X for Country II. Similarly, the vertical axis indicates Country I's imports of Good Y and Country II's exports of Good Y. Trading equilibrium occurs at Point E, and the equilibrium terms of trade, TOT_E, are indicated by the slope of the ray from the origin passing through E.

Why is Point E the trading equilibrium? At Point E, the quantity of exports that Country I wishes to sell (OX_E) exactly equals the quantity of imports that Country II wishes to buy (also OX_E). In addition, the quantity of imports that Country I wishes to buy (OY_E) equals exactly the quantity of exports that Country II wishes to sell (also OY_E). Thus, the relative price $(P_X/P_Y)_E$ is the market-clearing price, since the demand for and supply of Good X in the world market are equal, as are the demand for and the supply of Good Y.

Let us explore economically why TOT_E is the market-clearing price ratio. Suppose in Figure 1-10, the world prices are not at TOT_E but at some lower relative price of TOT_1. At this set of price, Country I would like to trade at Point

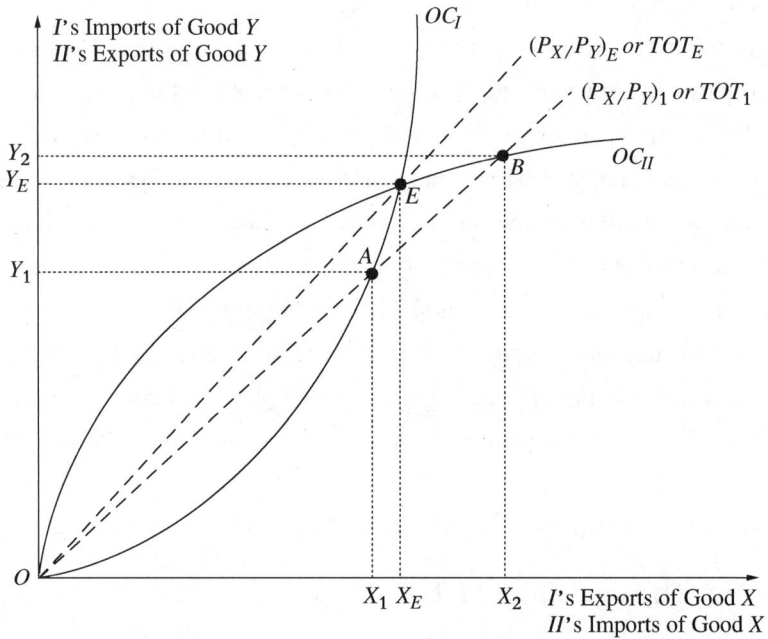

Figure 1-10   Trading Equilibrium

A, that is, it would like to sell OX_1 of Good X and buy OY_1 of Good Y. However, at this lower relative price of Good X, Country II would like to trade at Point B. It would like to buy OX_2 of Good X and sell OY_2 of Good Y. Therefore, at TOT_1, there is an excess demand for Good X which will bid up its price in the world market, while an excess supply of Good Y will bid down its price. With these changes in price, the relative price ratio $(P_X/P_Y)_1$ will rise, which means that the price line becomes steeper. As it does, both the excess demand for Good X and the excess supply of Good Y will be reduced. The price line will continue to rise until both the excess demand and the excess supply are eliminated at the equilibrium point E. It should be noted that in this two-commodity model, an excess demand for one good means that there must be an excess supply of the other; equilibrium in one good's market means that equilibrium exists in the other good's market, too.

Shifts of Offer Curves

The determination of the above equilibrium relative prices is carried out under the assumption that offer curves are fixed for each country. What we have done is develop a "snapshot" of the trading situation at a particular point in time. In practice, however, offer curves do not stay fixed. As time passes, changes in the two countries lead to changes in offer curves.

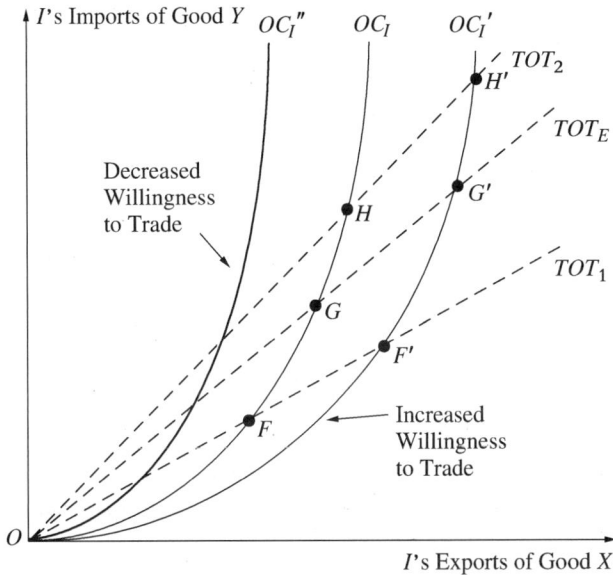

Figure 1-11　Shifts in Country I's Offer Curve

Suppose after reaching equilibrium as shown in Figure 1-10, the consumers of Country I change their tastes and decide that they would like to purchase more of Good Y. Since Y is the import, this means an increase in demand for imports. Country I now has greater willingness to trade and its offer curve will shift to reflect this change. The shift is analogous to an increase in demand in the ordinary demand-supply diagram. An increased willingness to trade in the offer curve analysis means that, at each possible terms of trade, the country is willing to supply more exports and demand more imports. In Figure 1-11, the offer curve shifts diagonally to the right from OC_I to OC_I'. Note that the shift is accomplished by plotting a point farther out on each potential price line than was originally plotted. A shift could occur of course for reasons other than a change in tastes for the imported good. Other reasons could include a rise in income that leads to an increased demand for imports or an improvement in productivity in Country I's export industries that causes an increased supply of exports. Similarly, a decrease in willingness to trade or a decrease in reciprocal demand is indicated by offer curve OC_I'', where the curve has shifted or pivoted inward to the left. This decrease could reflect a change in tastes away from the imported good, a decline in national income, or, of particular importance, the imposition of a tariff by Country I. An analogous procedure applies to Country II.

When offer curves shift, the equilibrium terms of trade and volume of trade change. These changes reflect the alteration of underlying market conditions. Suppose that Country I and Country II are in initial equilibrium in Figure 1-12 at TOT_E and at trading volumes OX_E of Good X and OY_E of Good Y. Now suppose that there is a shift in tastes by Country I toward its import Good Y. As noted above, this change in tastes will cause the offer curve OC_I to shift to OC_I'. With the increase in Country I's willingness to trade, the previous terms of trade, TOT_E, are no longer sustainable. TOT_E results in excess demand for Good Y and, correspondingly, excess supply of Good X. Country I is willing to buy OY_2 of Good Y and offer OX_2 of Good X in exchange. However, Country II has experienced no change in its offer curve, and it is willing to supply only OY_E of Good Y and offer OX_E of Good X at TOT_E. With excess demand of $Y_E Y_2$ for Good Y and the excess supply of $X_E X_2$ for Good X, the price of Y will rise in the world market and the price of X will fall. This change in relative price will continue until the excess demand for Y and the excess supply of X are eliminated at new equilibrium point E' with terms of trade TOT_1.

The change in terms of trade means that the price of the good that Country I sells has fallen relative to the price of the good that it buys; alternatively, the price of the good that Country I buys has increased relative to the price of the good that it sells. The economic explanation for the rise in the relative price of the imported good is that Country I's consumers value Good Y more highly than before and increase the demand for Good Y. Thus, with an unchanged supply schedule of exports of Country II, the price of the good has been bid up. The increased desire for imports has raised the volume of imports from the original OY_E to OY_1, and the quantity of exports exchanged for the new import quantity is OX_1, a larger amount

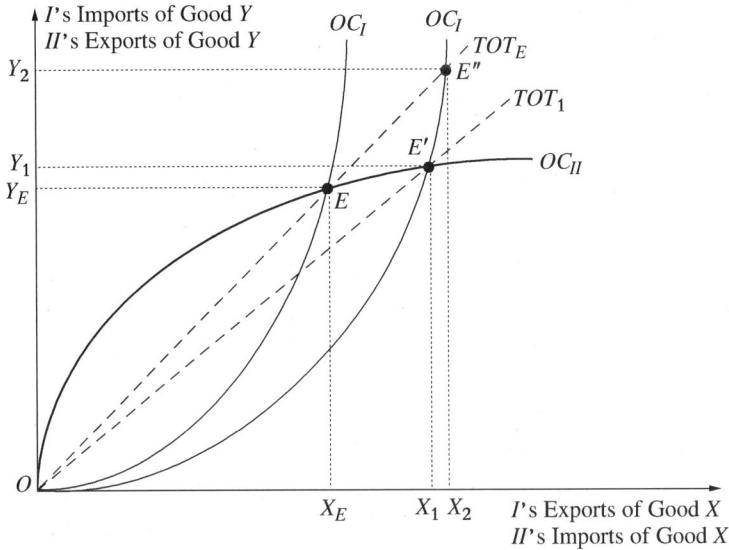

Figure 1-12   Increased Demand for Imports by Country *I*

than the original OX_E.

Obviously, other shifts could take place, and you need to reason how they would be handled in the offer curve diagram. For example, a decreased willingness to trade by Country *I* would shift its offer curve to the left and lead to higher (P_X/P_Y) and a smaller volume of trade. Further, an increased willingness to trade by Country *II* would shift its offer curve upward and, with no change in Country *I*'s offer curve, would also lead to higher equilibrium (P_X/P_Y). A decreased willingness to trade by Country *II* would shift its offer curve downward and produce a fall in (P_X/P_Y) and a reduction in the volume of trade.

Terms of Trade Estimates

The relative price ratio (P_X/P_Y) in the offer curve diagram is called as the commodity terms of trade, or net barter terms of trade, or simply, the terms of trade. The commodity terms of trade for any particular country are defined as the price of that country's exports divided by the price of its imports. Thus, the TOT for Country *I* would be (P_X/P_Y), while for Country *II* it would be P_Y/P_X. The economic interpretation of the terms of trade is that, as the price of exports rises relative to the price of imports, each unit of a country's exports is able to purchase a larger quantity of imports. Thus, more imports, which like any other goods bring utility to consumers, can be obtained with a given volume of exports, and the country's welfare on the basis of those price relations alone has improved.

In calculating the terms of trade for any given country, we need to recognize that a country exports and imports many goods. A price index must therefore be calculated for exports and imports. The price index is a weighted average of the prices of many goods, calculated for comparison with a base year. A base year for the exported price (P_X) and import price (P_Y) indices must be chosen. The base-year price indices are then set at values of 100, and other years can be compared with them.

Table 1-10 gives the commodity terms of trade for selected countries. With the year 1995 as the base year (index equal to 100), the table shows that by 2000 Greek index of export prices was 114, an increase of 14 percent. During the same period, the index of Greek import prices rose by 8 percent, to a level of 108. We find that Greek terms of trade rose by 6 percent $[(114/108) \times 100 = 106]$ over the period 1995-2000. This means that to purchase a given quantity of imports, Greece had to sacrifice 6 percent fewer exports; conversely, for a given number of exports, Greece could obtain 6 percent more imports.

Table 1-10   Commodity Terms of Trade, 2000 (1995 = 100)

Country	Export Price Index	Import Price Index	Terms of Trade
Greece	114	108	106
Switzerland	76	73	104
Canada	101	98	103
United Kingdom	89	87	102
Australia	86	86	100
United States	96	99	97
Japan	89	93	96
Germany	92	99	93

Source: International Monetary Fund, *IMF Financial Statistics*, Washington, DC, November 2001.

The commodity terms of trade are a useful concept. Over a long period, it illustrates how a country's share of the world gains from trade changes and gives a rough measure of the fortunes of a country in the world market. Table 1-11 shows historical movements in the commodity terms of trade for the industrial countries, oil-exporting countries, and non-oil-exporting developing countries.

Table 1-11   Commodity Terms of Trade: Annual Changes, in Percentages

Year	Industrial Countries	Oil-Exporting Countries	Non-Oil-Exporting Developing Countries
1983-1992 (average)	1.1	-7.5	-0.6
1993	2.0	-7.7	-0.7
1995	0.4	6.1	2.1
1997	-0.6	-0.6	-0.9
1999	0.1	31.2	-0.3
2000	-2.7	41.9	-2.5

Source: International Monetary Fund, *World Economic Outlook*, Washington, DC, October 2001.

1.7.3   Other Concepts of the Terms of Trade

Income Terms of Trade

A country's income terms of trade, sometimes judged to be more useful than the commodity terms of trade from an economic development perspective, are the commodity terms of trade multiplied by a quantity index of exports, that is, TOT_Y $= (P_X/P_M) \times Q_X$ or $(P_X \times Q_X)/P_M$. They are thus an index of total export earnings or value $(P_X \times Q_X)$ divided by the price index of imports (P_M). This measure attempts to quantify the trend of a country's export-based capacity of imported goods, as opposed to only the price relations between exports and imports. A rise in TOT_Y indicates that the country's export earnings now permit the country to purchase a greater quantity of imports. For developing countries, capital- and technology- intensive imports yield a stream of output in the future and can be critical for the development effort. A rise in TOT_Y can be very beneficial.

Single Factoral Terms of Trade

The single factoral terms of trade (TOT_{SF}) relate import price trends to productivity growth of the factors of production. The TOT_{SF} concept is the commodity terms of trade multiplied by an index of productivity in the export industries, that is, $TOT_{SF} = (P_X/P_M) \times O_X$, where O_X is the productivity index. If the single factoral terms of trade rise, the economic interpretation is that a greater quantity of imports can be obtained for a given unit of work effort in producing exports. In other words, a rise means that more imports can be purchased for a given amount of employment time of the factors of production in the export industries.

Calculation of the TOT_{SF} suffers from the difficulty of generating accurate productivity indexes. Since productivity generally tends to increase over time, TOT_{SF} will tend to show a more favorable (or less favorable) trend for any given country than will the commodity terms of trade.

Double Factoral Terms of Trade

The final TOT concept adjusts the single factoral terms of trade for productivity trends in a country's trading partners. Thus, the double factoral terms-of-trade ratio (TOT_{DF}) is the single factoral terms of trade divided by the index of productivity in the export industries of the trading partners, that is, $TOT_{DF} = (P_X/P_M) \times (O_X/O_M)$, where O_M represents the foreign productivity index for the home country's imports. A rise in TOT_{DF} indicates that given quantities of services of the home country's factors of production in its export industries are being exchanged for a greater quantity of the services of the factors of production in export industries in trading partner countries. In this sense, the exchange of factors between the partners has become more favorable for the home country. They have been occasionally calculated in practice, but the empirical difficulty of obtaining data on the productivity of foreign factors of production must be added to the difficulty of obtaining data on the productivity of home factors of production.

Chapter 2

New Classical Theories of International Trade

Key Concepts and Terms

Specific Factor Model	特定要素模型
Specific Factor	特定要素
Mobile Factor	流动要素
Value of Marginal Product (VMP)	边际产品价值
Marginal Product (MP)	边际产品
Factor Endowment Theory	要素禀赋理论
Heckscher-Ohlin Model	赫克歇尔—俄林模型
Capital-abundant Country	资本充裕国家
Land-abundant Country	土地充裕国家
Capital-intensive Product	资本密集产品
Land-intensive Product	土地密集产品
Rybczynski Theorem	罗伯津斯基定理
Factor Price Equalization Theory	要素价格均等化理论
Stolper-Samuelson Theorem	斯托尔帕—萨缪尔森定理
Leontief Paradox	列昂惕夫悖论
Input-output Table	投入—产出表

In Chapter 1, we have learned the difference in productivities causes international trade to occur. But where comes the productivity difference? This chapter tells us the answer lies in the difference in factor endowments.

2.1 Specific Factor Model

In the long run, factors may move across industries. But in the short run, moving labor across industries may require some length of time as workers might need to acquire new or different skills. In a large country such as China, this movement of labor may also require workers to relocate to another part of the country. Although not impossible, these work force adjustments take time. Moving capital from one industry in the economy to another industry may also be even more difficult. For example, capital equipment designed to produce machines may not be easily adapted to produce cloth. In the long run, reallocating capital from the cloth industry to the machine industry may mean expanding capital in the machine industry only as existing capital in the cloth industry wears out. In this way, new capital investment over time would eventually reallocate the capital between the two industries. Factor mobility between industries is realistic in the long run, but in the short run, factors of production may be somewhat immobile.

With imperfect factor mobility between industries, the gains and losses resulting from trade to the factors of production need to be modified. To examine why the payments received by the factors of production depend on the mobility of the factors of production, we return to our example. Assume that there are three factors of production: capital used to produce machines, capital used to produce cloth, and labor that can be used to produce either machines or cloth. Capital in this case is called a **specific factor** because its use is specific to either the production of machines or the production of cloth and cannot move between industries. Labor is called a variable or **mobile factor** because over time it can move between machine production and cloth production.

Remember, when trade opens up between the U.S. and India, the machine industry expands and the cloth industry contracts, both capital and labor in this industry suffer losses as employment contracts and factories are shut down. In the expanded machine industry, both labor and capital benefit as employment and profits increase. In fact, these initial industry-specific effects often dominate the political debate over trade policy within a country.

Now, suppose that labor can move between industries and capital is immobile between industries. In Figure 2-1, Point E illustrates the before-trade equilibrium for the U.S. In the figure, the total supply of labor in the U.S. is shown along the horizontal axis. The amount of labor employed in the machine industry is measured from the origin O rightward along the axis. In each industry, labor is combined with a fixed amount of specific capital to produce either cloth or machines. Under these conditions, labor is subject to diminishing returns in each industry. This means that the demand for labor in each industry is downward sloping and is equal to the value of the marginal product (VMP) of labor. (The value of the marginal product of labor is equal to the price of the product times the marginal product (MP) of labor.) The machine industry's demand for labor is represented by D_M, and the cloth industry's demand for labor is represented by D_C. (The cloth industry's demand for labor is measured leftward from O'.) By assuming that labor is mobile between industries, both the machine industry and the cloth industry will pay the same wage rate, W_0. This equilibrium occurs when OL labor is employed in the machine industry and $O'L$ labor is employed in the cloth industry.

When trade opens up between the U.S. and India, machine prices increase in the U.S., causing the demand for labor in the machine industry to increase to D_M'. (We illustrate the impact of trade on the labor market within the U.S. by allowing the price of machine to increase while the price of cloth has remained constant.) As a result, the machine production expands; employment decreases in the cloth industry and wage increases from W_0 to W_1.

The owners of the specific capital used to produce machines continue to benefit as the industry expands production. The owners of the specific capital used to produce cloth lose as production contracts. The effect on the mobile factor, labor, is uncertain. The price of machine has increased more than wages. Because of trade, U.S. labor faces higher machine prices and lower cloth prices. Whether workers are better or worse off depends on their consumption pattern. If labor consumes more machines than cloth, labor will be worse off as their real wage has decreased. If the reverse is true, labor will be better off. Thus, the mobile factor, labor, may gain or lose depending on its consumption pattern.

The results arising from the existence of specific factors are short-run effects. These short-run effects will diminish over time as factors of production move into

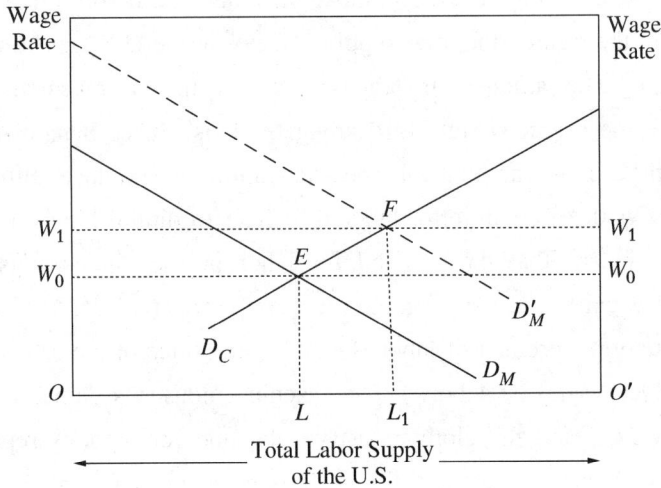

Figure 2-1 Specific Factor Model

the industry that has a comparative advantage. In the long run, the abundant factor of production (capital in the U.S.) gains, and the scarce factor of production (labor in the U.S.) loses. The difference is that some owners of sector-specific factors experience gains (owners of capital used to produce machines) or losses (owners of capital used to produce cloth) in the short run. Even with the existence of specific factors, the economy as a whole gains from trade.

The existence of specific factors can help explain why some groups resist free trade. In general, owners of the abundant factor of production in a country should be in favor of looser restrictions. With specific factors of production, both capital and labor in the industry with a comparative disadvantage suffer losses and may well resist free trade.

2.2　Factor Endowment Theory (H-O Model)

The Ricardian principle of comparative advantage explains why specialization and trade lead to gains for producers and consumers. It does not, however, in itself explain why the production possibilities frontiers (PPF) have different shapes from country to country, and thus why a country's comparative advantage is in one product rather than another.

Ricardo thought that comparative advantage depended on comparative differences in labor productivity — that is, differences in technology. However, he did not explain the basis for these differences. Ricardo essentially assumed the existence of comparative advantage in his theoretical model. Moreover, Ricardo's assumption of a single factor of production (labor) ruled out the explanation how trade affects the distribution of income within a country and why certain groups favor free trade, whereas other groups oppose it.

In the 1920s and 1930s, Swedish economists Eli Heckscher and Bertil Ohlin formulated a theory addressing two questions left largely unexplained by Ricardo: (1) What determines comparative advantage? (2) What effect does international trade have on the earnings of various factors of production (distribution of income) in trading countries? Because Heckscher and Ohlin maintained that factor (resource) endowments underlie a country's comparative advantage, their theory became known as the **factor endowment theory**. It is also known as the **Heckscher-Ohlin Model**, and Ohlin was awarded the 1977 Nobel Prize in economics for his contribution to the theory of international trade.

The factor endowment theory states that comparative advantage is explained exclusively by differences in relative national supply conditions. In particular, the theory highlights the role of countries' resource endowments (such as labor and capital) as the key determinant of comparative advantage. The theory implies that Brazil exports coffee because it has an abundance of the soil and climatic conditions required for coffee production; the United States and Canada export wheat because they are endowed with an abundance of temperate-zone land, which is well suited for wheat production; and India and China are huge exporters of shoes and garments because they are heavily endowed with labor.

The factor endowment theory relies on several simplifying assumptions: (1) countries have the same tastes and preferences (demand conditions); (2) they use factor inputs that are of uniform quality; and (3) they use the same technology. The last assumption is made explicitly to neutralize the possibility that trade is based on international technological variations by favoring the possibility that trade is based solely on differences in supplies of labor and capital.

According to the factor endowment theory, relative price levels differ among countries because (1) the countries have different relative endowments of factor inputs and (2) different commodities require that the factor inputs be used with different intensities in their production. Given these circumstances, a country will export that commodity for which a large amount of the relatively abundant (cheap) input is used. It will import that commodity in the production of which the relatively scarce (expensive) input is used. That is why land abundant countries (such as Australia) export labor-intensive goods, such as textiles.

The factor endowment theory is illustrated in Figure 2-2, which shows the PPFs of France and Germany. Assume that auto production is capital-intensive, requiring much capital and little land; wheat production is assumed to be land-intensive, requiring much land and little capital. Suppose that capital is relatively abundant in Germany and that land is relatively abundant in France. The abundance of capital in Germany causes its PPF to be biased toward the auto axis; the abundance of land in France causes its PPF to be biased toward the wheat axis.

According to the factor-endowment theory, demand conditions are assumed to be identical for each country. This is illustrated in Figure 2-2 by the community indifference curves (Curve I and Curve II) which are common for both France and Germany. In Figure 2-2(a), the points where community indifference curve I is tangent to the PPFs of Germany and France indicate the equilibrium locations for both countries. In the absence of trade, Germany locates at Point G on its PPF and France at Point F on its PPF. The relative price ratios at these points suggest that Germany has the comparative advantage in producing autos and France has the comparative advantage in producing wheat.

Figure 2-2(a) depicts the following assertion of the Heckscher-Ohlin model: Given identical demand conditions and input productivities, differences in the relative abundance of resources determine relative price levels and the pattern of trade. Capital is relatively cheaper in the capital abundant country, and land is relatively cheaper in the land abundant country. The capital abundant country thus exports the capital intensive product, and the land abundant country exports the land-intensive product.

Refer now to Figure 2-2 (b). With trade, each country continues to specialize in the production of the commodity of its comparative advantage until its commodity price equalizes with that of the other country. Specialization in production continues until France reaches F' and Germany reaches G', the points at which each country's PPF is tangent to the common relative price line t_1.

With trade, France maximizes its welfare by exchanging 10 bushels of wheat for 12 autos and achieves post-trade consumption at Point H along community indifference curve II. Similarly, Germany exchanges 12 autos for 10 bushels of wheat and achieves post-trade consumption at Point H. With trade, both countries achieve higher levels of satisfaction (community indifference curve II) than without trade (community indifference curve I).

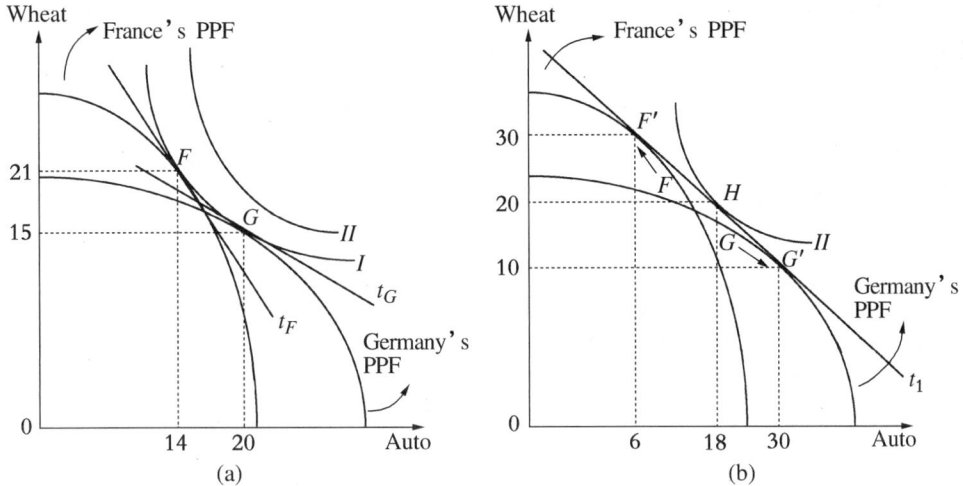

Figure 2-2 Comparative Advantage According to the Factor Endowment Model

In summary, the factor endowment model asserts that the pattern of trade is explained by differentials in resource endowments. A capital abundant country will have a comparative advantage in a capital-intensive product, while a labor abundant country will have a comparative advantage in a labor-intensive product. Here, we illustrate some examples of factor intensities for a variety of U.S. industries. See the following table.

Table 2-1 Capital/Labor Ratio: U.S. Industries, Selected Years
(Thousands of 1972 Dollars)

Industry	1960	1980	2000
Apparel	1.5	3.2	8.3
Chemicals	30.4	58.9	85.9
Electrical machines	6.4	13.0	35.3
Fabricated metals	8.7	13.2	22.1

continued

Industry	1960	1980	2000
Furniture	4.6	7.6	10.4
Instruments and related products	6.5	13.3	27.2
Leather products	2.3	4.3	14.6
Miscellaneous manufacturing	4.1	9.7	14.6
Nonelectrical machines	9.0	14.6	25.9
Paper products	20.2	38.4	58.9
Petroleum and coal	93.8	161.2	266.7
Primary metals	26.5	37.1	71.0
Printing and publishing	10.2	11.9	16.9
Rubber and plastics	10.3	18.8	24.7
Stone, clay, grass products	16.2	26.7	35.6
Textiles	8.4	14.3	27.3
Tobacco manufactures	9.0	31.9	100.1
Transportation equipment	10.5	20.3	21.3
Average	15.3	27.4	47.6

Source: E. R. Berndt & D. O. Wood, *Energy Price and Productivity Growth: A Survey*, working paper.

A number of interesting points emerge as we study the results in the table. First, there is considerable variation in capital/labor ratios across industries. In 1960, values for this ratio ranged from as low as in the apparel industry of $1,500 of capital per worker to as high as in the petroleum-and-coal industry of $93,800 of capital per worker. In 2000, these industries also represented the extremes in capital per worker, with the ratio in the apparel industry being $8,300 and the petroleum-and-coal ratio being $266,700 per worker. A second point to note is that over time, the capital/labor ratio has increased in all industries. This result reflects the fact that, for many, the capital stock of U.S. has increased more rapidly than the labor force. Third, the raking by industry has shown no dramatic changes over the forty-year period shown in the study.

2.3   Other New Classical Theories

In addition to the H-O Model which predicts the direction of comparative advantage, several other important theories explain economic behaviors in countries engaged in international trade. These theories refer to issues such as the effect of economic growth on trade and the impact of trade on the distribution of income in an economy.

2.3.1   Rybczynski Theorem

At constant world prices, if a country experiences an increase in the supply of one factor, it will produce more of the product whose production is intensive in that factor and less of the other product.

Accordingly, if Country A were to increase its capital stock above its initial endowment, holding everything else constant, it would produce more Good S than before and less Good T. This example is illustrated in Figure 2-3. Growth in Country A's capital stock leads to an outward shift in its PPF. Most of this shift occurs along the S axis, because S is in the capital-intensive industry. The new production point (after growth has occurred) is given by Point X_1, the point on the new PPF where its slope is equal to the (fixed) world price ρ.

Because S is Country A's exported good, an increase in the size of Country A's capital stock would lead producers in Country A to expand their exports. Conversely, if Country A's labor force were to increase, holding all other things constant, including world prices and the size of Country A's capital stock, Country A would produce more T relative to S and trade less.

The intuition behind the Rybczynski theorem is straightforward. It basically implies that the way in which a country grows has an impact on the production and trade mixes of the country. Countries with low savings rates that invest little in new plants and equipment will tend to produce and trade labor-intensive goods. Countries with high savings and investment rates will tend to produce and trade more capital-intensive goods.

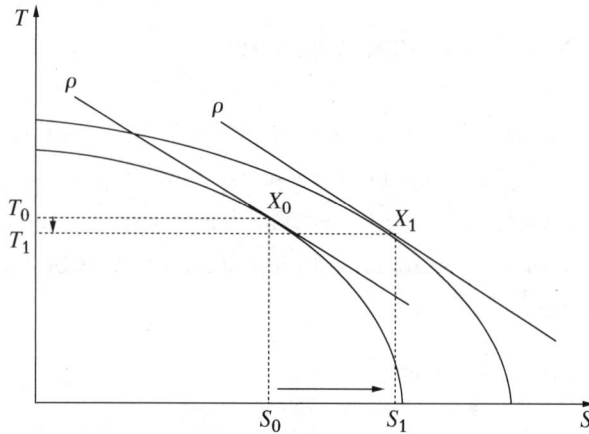

Figure 2-3　The Effect of an Increase in Country A's Capital Stock

2.3.2　Factor Price Equalization Theory

Perhaps the most controversial theory of the H-O model is concerned with the effect of international trade on factor prices. This theory is known as the **factor price equalization** theory.

Given all the assumptions of the H-O model, free international trade will lead to the international equalization of individual factor prices.

In other words, in countries that have high wages before trade begins, there will be tendency for wages to fall. In countries with initially low wages, trade will produce tendency for wages to rise. Under the strict assumptions of the H-O model, these tendencies will continue until the equalization of wages is achieved. The same will be true for rental rates on capital.

To understand this theory better, Let us try to prove that it is true. Recall our assumptions. Country A is assumed to be abundant in capital and scarce in labor. This would suggest that, initially, wages are high in Country A, while rents are low. In Country B, where capital is scarce and labor is abundant, we would expect just the opposite situation initially. Now, let trade occur. In Country A, there will be a tendency for the output of S to increase and for the output of T to contract. S industry employs relatively more capital per worker than T industry does. Consequently, there will be an initial mismatch between industry S's increased demand for factors and the factors that actually become available to S

industry as T industry contracts. In particular, we would expect that T would keep idle more labor and less capital than S initially desires. Hence, in factor markets there are an excess supply of labor at the initial wage and an excess demand for capital at the existing rental rate. For restoring equilibrium, we would expect that wages would fall in Country A, while rents would rise there.

We see from this discussion that there is a tendency for wages (rents) to fall when they are initially high and to rise when they are initially low. How do we know that they will equalize? The answer is simple. International trade leads to a common (product) price worldwide. We have assumed that markets are competitive and that technology is identical. Since each country will continue to produce some of both goods, and these goods will be produced at the same price using the same technology, it is straightforward to conclude that factor prices will equalize.

It is important to note how strict the conditions are for factor price equalization to occur. In particular, all of the assumptions of the H-O model must hold perfectly. The most important two are the assumptions of no barriers to trade and of access to identical technology. If workers everywhere have the same productivity, then free trade guarantees that they will earn the same wage. However, if there are restrictions on the ability to trade, then some workers may earn more than their equally productive foreign counterparts.

There are some supports, however, for the main predictions of the theorem. A recent study by Dan Ben-David examines how lowering trade barriers between countries has affected income levels in different countries. His analysis focuses on the effect of lowering trade barriers in Western Europe following the formation of the European Union. He shows in his study that trade liberalization leads to a marked reduction in the dispersion of incomes across countries. Since the technologies available to each of the countries in the study are quite similar, Ben-David's findings are in line with the model.

The factor price equalization theory predicts that some factor payments will rise and others fall with the introduction of trade. The next theory spells out in more detail the winners and losers from trade.

2.3.3   Stolper-Samuelson Theorem

Free international trade benefits the abundant factor and harms the scarce factor. To understand the implications of this theory, let us return to our proof of the factor price equalization theory. There, we showed that wages fall in Country A, the labor-scarce country, and rise in Country B, the capital scarce country. This, in fact, proves the theory.

The abundant factor enjoys an increase in its payment for productive efforts, while the scarce factor loses. The intuition behind this result is straightforward. Why are wages initially high in Country A? Because labor is relatively scarce and hence can exploit its scarcity power in the factor market. The introduction of international trade means that manufacturers using scarce labor in Country A must now compete with manufacturers using more abundant labor in Country B. International competitive pressures tend to force down wages in Country A. Thus, even though labor is immobile between countries, its price is equalized through competitive bidding for its services, embodied in the production of goods.

What are the implications of the Stolper-Samuelson theorem? First, we now have found the reason why some groups in a community oppose free international trade. In the classical model, international trade benefits everyone. This is true because no adjustment in wages is required to guarantee full employment as workers are displaced from import-competing industries toward export industries. In the H-O model, scarce factors must agree to a cut in their compensation to remain employed (in either industry).

The Stolper-Samuelson theorem provides insights into why governments may impose barriers to trade. Clearly, workers who expect their wages to fall because of trade should oppose trade. Similarly, so should capitalists in capital-scarce countries. Consequently, we would expect that scarce factors lobby their respective governments for measures to restrict the volume of international trade that could occur. On the other hand, abundant factors are apt to lobby for free trade policies.

Finally, it is important to remember that even though some interest groups lose from international trade, the country as a whole gains from international trade relative to autarky. After trade is established, each country consumes a bundle of goods that would have been unavailable in autarky. This implies a higher standard of living for each economy as a whole. To put it simply, the gainers gain from trade more than the losers lose. This is an interesting result that has a potential policy implication. It should be possible to develop a system of taxation and transfers that could compensate the losers for their loss while leaving the gainers better off than they would be in autarky. Such a system has never been implemented, but attempts at such programs (though highly imperfect) have been made in the United States and elsewhere.

2.3.4　Explaining Wage Inequality

As we have learned, economic theory suggests that free trade tends to undermine the real wages of those toward the bottom of income distribution. According to the H-O Model, the United States would export goods that are intensive in the use of its abundant factor (skilled labor) and import goods that intensively use its scarce factor (unskilled labor). Moreover, trade liberalization would reduce the wages of the scarce factor and increase those of the abundant factor. In other words, additional export opportunities would bid up wages of those primarily producing exported goods while increased competition from imports would tend to bid down wages of workers producing import-competing goods.

Economists agree that some combination of trade, technology, education, immigration, and union weakness has held down wages for unskilled workers. But blames are still tough, partly because income inequality is so pervasive. During the 1990s, economists attempted to disentangle the relative contributions of trade and other influences on the wage discrepancy between skilled workers and unskilled workers. Their approaches shared the analytical framework shown in Figure 2-4. This framework views wages of skilled workers "relative" to those of unskilled workers as the outcome of the interaction between supply and demand in the labor market.

The vertical axis of Figure 2-4 shows the wage ratio which is the wage of skilled workers divided by the wage of unskilled workers. The figure's horizontal axis shows the labor ratio, which equals to the quantity of skilled workers available divided by the quantity of unskilled workers. Initially, we assume that the supply curve of skilled workers relative to unskilled workers is fixed and is

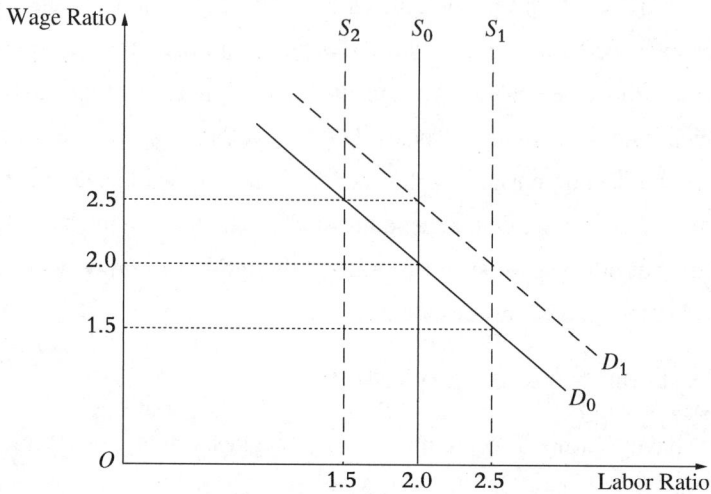

Figure 2-4 Inequality of Wages between Skilled and Unskilled Workers

denoted by S_0. The demand curve for skilled workers relative to unskilled workers is denoted by D_0. The equilibrium wage ratio is 2.0, found at the intersection at the supply and demand curves. It suggests that the wages of skilled workers are twice as much as the wages of unskilled workers.

In the figure, a shift in either the supply curve or demand curve of skilled workers available relative to unskilled workers will induce a change in the equilibrium wage ratio. Let us consider factors that can affect wage inequality.

• *International trade and technological change.* Trade liberalization and falling transportation and communication costs result in an increase in the demand curve of skilled workers relative to unskilled workers, say, to D_1 in Figure 2-4. Assuming a constant supply curve, the equilibrium wage ratio rises to 2.5, suggesting that the wages of skilled workers are 2.5 times as much as the wages of unskilled workers. Similarly, skill-biased technological improvements lead to an increase in the demand for skilled workers, thus promoting higher degrees of wage inequality.

• *Immigration.* Immigration of unskilled workers results in a decrease in the supply of skilled workers relative to unskilled workers. Assuming that the demand curve is constant, as the supply curve shifts from S_0 to S_2, the equilibrium wage ratio rises to 2.5, thus intensifying wage inequality.

• *Education and training.* As the availability of education and training increases, so does the ratio of skilled workers to unskilled workers, as seen by the increase in the supply curve from S_0 to S_1. If the demand curve remains constant, then the equilibrium wage ratio will fall from 2.0 to 1.5. Additional opportunities for education and training thus serve to reduce the wage inequality between skilled and unskilled workers.

To sum up, by increasing the demand for skilled workers relative to unskilled workers, expanding trade or technological improvements result in greater inequality of wages between skilled and unskilled workers. Also, immigration of unskilled workers intensifies wage inequality by decreasing the supply of skilled workers relative to unskilled workers. However, expanding opportunities for college education results in an increase in the supply of skilled workers relative to unskilled workers, thus reducing wage inequality.

2.4   Leontief Paradox

Perhaps the most famous test for the H-O Model in the history is the test conducted by Wassily Leontief in the early 1950s. At the time of conducting this test, Leontief was a member of the faculty at Harvard. He was already a world-famous economist, known especially for his empirical modeling of general equilibrium systems. The chief tool used in his analyses was an input-output table, a formulation so important that it won for him a Nobel Prize in economics in 1973.

An **input-output table** describes the flows of goods and services between every sector of the economy. Each industry in an economy depends upon other industries for its raw materials and intermediate inputs. For instance, computer production requires steel, plastics, semiconductors, paper (for packaging), and even computer services (for design and the like). Similarly, production in virtually every industry requires the use of computers. Thus, the computer industry buys products from other industries and also sells products to these same industries. Similar relationships between industries are found across every sector of an economy. An input-output table details these interindustry transactions that occur in the production process.

Leontief built his input-output table using data from 200 different U. S.

industries. In addition to the interindustry detail described in the table, the model detailed the labor and capital requirements of each of the 200 industries. During World War II, Leontief served as a consultant to the U.S. government, and the model was used extensively to plan production decisions for the economy. At the end of the war, however, economic planning by the government was no longer required. Consequently, Leontief turned his attention toward applying his model to new uses. One such use was to test the general validity of the H-O model.

At first, it might not seem very clear how one could use an input-output table to test the H-O model. In fact, the procedure is relatively simple and straightforward. Leontief began with data of U.S. exports and imports for 1947. He then considered the following experiment. Suppose that U.S. exports were decreased proportionately by $1 million and U.S. imports were increased proportionately by $1 million. What would be the capital and labor requirements necessary to carry out this change in production levels?

Before revealing the results of the test, let us first expect what Leontief might have found. Clearly, the United States in 1947 was the dominant economy in the world. The war had left the U.S. capital stock untouched, and had helped to rejuvenate the U.S. economy from the depression that had preceded the war. All of this would seem to imply that the United States, at least at that point in history, might well have been the most capital abundant country in the world. If so, the H-O model predicts that the United States should export capital intensive goods and import labor-intensive goods. In such a situation, Leontief's experiment would show that the amount of capital per worker idled by a hypothetical reduction in U.S. exports would exceed the amount of capital per worker needed to produce a hypothetical expansion of U.S. import-competing products. However, what Leontief found was exactly the opposite!

Using his input-output table with data for 1947, Leontief showed that to replace $1 million of U.S. imports by domestic output expansion would require 170 additional years per worker of labor and $3.1 million of capital. Reducing U.S. exports by $1 million would provide 182.3 years per worker of labor and $2.6 million in capital. Thus, according to the experiment, U.S. exports tended to be labor intensive relative to U.S. imports. Because this finding was so unexpected, it has become known as the **Leontief paradox**.

As its name suggests, the Leontief paradox was one of the most puzzling and troubling empirical findings ever uncovered by economists. From its first theoretical development, the H-O model had been regarded by economists as the most useful model to explain comparative advantage. The logical completeness of the model, its seeming agreement with casual observations about the trade flows, and the ease with which it could be manipulated to study the effects of trade on other aspects of the economy (e.g., factor payments), all served to enhance the model's reputation among economists. Then suddenly, the model appeared to be unable to explain trade patterns even in the presumably unambiguous case of the United States.

Attempted Reconciliations of Leontief's Findings

Not surprisingly, the immediate reaction among many economists was to attempt to resurrect the model by developing explanations for the Leontief paradox within the context of the model. Leontief was the first to try this. He argued that his results were due to the fact that the implicit assumption of the model that American workers were of equal productivity to their foreign counterparts was incorrect. Leontief's suggested reconciliation was to argue that because American workers were so productive relative to workers in the rest of the world, the United States should more properly be viewed as being relatively labor abundant. Under these alternative circumstances, then, Leontief's findings become consistent with the H-O Model.

How does Leontief's reconciliation square with the facts? Leontief was clearly guessing about the relative superiority of American labor. He had made his claim based on a presumption that the production orientation of American society, with its emphasis on entrepreneurship and organization, as well as the general education system, would produce relatively more efficient workers.

Jaroslav Vanek argued that tests based on a simple two-factor (capital and labor) model would be bound to produce the kind of results found by Leontief. This would be true because an important third factor, natural resources, had been omitted from the analysis. Vanek's argument proceeds as follows. Suppose the United States is relatively scarce in natural resources but relatively abundant in labor and capital. Under these circumstances, the H-O model would predict that the United States should import natural-resource-intensive products. But Leontief was not covering this in his data. Furthermore, natural resources, such as minerals, tend to be produced using capital-intensive techniques (e.g., mining and smelting). In this fashion the paradox may be explained. On a two-factor basis, U.S. imports appeared to be relatively capital intensive. On a three-factor basis, in fact, these products were relatively natural-resource intensive.

W. P. Travis, in the early 1960s, argued that the Leontief paradox could be explained by the prevailing U.S. tariff structure. Specifically, U.S. tariffs on labor-intensive products tended to be high, often exceeding 25 percent. Tariffs on capital-intensive products tended to be lower. This tariff structure, Travis claimed, could lead to a distortion in U.S. trade patterns away from natural comparative advantage, toward imports of relatively capital-intensive goods.

Another suggested reconciliation offered at the time was that the international equality of tastes could hold. The H-O model assumes tastes are identical across countries. As we have showed, if this is not the case, trade need not flow along the lines suggested by the H-O model. One way to test the hypothesis that tastes are identical is to examine consumption patterns across countries. Only limited statistics are available. What data there are, however, seem to suggest that expenditure patterns differ. Consider, for instance, the information presented in Table 2-2. This table summarizes consumption data for the year 1975 collected and first published by the United Nations.

The table illustrates a wide diversity of expenditure patterns that exist across countries. For instance, Indians spend almost 60 percent of their total consumption expenditures on food, while only about 14 percent of U.S. consumption is devoted to food. Similarly, the French and Dutch spend 11 percent of consumption on medical care, while the British spend only 1 percent. While some differences should be expected due to the fact that tariffs, transportation costs, and many government policies change relative prices from one country to the next, it is almost surely the case that the international equality of tastes is violated.

Table 2-2 Extremes in Consumption Patterns across Countries

(Percentages of Total Private Consumption Devoted to Each Category) [1]

Category	High	Low	Average[2]
Food	India (59.7)	United States (14.4)	33.3
Beverages	Ireland (14.4)	Libya (1.1)	5.1
Tobacco	Sri Lanka (6.6)	France (0.9)	2.9
Clothing and shoes	Ghana (14.2)	Jamaica (4.3)	8.8
Rent, fuel, power	Israel (20.7)	Sri Lanka (6.8)	13.6
Furniture	Belgium (15.0)	Korea (3.2)	8.4
Medical care	Netherlands and France (11.2)	United Kingdom (1.0)	4.9
Transportation and communication	Cyprus (19.6)	Philippines (2.2)	11.2
Recreation	Singapore (12.3)	Sri Lanka (2.6)	6.8

[1] Data are based on information from national account statistics for 39 countries for the year 1975.

[2] Numbers are computed as simple averages for the individual levels of the 39 countries.

Source: Compiled from information in Leamer, *Sources of International Comparative Advantage: Theory and Evidence*, Bosten: MIT Press, 1984, Table 1.6, p.40.

Finally, one additional explanation should not be neglected. In his tests, Leontief used the U.S. input-output table to construct the factor requirements for both U.S. exports and U.S. import-competing goods. The assumption he then made was that foreign goods would be produced using technologies identical with those found in U.S. import-competing industries. While this assumption is consistent with the identical-technology assumption of the H-O model (the technology sets available to each country are identical), it is true in the H-O model only if factor prices are equalized internationally or if there is no possibility for industries in different countries to substitute between labor and capital in the production process as factor prices change. If these conditions fail to hold (which is certainly the case) and if labor is relatively more expensive in the United States than in the rest of the world (which was probably the case at the time of his study), then Leontief's procedure would estimate that U.S. imports are relatively more capital intensive than the techniques actually used to produce these goods in the rest of the world. This is true because foreign producers, reacting to their relatively lower labor costs, use more labor-intensive production methods than those are employed in the United States, where labor is relatively more expensive.

Chapter 3

Modern Trade Theories

Key Concepts and Terms

Economies of Scale	规模经济
Interindustry Trade	产业间贸易
Intraindustry Trade	产业内贸易
Intraindustry Specialization	产业内分工
Homogeneous Goods	同质商品
Technological Gap Theory	技术差距理论
Product Life Cycle Theory	产品生命周期理论
Theory of Overlapping Demands	重叠需求理论
Product Differentiation	产品差异
Monopolistically Competitive Market	垄断竞争市场
Oligopoly	寡头
Average Cost	平均成本
Marginal Cost	边际成本
Marginal Revenue	边际收益
Reciprocal Dumping Model	相互倾销模型
Price Discrimination	价格歧视

Though the theories we learned in the previous chapters have given clear explanations for interindustry trade, that is, each country exports and imports quite different products, about one-fifth of the world trade consists of intraindustry trade, that is, two-way exchanges of goods within standard industrial classifications. Intraindustry trade plays a particularly large role in the trade in manufactured goods among advanced industrial countries which accounts for most of world trade. Over time, the industrial countries have become increasingly similar in their levels of technology and in the availability of capital and skilled labor. Since the major trading countries have become similar in technology and resources, there is often no clear comparative advantage within an industry, and much of international trade therefore takes the form of two-way exchanges within industries — probably driven in large part by economies of scale — rather than interindustry specialization driven by comparative advantage.

3.1   Existence of Intraindustry Trade

Interindustry trade is based on interindustry specialization: Each country specializes in a particular industry (say, steel) in which it enjoys a comparative advantage. As resources shift to the industry with a comparative advantage, some other industries having comparative disadvantages (say, electronics) will contract. Resources thus move geographically to the industry where comparative costs are lowest. As a result of specialization, a country experiences a growing dissimilarity between the products that it exports and the products that it imports.

Although some interindustry specialization occurs, this generally has not been the type of specialization that industrialized countries have undertaken in the post-World War II era. Rather than emphasizing entire industries, industrial countries have adopted a narrower form of specialization. They have practiced intraindustry specialization, focusing on the production of particular products or groups of products within a given industry (for example, subcompact autos rather than autos). With intraindustry specialization, the opening up of trade does not generally result in the elimination or wholesale contraction of entire industries within a country. However, the range of products produced and sold by each country changes.

Advanced industrial countries have increasingly emphasized **intraindustry trade** — two-way trade in a similar commodity. For example, computers manufactured by IBM are sold abroad, while the United States imports computers produced by Hitachi of Japan. Table 3-1 provides examples of intraindustry trade for the United States. As the table indicates, the United States is involved in two-way trade in many manufactured goods such as chemicals and motor vehicles.

Table 3-1　Intraindustry Trade in the U.S., 2002（in Billion of Dollars）

Category	Exports	Imports
Motor vehicles	60.39	168.1
Electrical machinery	82.7	81.2
Office machines	39.7	76.9
Telecommunications equipment	24.9	66.3
Power-generating equipment	34.4	34.0
Industrial machinery	31.8	35.2
Scientific instruments	29.2	20.9
Transportation equipment	46.1	20.2
Chemicals	16.8	30.2
Apparel and clothing	8.0	63.8

Source: U. S international Trade Administration, *U.S. Manufacturers Trade 1997-2002*, at http://www. ita. doc. gov. See also U. S Department of Commerce, Bureau of Economic Analysis, *U. S Trade in Goods 2000*, at http://www. bea. doc. gov.

　　The existence of intraindustry trade appears to be incompatible with the models of comparative advantage previously discussed. In the Ricardian and Heckcher-Ohlin models, a country would not simultaneously export and import the same product. However, take California for instance. It is a major importer of French wines as well as a large exporter of its wines. Intraindustry trade involves flows of goods with similar factor requirements. Countries that are net exporters of manufactured goods embodying sophisticated technology also purchase such goods from other countries. Much of intraindustry trade is conducted among industrial countries, especially those in Western Europe whose resource endowments are similar. The firms that produce these goods tend to be oligopolies, with a few large firms constituting each industry.

　　Intraindustry trade includes trade in homogeneous goods as well as in differentiated products. For homogenous goods, the reasons for intraindustry trade are easy to grasp. A country may export and import the same product because of transportation costs. Canada and the United States, for example, share a border of several thousand miles. To minimize transportation costs (and thus total costs), a buyer in Albany, New York, may import cement from a firm in Montreal, Quebec, while a manufacturer in Seattle, Washington, sells cement to a buyer in

Vancouver, British Columbia. Such trade can be explained by the fact that it is less expensive to transport cement from Montreal to Albany than to ship cement from Seattle to Albany.

Another reason for intraindustry trade in homogeneous goods is seasonal. The seasons in the Southern Hemisphere are opposite to those in the Northern Hemisphere. Brazil may export seasonal items (such as agricultural products) to the United States at one time of the year and import them from the United States at another time during the same year. Differentiation in time also affects electricity suppliers. Because of heavy fixed costs in electricity production, utilities attempt to keep plants operating close to full capacity, meaning that it may be less costly to export electricity at off-peak times when domestic demand is inadequate to ensure full-capacity utilization, and import electricity at peak times.

Although some intraindustry trade occurs in homogeneous products, available evidence suggests that most intraindustry trade occurs in differentiated products. Within manufacturing, the levels of intraindustry trade appear to be especially high in machinery, chemicals, and transportation equipment. A significant share of the output of modern economies consists of differentiated products within the same broad product group. Within the automobile industry, a Ford is not identical to a Honda or a Toyota. Two-way trade flows can occur in differentiated products within the same broad product group.

For industrial countries, intraindustry trade in differentiated manufactured goods often occurs when manufacturers in each country produce for the "majority" consumer tastes within their country while ignoring "minority" consumer tastes. This unmet need is fulfilled by imported products. For example, most Japanese consumers prefer Toyotas to General Motors vehicles; yet some Japanese consumers purchase vehicles from General Motors, while Toyotas are exported to the United States. Intraindustry trade increases the range of choices available to consumers in each country, as well as the degree of competition among manufacturers of the same class of product in each country.

Intraindustry trade in differentiated products can also be explained by overlapping demand segments in trading countries. When U.S. manufacturers look overseas for markets in which to sell, they often find them in countries having market segments that are similar to the market segments in which they sell in the

United States, for example, luxury automobiles sold to high-income buyers. Countries with similar income levels can be expected to have similar tastes, and thus sizable overlapping market segments; they would be expected to engage heavily in intraindustry trade.

Besides marketing factors, economies of scale associated with differentiated products also explain intraindustry trade. A country may enjoy a cost advantage over its foreign competitor by specializing in a few varieties and styles of a product (for example, subcompact autos with a standard transmission and optional equipment), while its foreign competitor enjoys a cost advantage by specializing in other variants of the same product (subcompact autos with automatic transmission, air-conditioning, cassette player, and other optional equipment). Such specialization permits longer production runs, economies of scale, and decreasing unit costs. Each country exports its particular type of auto to the other country, resulting in two-way auto trade.

With intraindustry specialization, fewer adjustment problems are likely to occur than with interindustry specialization, because intraindustry specialization requires a shift of resources within an industry instead of between industries. Interindustry specialization results in a transfer of resources from import-competing to export-expanding sectors of the economy. Adjustment difficulties can occur when resources, notably labor, are occupationally and geographically immobile in the short run; massive structural unemployment may result. In contrast, intraindustry specialization often occurs without requiring workers to exit from a particular region or industry (as when workers are shifted from the production of large-size automobile to subcompacts); the probability of structural unemployment is thus lessened.

3.2   Technological Gap, Product Life Cycle and International Trade

Before the emergence of the theories of technological gap and product cycle, the international trade theories have only studied the trading behavior statically. They only explained the causes of trade and the distribution of benefits. However, the initial trade theories couldn't make reasonable explanations on some economical phenomenon. For example, the importing and exporting countries and districts vary with time, and the U. S. once was both the large car exporting country and car importing country.

3.2.1 Technological Gap Theory

The traditional trade theories haven't taken into account the technology change, while technology is one of the most important determinants of one country's economical activities and trade pattern. R. Posner, an American economist, put forward the technological gap theories in 1961 and tried to explain the international trade problems from the perspective of technology changes.

Different countries don't conform with each other in technological progress. The countries with advanced technology can enjoy the comparative advantage of exporting tech-intensive products, stand in the monopolistic status around the world market and become the main manufacturing countries and exporting countries. When some country has developed the new products through technological innovation, it may export such products to other countries by means of the comparative advantage formed by the technological gap. Such technological gap will continue until the foreign countries can grasp the advanced technology gradually through the import of this new product or technology cooperation. And the technological gap will not disappear until the importing countries can use their native cheap labor to imitate production and export. The innovating country will invent new technology, process new products, and export in quantity to earn monopolistic profits. Then it can produce a new technological gap. At the same time, the foreign producers continue to imitate, produce and export. With the circles on, trade continues steadily. Thus, technological gap is the real cause of international trade and determines the flow of international trade.

R. Posner thought that there is a time lag from the introduction of new technology or the development of new products to the consumers' response in foreign countries. In Posner's analysis, the process of such response lag can be divided into the demand lag of consumers and imitation lag of producers (See Figure 3-1). The stage of **demand lag**, T_0-T_1, means the time lag from the invention of new products in innovating countries to the acceptance of importing countries, which depends on income factors and the consumers' cognition of new

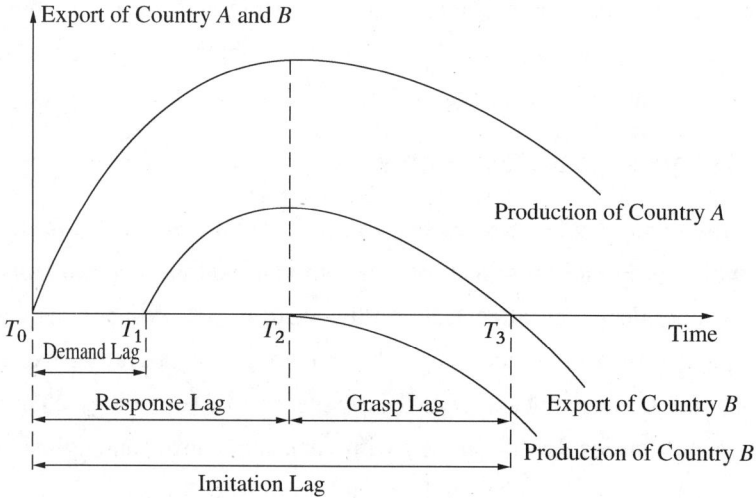

Figure 3-1 The Period of Technological Gap

products in imitation countries. The stage of **imitation lag**, T_0-T_3, means the time interval from the invention of new products in innovating countries to generic production until the import is zero. After this, imitation countries will export on the basis of low costs. The stage of imitation lag can be divided into response lag and grasp lag. The stage of **response lag**, T_0-T_2, means the time lag from the invention of new products to imitation of importing countries, which depends on the response of manufacturers in imitation countries and the scale economy, price, market and tariffs, etc. The stage of **grasp lag**, T_2-T_3, is from imitation to no import until the generic production can meet domestic demand and turn to export, which depends on the imitation country's access to technology channels and the ability to digest technology. T_1-T_3 is the trading period caused by technological gap. During this period, the earlier innovator can make more benefits through export to the countries whose demand lag is smaller than response lag.

The technological gap theory explains the causes of trade among different countries from the perspective of comparative advantage, and proves that leading technology can form comparative advantage even among the countries with close endowments and tastes. However, this theory hasn't explained the transfer of trade flow and the causes of the emergence and disappearance of technological gap. Thus, Vernon put forward the product life cycle theory.

3.2.2   Product Life Cycle Theory

In 1966, Vernon, an American economist, put forward the theory of product cycle. He advocates that products have life cycle just similar with life form. The life cycle of products means all products will experience the course of innovation, growth, maturity and decline. The introduction of new products requires highly skilled workers. When the product is matured, widespread and standardized, a lot of technologies will flow to machines and production assembling lines and only the non-skilled workers hold the production. Then, comparative advantage will transfer from advanced inventing countries to backward countries with low labor cost. Such transfer may be caused by foreign direct investment of inventing countries. Therefore, inventing countries produce and export products before standardization, while lagging countries produce and export after standardization. The transfer of comparative advantages can be divided into three stages:

   • *The stage of new products.* Technology is at the stage of invention, which needs advanced scientific knowledge and a large amount of research and development funds. The new products are so knowledge-intensive that few countries have strength to own comparative advantage of new products. Hence, new products usually arise in a few developed countries.

   • *The stage of mature technique.* The main goal is mass production. Equipment and skilled labor are then needed. The products turn from knowledge-intensive to technology-intensive or resource-intensive. Countries abundant in capital and skilled labor begin to enjoy the comparative advantage of production and become the main manufacturer and exporter taking the place of inventing countries.

   • *The stage of standardization.* On one hand, the new technique has gone through the life cycle and entered into machinery and production assembling line, so the production course is normalized and the operation becomes simpler. On the other hand, the machinery itself has also become standardized products and turns cheaper. Thus, technique and capital have lost importance to this stage, while the labor cost has become one of the main determinants of comparative advantage. The products become labor-intensive then. The comparative advantage of the product has transferred to developing countries abundant in labor.

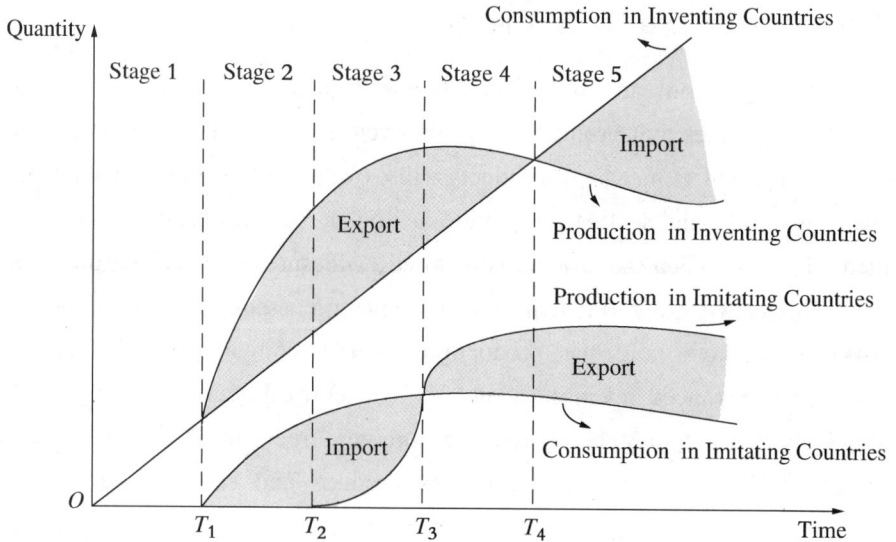

Figure 3-2　Model of Product Life Cycle

In Figure 3-2, the life cycle of the product can be divided into five stages. The first stage (O-T_1) is the introduction of new products. New products could only be produced and consumed in inventing countries, and arise in developed countries as well. The successful research of new products not only needs a lot of R & D fees and qualified labor, but also needs favorable environment for innovation and the required capacity for new products. Nevertheless, all these are lacking in developing countries. In other words, developed countries have the comparative advantage in technology. Once the products are exported, they can earn monopolistic profits in international trade. The second stage (T_1-T_2) is the growing period of products. The new products have been improved in inventing countries and begin to export to foreign countries. Because the foreign countries haven't begun to imitate, the inventing countries still monopolize in the international market. During the first two stages, the products need a lot of input of technique and labor, so the products are knowledge (tech)-intensive. The gap of technological innovation has become the determinant of trade pattern. The third stage (T_2-T_3) is the maturing period of products. The production in innovating countries has become standardized and the input of capital has increased heavily, which make the products more capital-intensive. As the demand continues to increase, in addition to continual production and export of the innovating countries, other foreign manufacturers begin to imitate and meet part of the native consumer demand but still need to import. Now the capital-intensive technique gap has become the main cause of trade. At the fourth stage (T_3-T_4) , because the products have been standardized and don't require skilled labor, the innovating country can manufacture the identical cheaper products than the inventing country by native cheap non-skilled labor, sell in the international market and compete with inventing country. Price competition leads the output of the inventing country to decrease and technological gap vanishes gradually. Then, technology and brand will give place to cost and price advantage, which makes the developing countries abundant in cheap labor own comparative advantage during production. At the fifth stage (after T_4) , imitation countries begin to sell products to the inventing country, and the output of the inventing country will decrease so substantially as to come to a full stop. And the life cycle of the products will finish. Inventing countries will restart to invent innovative technologies and products. The fourth and fifth stages are declining stages of products when the products have become the labor-intensive and the wage gap of non-tech labor has been the real cause of trade.

From Figure 3-2, we can see that comparative advantage transfers or spreads from innovating countries to countries densely using the cheap factors. The flow of trade reversed to that of the comparative advantage. Namely, more technology transmission and diffusion, more products will flow to the innovating country and those countries with similar technology.

As time passes, the manufacturer realizes that he should locate production operation closer to the foreign markets in order to protect his export profits. The domestic industry enters its mature stage as innovating businesses establish branches abroad. A reason for locating production operations abroad is that the cost advantage initially enjoyed by an innovator is not likely to last indefinitely. Over time, the innovating country may find its technology becoming more commonplace. At the same time, transportation costs and tariffs begin to play an increasingly important role in influencing selling costs. The innovator may also find that the foreign market is large enough to permit mass-production operations.

Although an innovating country's monopoly position may be prolonged by legal patents, it is likely to be broken down over time, because knowledge tends to be a free good in the long run. The benefits an innovating country achieves from its technological gap are short-lived, as import competition from foreign producers begins. Once the innovative technology becomes fairly commonplace, foreign producers begin to imitate the production process. The innovating country gradually loses its comparative advantage, and its export cycle enters a declining phase.

The trade cycle is complete when the production process becomes so standardized that it can be easily used by other countries. The technological breakthrough therefore no longer benefits the innovating country only. In fact, the innovating country may itself become a net importer of the product as its monopoly position is eliminated by foreign competition. Textiles and paper products are generally considered to have run the full course of the trade cycle. The spread of automobile production into many parts of the world implies that its production process is close to becoming standardized.

3.3　Theory of Overlapping Demands

The relationship between demand conditions and international trade patterns has been analyzed by Staffan Linder. According to Linder, the factor endowment theory has considerable explanatory power for trade in primary products (natural resources) and agriculture goods, not for trade in manufactured goods, because the main force influencing manufactured-good is domestic demand conditions. Because much of international trade involves manufactured goods, demand conditions play an important role in explaining overall trade patterns.

Linder states that firms within a country are generally motivated to manufacture goods for which there is a large domestic market. This market determines the set of goods that these firms will have to sell when they begin to export. The foreign markets are with consumer tastes similar to those of domestic consumers. A country's exports are thus an extension of production for the domestic market.

Going further, Linder contends that tastes of consumers are conditioned strongly by their income levels. Thus, a country's average or per capita income will yield a particular pattern of tastes. Countries with high per capita incomes will demand high-quality manufactured goods (luxuries), while countries with low per capita incomes will demand low-quality manufactured goods (necessities). The Linder hypothesis explains which types of countries will most likely trade with each other. Countries with similar per capita incomes will have overlapping demand structures and will likely consume similar types of manufactured goods. Wealthy (industrial) countries will likely trade with other wealthy countries, and poor (developing) countries will likely trade with other poor countries. The Linder hypothesis is thus known as the **theory of overlapping demands**.

Linder does not rule out all trade in manufactured goods between wealthy and poor countries. Because of unequal income distribution within countries, there will always be some overlapping of demand structures; some people in poor countries are wealthy, and some people in wealthy countries are poor. However, the potential for trade in manufactured goods is small when the extent of demand overlap is limited.

Linder's theory is in rough accord with the facts. A high proportion of international trade in manufactured goods takes place among the relatively high-income (industrial) countries: Japan, Canada, the United States, and the European countries. Moreover, much of this trade involves the exchange of similar products: Each country exports products that are much like the products it imports.

3.4   Economies of Scale, Imperfect Competition, and International Trade

The analysis of trade based on economies of scale presents certain problems that we have so far avoided. Up to now we have assumed that markets are perfectly competitive, so that all monopoly profits are always competed away. When there are increasing returns, however, large firms usually have an advantage over small ones, so that markets tend to be dominated by one firm (monopoly) or, more often, by a few firms (oligopoly). When increasing returns enter the trade picture, then, markets usually become imperfectly competitive.

3.4.1 Economies of Scale and International Trade

The models of comparative advantage are based on the assumption of constant returns to scale. That is, we assume that if inputs to an industry are doubled, industry output would double as well. In practice, however, many industries are characterized by economies of scale (also referred to as increasing returns), so that the more efficient production is, the larger the scale at which it takes place. Where there are economies of scale, doubling the inputs to an industry will more than double the industry's production.

A simple example can help convey the significance of economies of scale for international trade. Table 3-2 shows the relationship between input and output of a hypothetical industry. Widgets are produced using only one input, labor. The table shows how the amount of labor required depends on the number of widgets produced. To produce 10 widgets, for example, requires 15 hours of labor, while to produce 25 widgets requires 30 hours. The presence of economies of scale may be seen from the fact that doubling the input of labor from 15 to 30 more than doubles the industry's output — in fact, output increases 2.5 times. Equivalently, the existence of economies of scale may be seen by looking at the average amount of labor used to produce each unit of output: If output is only 5 widgets, the average labor input per widget is 2 hours, while if output is 25 units, the average labor input falls to 1.2 hours.

Table 3-2   Relationship of Input to Output for a Hypothetical Industry

Output	Total Labor Input	Average Labor Input
5	10	2
10	15	1.5
15	20	1.3
20	25	1.25
25	30	1.2
30	35	1.17

We can use this example to see why economies of scale provide an incentive for international trade. Imagine a world consisting of two countries, the U.S. and the U.K., both of whom have the same technology for producing widgets, and suppose that initially each country produces 10 widgets. According to Table 3-2, this requires 15 hours of labor in each country, so in the world as a whole 30 hours of labor produces 20 widgets. But now suppose that we concentrate world production of widgets in one country, say, the U.S., and let the U.S. employ 30 hours of labor in the widget industry. In a single country, these 30 hours of labor can produce 25 widgets. So by concentrating production of widgets in the U.S., the world economy can use the same amount of labor to produce 25 percent more widgets.

But where does the U.S. find the extra labor to produce widgets, and what happens to the labor that was employed in the U.K. widget industry? To get the labor to expand its production of some goods, the U.S. must decrease or abandon the production of others; these goods will then be produced in the U.K. instead, using the labor formerly employed in the industries whose production has expanded in the U.S.. Imagine that there are many goods subject to economies of scale in production, and give them numbers: 1, 2, 3, etc.. To take advantage of economics of scale, each of the countries must concentrate on producing only a limited number of goods. Thus, for example, the U.S. might produce Goods 1, 3, 5, and so on, while the U.K. produces 2, 4, 6, and so on. If each country produces only some of the goods, then each good can be produced at a larger scale than would be the case if each country tried to produce everything, and the world economy can therefore produce more of each good.

How does international trade enter the story? Consumers in each country will still want to consume a variety of goods. Suppose that Industry A ends up in the U.S. and Industry B in the U.K.; then the U.S. consumers of Good Y will have to buy goods imported from the U.K., while the U.K. consumers of Good X will have to import it from the U.S.. International trade plays a crucial role. International trade makes it possible for each country to produce a restricted range of goods and to take advantage of economies of scale without sacrificing variety in consumption. Indeed, as well as seen below, international trade typically leads to an increase in the variety of goods available.

Our example, then, suggests how mutually beneficial trade can arise as a result of economies of scale. Each country specializes in producing a limited range of products, which enables it to produce these goods more efficiently than if it tried to produce everything for itself; these specialized economies then trade with each other so as to be able to consume the full range of goods.

How do economies of scale underline a country's comparative advantage? Adam Smith gave the answer in his 1776 classic, *The Wealth of Nations* which stated that the division of labor is limited by the size of the market. By widening the size of a firm's market, international trade permits the firm to take advantage of longer production runs which lead to increasing efficiency. An example is Boeing which has sold more than half of its jet planes overseas in recent years. Without exports, Boeing would have found it difficult to cover the large design and tooling costs of its jumbo jets, and the jets might not have been produced at all.

Figure 3-3 illustrates the effect of economies of scale on trade. Assume that a U.S. auto firm and a Mexican auto firm are each able to sell 100,000 vehicles in their respective countries. Also assume that identical cost conditions result in the same long-run average cost curve for the two firms. Note that scale economies result in decreasing unit costs over the first 275,000 autos produced.

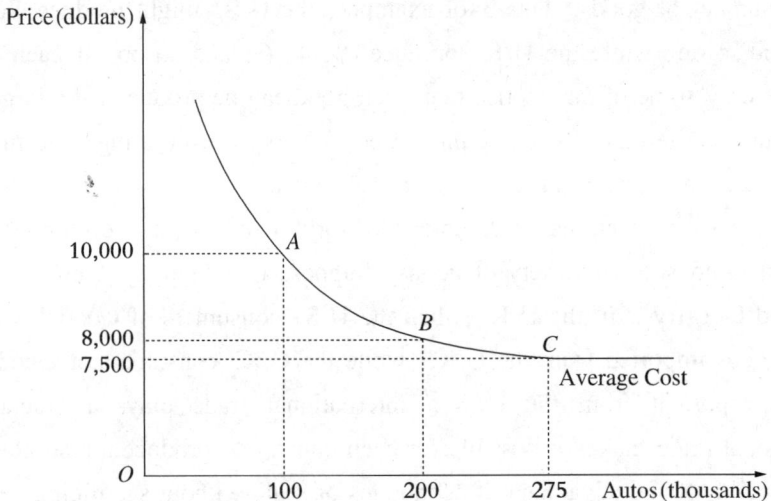

Figure 3-3   Economies of Scale as a Basis for Trade

By adding to the size of the domestic market, international trade permits longer production runs by domestic firms, which can lead to greater efficiency and reductions in unit costs.

Initially, there is no basis for trade, because each firm realizes a production cost of $10,000 per auto. Suppose that rising income in the U.S. results in demand for 200,000 autos, while the Mexican auto demand remains constant. The larger demand allows the U.S. firm to produce more output and take advantage of economies of scale. The firm's cost curve slides downward until its cost equals $8,000 per auto. Compared to the Mexican firm, the U.S. firm can produce autos at a lower cost. With free trade, the U.S. will now export autos to Mexico.

Economies of scale thus provide additional cost incentives for specialization in production. Instead of manufacturing only a few units of each and every product that domestic consumers desire to purchase, a country specializes in the manufacture of large amounts of a limited number of goods and trades for the remaining goods. Specialization in a few products allows a manufacturer to benefit from longer production runs which lead to decreasing average costs.

How might trade operate with economies of scale? Figure 3-4 represents the production possibilities frontiers (PPFs) of the U. S. and South Korea for computers and steel. Note that the two countries' PPFs are bowed inward (convex from the diagram's origin), indicating that the cost of producing steel becomes less and less in terms of computers sacrificed. At each point, the (absolute) slope of the PPF reflects the cost of steel in terms of computers sacrificed.

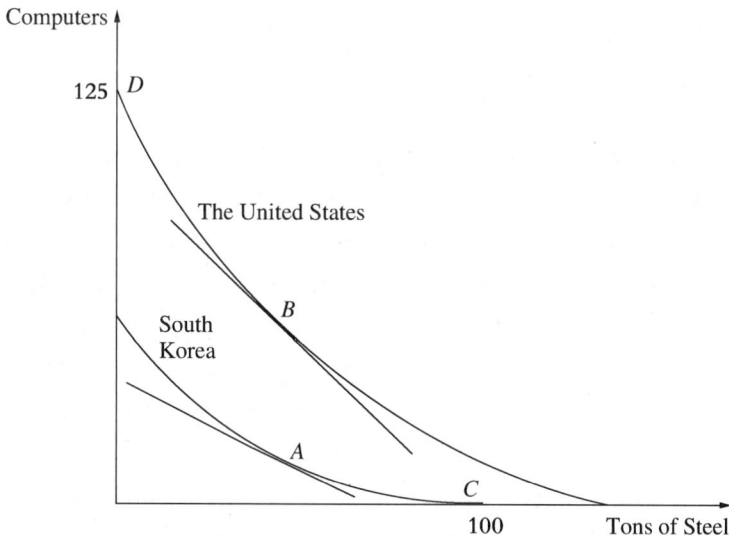

Figure 3-4　Trade and Specialization under Decreasing Costs

With deceasing costs, a country has the cost incentive to specialize completely in the period of its comparative advantage. Devoting additional resources to steel (computer) production results in economies of large-scale production and falling unit cost. With specialization, South Korea produces 100 tons of steel at Point C while the U.S. produces 125 computers at Point D.

Without trade, suppose South Korea and the U.S. desire both computers and steel. Both countries would have to manufacture some of each good at inefficient points, such as Point A for South Korea and Point B for the United States. Reflecting the (absolute) slopes of the PPFs at these points, South Korea has a comparative advantage in steel, while the U.S. has a comparative advantage in computers. The two countries should not remain for long at these inefficient production points. They can reduce costs by specializing completely in the production of the goods of their comparative advantage.

As South Korea moves to the right of Point A along its PPF, the relative cost of steel continues to decrease until South Korea totally specializes in steel production at Point C. Similarly, as the United States moves to the left of Point B along its PPF, the relative cost of computers continues to fall until the United States totally specializes in computers. Both countries can attain consumption points that are superior to those attained in the absence of trade.

3.4.2 Monopolistic Competition and Trade

Monopolistic Competition

Monopolistic profits rarely go uncontested. A firm making high profits normally attracts competitors. Thus situations of pure monopoly are rare in practice. Instead, the usual market structure in industries characterized by internal economies of scale is one of oligopoly: several firms, each of them large enough to affect prices, but none with an uncontested monopoly. However, there is a special case of oligopoly, known as monopolistic competition, which is relatively easy to analyze. Since the 1980s, monopolistic competition models have been widely applied to international trade.

In monopolistic competition models, two key assumptions are made to get around the problem of interdependence. First, each firm is assumed to be able to differentiate its product from that of its rivals. That is, because they want to buy this firm's particular product, the firm's customers will not rush to buy other firm's products because of a slight price difference. Product differentiation assures that each firm has a monopoly power in its particular product within an industry and is therefore somewhat insulated from competition. Second, each firm is assumed to take the prices charged by its rivals as given — that is, it ignores the impact of its own price on the prices of other firms. As a result, the monopolistic competition model assumes that even though each firm is in reality facing competition from other firms, it behaves as if it were a monopolist — hence the model's name.

Are there any monopolistically competitive industries in the real world? Some industries may be reasonable approximations. For example, the automobile industry in Europe, where a number of major producers (Ford, General Motors, Volkswagen, Renault, Peugeot, Fiat, Volvo — and more recently Nissan) offer substantially different yet nonetheless competing automobiles, may be fairly well described by monopolistically competitive assumptions. The main appeal of the monopolistic competition model is not, however, its realism, but its simplicity. As we will see in the next section of this chapter, the monopolistic competition model gives us a very clear view of how economies of scale can give rise to mutually beneficial trade.

Before we can examine trade, however, we need to develop a basic model of monopolistic competition. Let us therefore imagine an industry consisting of a number of firms. These firms produce differentiated products, that is, goods that are not exactly the same but that are substitutes for one another. Each firm is therefore a monopolist in the sense that it is the only firm producing its particular good, but the demand for its good depends on the number of other similar products available and on the prices of other firms in the industry.

Assumptions of the Model

We begin by decreasing the demand facing a typical monopolistically competitive firm. In general, we would expect a firm to sell more: the larger the total demand for its industry's product is, the higher prices its rivals will charge. On the other hand, we expect the firm to sell less: the greater the number of firms in the industry is, the higher its own price will be. A particular equation for the demand facing a firm that has these properties is

$$Q = S \times [\, 1/n - b \times (P - \bar{P}) \,] \qquad\qquad (3\text{-}1)$$

where Q is the firm's sales, S is the total sales of the industry, n is the number of firms in the industry, b is a constant term representing the responsiveness of a firm's sales to its price, P is the price charged by the firm itself, and $\bar{P}$ is the average price charged by its competitors.

Equation 3-1 may be rewritten as

$$Q = S/n - S \times b \times (P - \bar{P}) \qquad (3\text{-}2)$$

If $P = \bar{P}$, Equation 3-2 reduces to $Q = S/n$. If $P > \bar{P}$, then $Q < S/n$. And if $P < \bar{P}$, we have $Q > S/n$. Then Equation 3-1 may be given the following intuitive justification. If all firms charge the same price, each will have a market share. A firm charging less will occupy a larger share.

It is helpful to assume that total industry sales S are unaffected by the average price $\bar{P}$ charged by firms in the industry. That is, we assume that firms can gain customers only at each other's expense. This is an unrealistic assumption, but it simplifies the analysis and helps focus on the competition among firms. In particular, it means that S is a measure of the size of the market and that if all firms charge the same price, each sells S/n units.

Next we turn to the costs of a typical firm. Here we simply assume that total and average costs of a typical firm are described by

$$C = F + c \times Q \qquad (3\text{-}3)$$

where F is a fixed cost that is independent of the firm's output, c is the firm's marginal cost, and Q is once again the firm's output. Equation 3-3 is also called a linear cost function. The fixed cost in a linear cost function gives rise to economies of scale, because the larger the firm's output is, the less the fixed cost per unit will be. Specially, the firm's average cost is

$$AC = F/Q + c \qquad (3\text{-}4)$$

This average cost declines as Q increases, because the fixed cost is spread over a larger output.

Market Equilibrium

To model the behavior of this monopolistically competitive industry, we will assume that all firms in this industry are symmetric, that is, the demand function and cost function are identical for all firms (even though they are producing and selling somewhat differentiated products). When the individual firms are symmetric, the state of the industry can be described without enumerating the features of all firms in detail: all we really need to know to describe the industry is how many firms there are and what price the typical firm charges. To analyze the industry, for example to assess the effects of international trade, we need to determine the number of firms n and the average price they charge $\overline{P}$. Once we have a method for determining n and $\overline{P}$, we can analyze how they are affected by international trade.

Our method for determining n and $\overline{P}$ involves three steps. First, we derive a relationship between the number of firms and the average cost of a typical firm. We show that this curve is upward sloping, that is, the more firms there are, the lower the output of each firm, and thus the higher its cost per unit of output. Next, we show the relationship between the number of firms and the price each firm charges which must equal $\overline{P}$ in equilibrium. We show that this curve is downward sloping: the more firms there are, the more intense competition among firms is, and as a result, the lower the prices they charge. Finally, we argue that when the price exceeds average cost, additional firms will enter the industry,

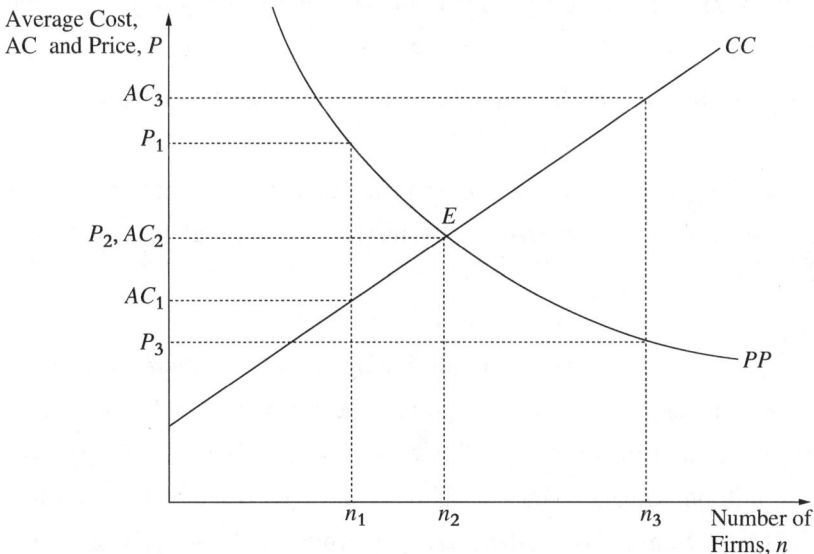

Figure 3-5　Equilibrium in Monopolistically Competitive Market

while when the price is less than average cost, firms will exit. So in the long run the number of firms is determined by the intersection of the curve that relates average cost to n and the curve that relates price to n.

The number of firms in a monopolistically competitive market, and the prices they charge, are determined by two relationships. On one side, the more firms there are, the more intensely they compete, and hence the lower is the industry price. This relationship is represented by PP. On the other side, the more firms there are, the less each firm sells and therefore the higher is its average cost. This relationship is represented by CC. If price exceeds average cost(PP curve is above CC curve), the industry will be making profits and additional firms will enter the industry; if price is less than average cost, the industry will be incurring losses and firms will leave the industry. The equilibrium price and number of firms occur when price equals average cost, at the intersection of PP and CC.

(1) *The number of firms and average cost.* As a first step toward determining n and $\overline{P}$, we ask how the average cost of a typical firm depends on the number of firms in the industry. Since all firms are symmetric in this model, in equilibrium they will all charge the same price. But when all firms charge the same price, so that $P = \overline{P}$, Equation 3-2 tells us that $Q = S/n$; that is, each firm's output Q is a $1/n$ share of the total industry sales S. But we saw in Equation 3-4 that average cost depends inversely on a firm's output. We therefore conclude that average cost depends on the size of the market and the numbers of firms in the industry:

$$AC = F/Q + c = n \times F/S + c \qquad (3\text{-}5)$$

Equation 3-5 tells us that given other things equal, the more firms there are in the industry, the higher the average cost is. The reason is that the more firms there are, the less each firm produces. For example, imagine an industry with total sales of 1 million widgets annually. If there are five firms in the industry, each will sell 200,000 annually. If there are ten firms, each will sell only 100,000, and therefore each firm will have higher average cost. The upward-sloping curve CC in Figure 3-5 shows the relationship between n and average cost AC.

(2) *The number of firms and the price.* Meanwhile, the price the typical firm charges also depends on the number of firms in the industry. In general, we would expect that the more firms there are, the more intensive the competition will be among them, and hence the lower the price will be. This turns out to be true in this model, but proving it takes a moment. The basic trick is to show that each firm faces a straight-line demand curve.

First recall that in the monopolistic competition model, firms are assumed to take each others' prices as given, that is, each firm ignores the possibility that if it charges its price, other firms will also change theirs. If each firm treats $\overline{P}$ as given, we can rewrite the demand curve in the form as follows

$$Q = (S/n + S \times b \times \overline{P}) - S \times b \times P \tag{3-6}$$

where b is the parameter that measured the sensitivity of each firm's market share to the price it charges. Now this is in the same form as $Q = A - B \times P$, with $(S/n + S \times b \times \overline{P})$ in place of the constant term A and $(S \times b)$ in place of the slope coefficient b. If we plug these values back into the formula for marginal revenue $MR = P - Q/b$, we have a marginal revenue for a typical firm of

$$MR = P - Q/(S \times b) \tag{3-7}$$

Profit-maximizing firms will set marginal revenue equal to their marginal cost, here, c, so that

$$MR = P - Q/(S \times b) = c \tag{3-8}$$

which can be rearranged to give the following equation for the price charged by a typical firm

$$P = c + Q/(S \times b) \tag{3-9}$$

We have already noted, however, that if all firms charge the same price, each will sell an amount $Q = S/n$. Plugging this back into Equation 3-9 gives us a relationship between the number of firms and the price each firm charges.

$$P = c + 1/(b \times n) \tag{3-10}$$

Equation 3-10 says algebraically that the more firms there are in the industry, the lower the price each firm will charge. Equation 3-10 is shown in Figure 3-5 as the downward-slopping curve *PP*.

(3) *The equilibrium number of firms.* Let us now ask what Figure 3-5 means. We have summarized an industry by two curves. The downward-sloping

curve PP shows that the more firms there are in the industry, the lower price each firm will charge. This makes sense: the more firms there are, the more competition each firm faces. The upward-sloping curve CC tells us that the more firms there are in the industry, the higher average cost each firm has. This also makes sense: if the number of firms increases, each firm will sell less; so firms will not be able to move as far down their average cost curve.

The two curves intersect at Point E, corresponding to the number of firms n_2. The significance of n_2 is that it is the zero-profit number of firms in the industry. When there are n_2 firms in the industry, their profit-maximizing price is p_2 which is exactly equal to their average cost AC_2.

What we will now argue is that in the long run, the number of firms in the industry tends to move toward n_2, so that Point E describes the industry's long-run equilibrium.

To see why, suppose that n were less than n_2, say n_1. Then the price charged by firms would be P_1, while their average cost would be only AC_1. Thus firms would be making monopolistic profits. Conversely, suppose that n were greater than n_2, say n_3. Then firms would charge only the price P_3, while their average cost would be AC_3. Firms would be suffering losses.

Over time, firms will enter an industry that is profitable, and exit the one in which they lose money. The number of firms will rise over time if it is less than n_2, and fall if it is greater than n_2. This means that n_2 is the equilibrium number of firms in the industry and P_2 is the equilibrium price.

We have now developed a model of a monopolistically competitive industry in which we can determine the equilibrium number of firms and the average price that firms charge. We can use this model to derive some important conclusions about the role of economies of scale in international trade. But before we do, we should take a moment to note some limitations of the monopolistic competition model.

Limitations of the Monopolistic Competition Model

The monopolistic competition model captures certain key elements of markets where there are economies of scale and thus imperfect competition. However, few industries are well described by monopolistic competition. Instead, the most common market structure is one of small group oligopoly, where only a few firms are actively engaged in competition model. That each firm will behave as if were a true monopolist is likely to break down. Instead, firms will be aware that their actions influence the actions of other firms and will take this interdependence into account.

Two kinds of behavior arise in the general oligopoly setting that is excluded by assumption from the monopolistic competition model. The first is collusive behavior. Each firm may keep its price higher than the apparent profit-maximizing level as part of an understanding that other firms will do the same. Since each firm's profits are higher if its competitors charge high prices, such an understanding can raise the profits of all the firms (at the expense of consumers). Collusive price-setting behavior may be managed through explicit agreements or through tacit coordination strategies, such as allowing one firm to act as a price leader for the industry.

Firms may also engage in strategic behavior, that is, they do things that seem to lower profits but that affect the behavior of competitors in a desirable way. For example, a firm may build extra capacity not to use it but to deter potential rivals from entering its industry.

These possibilities for both collusive and strategic behavior make the analysis of oligopoly a complex matter. There is no one generally accepted model of oligopoly behavior, which makes modeling trade in monopolistic industries problematic.

The monopolistic competition approach to trade is attractive because it avoids these complexities. Even though it may leave out some features of the real world, the monopolistic competition model is widely accepted as a way to provide at least a first cut at the role of economies of scale in international trade.

Monopolistic Competition and Trade

Underlying the application of the monopolistic competition model to trade is the idea that trade increases market size. In industries where there are economies of scale, both the variety of goods that a country can produce and the scale of its production are constrained by the size of the market. By trading with each other, and therefore forming an integrated world market that is bigger than any individual national market, countries are able to loosen these constraints. Each country can specialize in producing a narrower range of products than it would in the absence of trade; yet by buying goods that it does not make from other countries, each country can simultaneously increase the variety of goods available to its consumers. As a result, trade offers an opportunity for mutual gains even when countries do not differ in their resources or technology.

Suppose, for example, that there are two countries, each with an annual market for 1 million automobiles. By trading with each other, these countries can create a combined market of 2 million autos. In this combined market, more varieties of automobiles can be produced, at lower average costs, than in either market alone.

The monopolistic competition model can be used to show that trade improves the trade-off between scale and variety that individual countries face. We will begin by showing how a larger market leads, in the monopolistic competition model, to both a lower average price and the availability of a greater variety of goods. Applying this result to international trade, we observe that trade creates a world market larger than any of the national markets that comprise. Integrating markets through international trade therefore has the same effects as growth of a market within a single country.

The Effects of Increased Market Size

The number of firms in a monopolistically competitive industry and the prices they charge are affected by the size of the market. In larger markets, there usually will be both more firms and more sales per firm; consumers in a large market will be offered both lower prices and a greater variety of products than consumers in small markets.

To see this in the context of our model, look again at CC curve in Figure 3-5, which shows that the higher the average costs per firm are, the more firms there are in the industry. Examining Equation 3-5, we see that an increase in total sales S will reduce average costs for any given number of firms n. The reason is that if the market grows while the number of firms is held constant, sales per firm will increase and the average cost of each firm will therefore decline. Thus if we compare two markets, one with higher S than the other, CC curve in the larger market will be below that in the smaller one.

Meanwhile, PP curve in Figure 3-5, which relates the price charged by firms to the number of firms, does not shift. The definition of that curve was given in Equation 3-10. The size of the market does not enter into this equation, so an increase in S does not shift PP curve.

Figure 3-6 uses this information to show the effect of an increase in the size of the market on long-run equilibrium. Initially, equilibrium is at Point 1, with a price P_1 and a number of firms n_1. An increase in the size of the market, measured by industry sales S, shifts the CC curve downward from CC_1 to CC_2, while it has no effect on PP curve. The new equilibrium is at Point 2: The number of firms increases from n_1 to n_2, while the price falls from P_1 to P_2.

Clearly, consumers would prefer to be part of a larger market rather than a small one. At Point 2, a greater variety of products is available at a lower price than at Point 1.

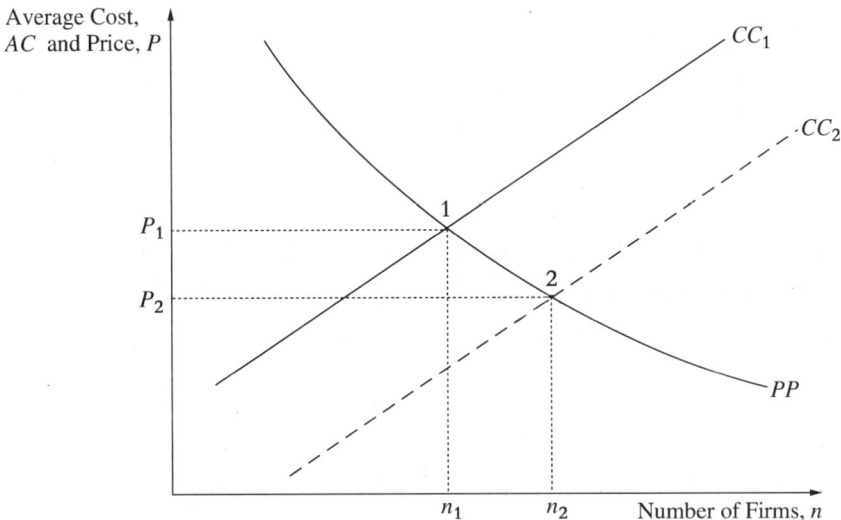

Figure 3-6   Effects of Larger Market

An increase in the size of the market allows each firm, given other things equal, to produce more and thus have lower average cost. This is represented by a downward shift from CC_1 to CC_2. The result is a simultaneous increase in the number of firms (and hence in the variety of goods available) and a fall in the price of each.

Gains from an Integrated Market: A Numerical Example

International trade can create a larger market. We can illustrate the effects of trade on prices, scale, and the variety of goods available with a specific numerical example.

Imagine that automobiles are produced by a monopolistically competitive industry. The demand curve facing any given producer of automobiles is described by Equation 3-1, with $b = 1/30,000$. Thus the demand facing any one producer is given by

$$Q = S \times [1/n - (1/30,000) \times (P - \bar{P})]$$

where Q is the number of automobiles sold per firm, S the total sales of the industry, n the number of firms, P the price that a firm charges, and $\bar{P}$ the average price of other firms. We also assume that the cost function for producing automobiles is described by Equation 3-3, with a fixed cost $F = \$750,000,000$ and a marginal cost $c = \$5,000$ per automobile. The total cost is

$$C = 750,000,000 + (5,000 \times Q)$$

The average cost curve is therefore

$$AC = (750,000,000/Q) + 5,000$$

Now suppose there are two countries, Home and Foreign. Home has annual sales of 900,000 automobiles; Foreign has annual sales of 1.6 million. The two countries are assumed, for the moment, to have the same costs of production.

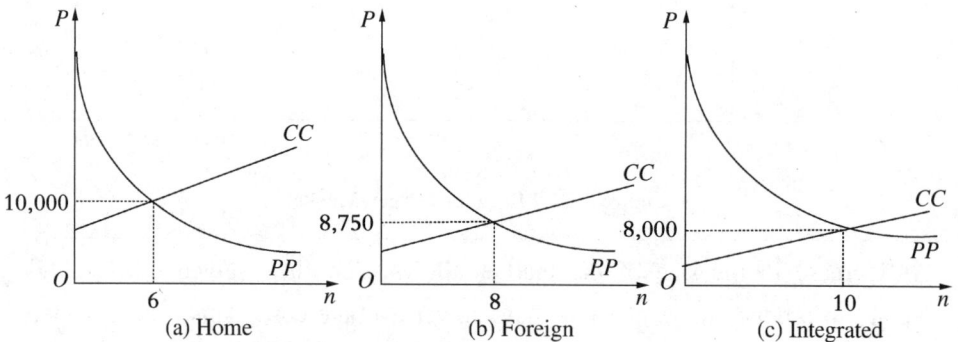

Figure 3-7　Equilibrium in the Automobile Market

(a) The home market. With a market size of 900,000 automobiles, Home's equilibrium, determined by the intersection of the *PP* and *CC* curve, occurs with 6 firms and an industry price of $10,000 per auto.

(b) The foreign market. With a market size of 1.6 million automobiles, Foreign's equilibrium occurs with 8 firms and an industry price of $8,750 per car.

(c) The combined market. Integrating the two markets creates a market for 2.5 million autos. This market supports 10 firms and the price of an auto is only $8,000.

Figure 3-7(a) shows *PP* and *CC* curves for Home's auto industry. We find that in the absence of trade, Home would have six automobile firms, selling autos at a price of $10,000 each. To confirm that this is the long-run equilibrium, we need to show that in the pricing equation 3-10.

$$P = \$10,000 = c + 1/(b \times n) = \$5,000 + 1/[(1/30,000) \times 6] = \$5,000 + \$5,000$$

So the condition for profit maximization — that marginal revenue equal marginal cost — is satisfied. Each firm sells 900,000 units/6firms = 150,000 units/firm. Its average cost is therefore

$$AC = (750,000,000/150,000) + 5,000 = \$10,000$$

Since the average cost of $10,000 per unit is the same as the price, all monopoly profits have been competed away. Thus six firms, selling each unit at a price of $10,000, with each firm producing 150,000 cars, is the long-run equilibrium in Home's market.

What about Foreign? By drawing *PP* and *CC* curves (Figure 3-7(b)) we find that when the market is for 1.6 million automobiles, the curves intersect at $n=8$, $P=8,750$. That is, in the absence of trade, Foreign's market would support 8 firms, each producing 200,000 automobiles, and selling them at a price of $8,750. We can again confirm that this solution satisfies the equilibrium conditions:

$$P = \$8,750 = c + 1/(b \times n) = \$5,000 + 1/[(1/30,000) \times 8] = \$5,000$$

+ $ 3,750

And,

$$AC = (\$ 750,000,000/200,000) + \$ 5,000 = \$ 8,750$$

Now suppose it is possible for Home and Foreign to trade automobiles with one another without transaction costs. This creates a new, integrated market (Figure 3.7(c)) with total sales of 2.5 million. By drawing PP and CC curves one more time, we find that this integrated market will support 10 firms, each producing 250,000 cars and selling them at a price of $ 8,000. The conditions for profit maximization and zero profits are again satisfied:

$$P = \$ 8,000 = c + 1/ (b \times n) = \$ 5,000 + 1/[(1/30,000) \times 10] = \$ 5,000$$
+ $ 3,000

And,

$$AC = (\$ 750,000,000/250,000) + \$ 5,000 = \$ 8,000$$

We summarize the results of creating an integrated market in Table 3-3. The table compares each market alone with the integrated market. The integrated market supports more firms, each producing at a larger scale and selling at a lower price than either national market did on its own.

Table 3-3   Hypothetical Example of Gains from Market Integration

	Home Market (Before Trade)	Foreign Market (Before Trade)	Integrated Market (After Trade)
Total sales of autos	900,000	1,600,000	2,500,000
Number of firms	6	8	10
Sales per firm	150,000	200,000	250,000
Average cost	10,000	8,750	8,000
Price	10,000	8,750	8,000

Clearly everyone is better off as a result of integration. In the larger market, consumers have a wider range of choice, yet each firm produces more and is therefore able to offer its product at a lower price.

To realize these gains from integration, the countries must engage in international trade. To achieve economies of scale, each firm must concentrate its production in one country — either Home or Foreign. Yet it must sell its output to customers in both markets. So each product will be produced in only one country and export to the other.

3.5   Reciprocal Dumping Model

The monopolistic competition model helps us understand how increasing returns promote international trade. As we noted earlier, however, this model assumes away many of the issues that can arise when firms are imperfectly competitive. Although it recognizes that imperfect competition is a necessary consequence of economies of scale, the monopolistic competition analysis does not focus on the possible consequence of imperfect competition itself for international trade.

In reality, imperfect competition has some important consequences for international trade. The most striking one is that firms do not necessarily charge the same price for goods that are exported or sold to domestic buyers.

3.5.1   Economics of Dumping

In imperfectly competitive markets, firms sometimes charge one price for a good when that good is exported and a different price for the same good when it is sold domestically. In general, the practice of charging different customers different prices is called **price discrimination**. The most common form of price discrimination in international trade is **dumping**, a pricing practice in which a firm charges a lower price for exported goods than it does for the same goods sold domestically. Dumping is a controversial issue in trade policy, where it is widely regarded as an "unfair" practice and is subject to special rules and penalties.

Dumping can occur only if two conditions are met. First, the industry must be imperfectly competitive, so that firms set prices rather than taking market prices as given. Second, markets must be segmented, so that domestic residents cannot easily purchase goods intended for export. Given these conditions, a monopolistic firm may find that it is profitable to engage in dumping.

An example may help to show how dumping can be a profit-maximizing strategy. Imagine a firm that currently sells 1,000 units of a good at home and 100 units abroad. Currently selling the good at $20 per unit domestically, it gets only $15 per unit on export sales. One might imagine that the firm would conclude that additional domestic sales are much more profitable than additional exports.

Suppose, however, that to expand sales by one unit, in either market, would require reducing the price by $0.01. Reducing the domestic price by a penny, then, would increase sales by one unit — directly adding $19.99 in revenue, but reducing the receipts on the 1,000 units that would have sold at the $20 price by $10. So the marginal revenue from the extra unit sold is only $9.99. On the other hand, reducing the price charged to foreign customers and thereby expanding exports by one unit would directly increase revenue by only $14.99. The indirect cost of reduced receipts on the 100 units that would have been sold at the original price, however, would be only $1, so that marginal revenue on export sales would be $13.99. It would therefore be more profitable in this case to expand exports rather than domestic sales, even though the price received on exports is lower.

This example could be reversed, with incentive being to charge less on domestic than foreign sales. However, price discrimination in favor of exports is more common. Since international markets are imperfectly integrated due to both transportation cost and protectionist trade barriers, domestic firms usually have a larger share of home markets that affected by their pricing than their foreign sales. A firm with a 20 percent share typically see themselves as having less monopoly power, and a greater incentive to keep their prices low, on exports than on

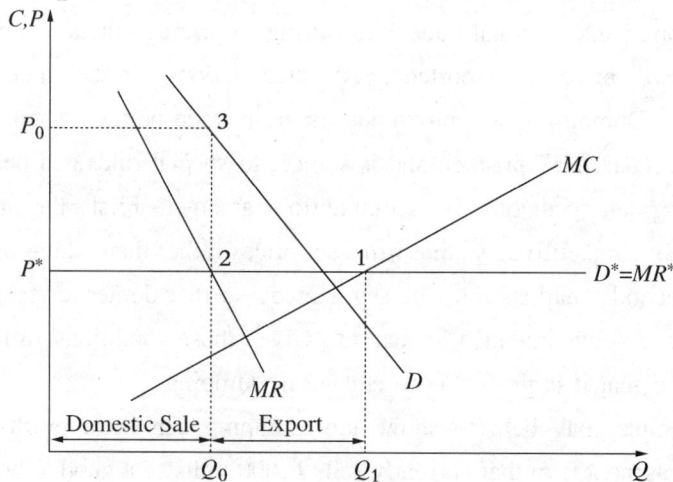

Figure 3-8   Dumping

domestic sales. A firm with a 20 percent market share need not cut its price as much to double its sales as a firm with an 80 percent share. So firms typically see themselves as having less monopoly power, and they have a greater incentive to keep their prices low, on exports rather than on domestic sales.

The figure shows a monopolist that faces a demand curve D for domestic sales, but which can also sell as much as it likes at the export price P^*. Since an additional unit can always be sold at P^*, the firm increases output until the marginal cost equals P^*; this profit-maximizing output is shown as Q_1. Since the firm's marginal cost at Q_1 is P^*, it sells output on the domestic market up to the point where marginal revenue equals P^*; this profit-maximizing level of domestic sales is shown as Q_0. The rest of its output, Q_1-Q_0 is exported. P_0 is the price at which domestic consumers demand Q_0. Since $P_0 > P^*$, the firm sells exports at a lower price than it charges domestic consumers.

Figure 3-8 offers a diagrammatic example of dumping. It shows an industry in which there is a single monopolistic domestic firm. The firm sells in two markets: a domestic market, where it faces the demand curve D, and an export market. In the export market we take the assumption that sales are highly responsive to the price the firm charges to an extreme, assuming the firm can sell as much as it wants at the price P^* which is thus the demand curve for sales in the foreign market. We assume the markets are segmented, so that the firm can charge a higher price for domestically sold goods than it does for exports. MC is the marginal cost curve for total output, which can be sold on either market.

To maximize profits, the firm must set marginal revenue equal to marginal cost in each market. Marginal revenue on domestic sales is defined by the curve MR, which lies below the domestic demand curve D. Export sales take place at a constant price P^*. To set marginal cost equal to marginal revenue in both market it is necessary to produce the quantity Q_1, to sell Q_0 on the domestic market, and to export $Q_1 - Q_0$. The cost of producing an additional unit in this case is equal to P^*, the marginal revenue from exports, which in turn is equal to the marginal revenue for domestic sales.

The quantity Q_0 will be demanded domestically at a price of P_0, which is above the export price P^*. Thus the firm is indeed dumping, selling more cheaply abroad than at home.

In both our numerical example and Figure 3-8, the reason the firm chooses to dump is the difference in the responsiveness of sales to price in the export and domestic markets. In Figure 3-8 we assume the firm can increase exports without cutting its price, so marginal revenue and price coincide on the export market. Domestically, by contrast, increased sales do lower the price. This is an extreme example of the general condition for price discrimination presented in microeconomics courses: Firms will price-discriminate when sales are more price-responsive in one market than in another.

The situation shown in Figure 3-8 is simply an extreme version of a wider class of situations in which firms have an incentive to sell exports for a lower price than the price they charge domestic customers.

3.5.2　Reciprocal Dumping

The analysis of dumping suggests that price discrimination can actually give rise to international trade. Suppose there are two monopolies, each producing the same good, one in Home and one in Foreign. To simplify the analysis, assume that these two firms have the same marginal cost. Suppose also that there are some costs of transportation between the two markets, so that if the firms charge the same price there will be no trade. In the absence of trade, each firm's monopoly would be uncontested.

If we introduce the possibility of dumping, however, trade may emerge. Each firm will limit the quantity it sells in its home market, recognizing that if it tries to sell more it will drive down the price on its existing domestic sales. If a firm can sell a little bit in the other market, however, it will add to its profits even if the price is lower than in the domestic market, because the negative effect on the price of existing sales will fall on the other firm, not on itself. So each firm has an incentive to "raid" the other market, selling a few units at a price that is lower than the home market price but still above marginal cost.

If both firms do this, however, the result will be the emergence of trade even though there is (by assumption) no initial difference in the price of the good in the two markets and there are some transportation costs. Even more peculiarly, there will be two-way trade in the same product. For example, a cement plant in Country *A* might be shipping cement to Country *B* while a cement plant in Country *B* is doing the reverse. The situation in which dumping leads to a two-way trade in the same product is known as reciprocal dumping.

This may be seen like a strange case, and it is admittedly probably rare in international trade for exactly identical goods to be shipped in both directions at once. However, the reciprocal dumping effect probably tends to increase the volume of trade in goods that are not quite identical.

Is such peculiar and seemingly pointless trade socially desirable? The answer is ambiguous. It is obviously wasteful to ship the same good or close substitutes back and forth when transportation is costly. However, notice that the emergence of reciprocal dumping in our story eliminates what were initially pure monopolies, leading to some competition. The increased competition represents a benefit that may offset the waste of resources in transportation. The net effect of such peculiar trade on a country's economic welfare is therefore uncertain.

Chapter 4

Tariffs and Nontariff Barriers

Key Concepts and Terms

Infant Industry Argument	幼稚产业论
Terms of Trade Argument	贸易条件论
Domestic Market Failure Argument	国内市场失灵论
Theory of the Second Best	次优理论
Strategic Trade Policy	战略贸易政策
Protective Tariff	保护性关税
Revenue Tariff	收入性关税
Specific Tariff	从量税
Ad Valorem Tariff	从价税
Compound Tariff	混合税
Nominal Tariff Rate	名义关税率
Effective Rate of Protection	有效保护率
Value Added	增加值
Tariff Escalation	关税升级
Consumer Surplus	消费者剩余
Producer Surplus	生产者剩余
Redistributive Effect	再分配效应
Protective Effect	保护效应
Revenue Effect	收入效应
Consumption Effect	消费效应
Terms of Trade Effect	贸易条件效应
Nontariff Trade Barriers	非关税壁垒
Import Quota	进口配额

Tariff-rate Quota	关税配额
Voluntary Export Restraint	自愿出口限制
Export Subsidy	出口补贴
Domestic Content Requirement	本国成分要求
Sporadic Dumping	偶然性倾销
Predatory Dumping	掠夺性倾销
Persistent Dumping	持续性倾销

As we have learned in the previous chapters, all countries can benefit in the long run if they take part in international specialization and free trade. They can enjoy lower prices, higher production or a wider variety of products. But in reality, restrictions on goods, services and capital flows are widespread. In this chapter, we will introduce restrictions on trade and analyze their effects on economy.

4.1   Theories for Trade Protection

4.1.1   Infant Industry Argument

One of the more commonly accepted cases for tariff protection is the **infant industry argument**. This argument does not deny the validity of the case for free trade. However, it contends that for free trade to be meaningful, trading countries should temporarily shield their newly developing industries from foreign competition. Otherwise, mature foreign businesses, which are at the time more efficient, can drive infant domestic businesses out of the market. Only after the infant companies have had time to become efficient producers, should the tariff barriers be lifted and free trade take place.

Although there is some truth in the infant industry argument, it must be qualified in several respects. First, once a protective tariff is imposed, it is very difficult to remove, even after industrial maturity has been achieved. Special interest groups can often convince policy makers that further protection is justified. Second, it is very difficult to determine which industries will be capable of realizing comparative advantage potential and thus merit protection. Third, the infant industry argument generally is not valid for mature, industrialized countries such as the United States, Germany, and Japan. Finally, there may be other ways of insulating a developing industry from cutthroat competition. Rather than adopt a protective tariff, the government could grant a subsidy to the industry.

4.1.2   Terms of Trade Argument

One argument for deviating from free trade comes directly out of cost-benefit analysis. For a large country that is able to affect the prices of foreign exporters, a tariff lowers the price of imports and thus generates a terms-of-trade benefit. This benefit must be set against the costs of tariff, which arise because the tariff distorts production and consumption incentives. It is possible, however, that in some cases the terms-of-trade benefits of a tariff outweigh its costs, so there is the **terms of trade argument** for a tariff.

The terms of trade argument against free trade have some important limitations, however. Most small countries have very little ability to affect the world prices of either their imports or other's exports, so that the terms of trade argument is of little practical importance. For large countries, the problem is that the terms of trade argument amounts to an argument for using national monopoly power to extract gains at other countries' expense. Such a predatory policy would probably bring retaliation from other large countries. A cycle of retaliatory trade moves would, in turn, undermine the attempts at international trade policy coordination.

The terms of trade argument against free trade, then, is intellectually impeccable but of doubtful usefulness. In practice, it is emphasized more by economists as a theoretical proposition than used by governments as a justification for trade policy.

4.1.3   Domestic Market Failure Argument

Leaving aside the issue of the terms of trade, the basic theoretical case for free trade rested on cost-benefit analysis using the concepts of consumer and producer surplus. Many economists have made a case against free trade based on the counterargument that these concepts, producer surplus in particular, do not properly measure costs and benefits.

Why might producer surplus not properly measure the benefits of producing a good? There are a variety of reasons, including the possibility that the labor used in a sector would otherwise be unemployed or underemployed, the existence of defects in the capital or labor markets that prevent resources from being transferred as rapidly as they should be to sectors that yield high returns, and the possibility of technological spillovers from industries that are new or particularly innovative. These can all be classified a under general heading of **domestic market failures**. Then there is a marginal social benefit to additional production that is not captured by the producer surplus measure. This marginal social benefit can serve as a justification for tariffs or other trade policies.

The domestic market failure argument against free trade is a particular case of a more general concept known in economics as the **theory of the second best**. This theory states that a hands-off policy is desirable in any one market only if all other markets are working properly. If they are not, a government intervention that appears to distort incentives in one market may actually increase welfare by offsetting the consequences of market failures elsewhere. For example, if the labor market is malfunctioning and fails to deliver full employment, a policy of subsidizing labor-intensive industries, which would be undesirable in a full-employment economy, might turn out to be a good idea. It would be better to fix the labor market, for example, by making wages more flexible, but if for some reason this cannot be done, intervening in other markets may be a "second-best" way of alleviating the problem.

When economists apply the theory of the second best to trade policy, they argue that imperfections in the internal functioning of an economy may justify interfering in its external economic relations. This argument accepts that international trade is not the source of the problem but suggests nonetheless that trade policy can provide at least a partial solution.

4.1.4 Strategic Trade Policy

During the 1980s, a new argument for industrial targeting received substantial theoretical attention. Originally proposed by the economists Barbara Spencer and James Brander of the University of British Columbia, this argument locates the market failure that justifies government intervention in the lack of perfect competition. In some industries, they point out there are only a few firms in effective competition. Because of the small number of firms, the assumption of perfect competition does not apply. In particular, there will typically be excess returns; that is, firms will make profits above what equally risky investments elsewhere in the economy can earn. There will be an international competition over who gets these profits.

The theory of **Strategic trade policy** that, in this case, it is possible in principle for a government to alter the rules of the game to shift these excess returns from foreign to domestic firms. In the simplest case, a subsidy to domestic firms, by deterring investment and production by foreign competitors, can raise the profits of domestic firms by more than the amount of the subsidy. Setting aside the effects on consumers—for example, when the firms are selling only in foreign markets—this capture of profits from foreign competitors would mean the subsidy raises national income at other countries' expense.

4.2　Tariffs

A tariff is simply a tax (duty) levied on a product when it crosses national boundaries. The most widespread tariff is the **import tariff**, which is a tax levied on an imported product. A less common tariff is an **export tariff**, which is a tax imposed on an exported product. Export tariffs have often been used by developing countries.

Tariffs may be imposed for protection or revenue purposes. A **protective tariff** is designed to insulate import-competing producers from foreign competition. Although a protective tariff generally is not intended to totally prohibit imports from entering the country, it does place foreign producers at a competitive disadvantage when selling in the domestic market. A **revenue tariff** is imposed for the purpose of generating tax revenues and may be imposed on either exports or imports. Over time, tariff revenues have decreased as a source of government revenue for industrial countries. However, some developing countries currently rely on tariffs as a major source of government revenue.

4.2.1   Types of Tariffs

Tariffs can be specific, ad valorem, or compound.

Specific Tariff

A specific tariff is expressed in terms of a fixed amount of money per physical unit of the imported product. For example, a U.S. importer of German computers may be required to pay a duty to the U.S. government of $100 per computer, regardless of the computer's price.

As a fixed monetary duty per unit of the imported product, a specific tariff is relatively easy to apply and administer, particularly to standardized commodities and staple products where the value of the dutiable goods cannot be easily observed.

A main disadvantage of a specific tariff is that the degree of protection affords domestic producers to vary inversely with changes in import prices. For example, a specific tariff of $1,000 on autos will discourage imports priced at $20,000 per auto to a greater degree than those priced at $25,000. During times of rising import prices, a given specific tariff loses some of its protective effect. The result is to encourage domestic firms to produce less expensive goods, for which the degree of protection against imports is higher. On the other hand, a specific tariff has the advantage of providing domestic producers more protection during a business recession when cheaper products are purchased. Specific tariffs thus cushion domestic producers progressively against foreign competitors who cut their prices.

Ad Valorem Tariff

An ad valorem (of value) tariff, much like a sales tax, is expressed as a fixed percentage of the value of the imported product. Suppose that an ad valorem duty of 15 percent is levied on imported trucks. A U.S. importer of a Japanese truck valued at $20,000 would be required to pay a duty of $3,000 to the government ($20,000 × 15% = $3,000).

Ad valorem tariffs usually lend themselves more satisfactorily to manufactured goods, because they can be applied to products with a wide range of grade variations. As a percentage applied to a product's value, an ad valorem tariff can distinguish among small differentials in product quality to the extent that they are reflected in product price. Under a system of ad valorem tariffs, a person importing a $20,000 Honda would have to pay a higher duty than a person importing a $19,900 Toyota. Under a system of specific tariffs, the duty would be the same.

Another advantage of an ad valorem tariff is that it tends to maintain a constant degree of protection for domestic producers during periods of changing prices. If the tariff rate is 20 percent ad valorem and the imported product price is $200, the duty is $40; if the product's price increases, say, to $300, the duty collected rises to $60; if the product price falls to $100, the duty drops to $20.

An ad valorem tariff yields revenues proportionate to values, maintaining a constant degree of relative protection at all price levels. An ad valorem tariff is similar to a proportional tax in that the real proportional tax burden or protection does not change as the tax base changes. In recent decades, in response to global inflation and the rising importance of world trade in manufactured products, ad valorem duties have been used more often than specific duties.

Determination of duties under the ad valorem principle at first appears to be simple, but in practice it has suffered from administrative complexities. The main problem has been trying to determine the value of an imported product, a process referred to as customs valuation. Import prices are estimated by customs appraisers, who may disagree on product values. Moreover, import prices tend to fluctuate over time, which makes the valuation process rather difficult.

Another customs valuation problem stems from variations in the methods used to determine a commodity's value. For example, the United States has traditionally used free-on-board (FOB) valuation, whereby the tariff is applied to a product's value as it leaves the exporting country. But European countries have traditionally used a cost-insurance-freight (CIF) valuation, whereby ad valorem tariffs are levied as a percentage of the imported commodity's total value as it arrives at its final destination. The CIF price thus includes transportation costs, such as insurance and freight.

Compound Tariff

A compound tariff is a combination of specific and ad valorem tariffs. For example, a U.S. importer of televisions might be required to pay a duty of $ 20 plus 5 percent of the value of the television.

Compound duties are often applied to manufactured products embodying raw materials that are subject to tariffs. In this case, the specific portion of the duty neutralizes the cost disadvantage of domestic manufactures that results from tariff protection granted to domestic suppliers of raw materials, and the ad valorem portion of the duty grants protection to the finished-goods industry. In the United States, for example, there is a compound duty on woven fabrics (48. 5 cents per kilogram plus 38 percent). The specific portion of the duty (48. 5 cents) compensates U.S. fabric manufacturers for tariff protection granted to U.S. cotton producers, while the ad valorem portion of the duty (38 percent) provides protection for their own woven fabrics.

Table 4-1 Selected U.S. Tariffs

Product	Duty Rate
Live chickens	0. 9 cents each
Hams	1. 4 cents/kg
Butter	12. 3 cents/kg
Rice wine of sake	3 cents/liter
Cheddar cheese	16%
Caviar	15%
High-quality beef cuts	4%
Photographic film in rolls, 35mm	3. 7%
Tire of rubber for motor vehicles, radial	4%
Bicycles	11%
Mushrooms	8. 8 cents/kg +20%
Cigars, each valued at less than 15 cents	$ 1. 89/kg +4. 7%
Cigarettes, paper wrapped	41. 7cents/kg +0. 9%
Women's or girl's overcoats made of wool	55. 9cents/kg +16. 4%

Source: U.S. International Trade Commission, *Tariff Schedules of the United States*, Washington, D.C.: U.S. Government Printing Office, 2004.

4.2.2　Effective Rate of Protection

A main objective of an import tariff is to protect domestic producers from foreign competition. By increasing the domestic price of an import, a tariff serves to make home-produced goods more attractive to resident consumers. Output in the import-competing industry can thus expand beyond what would exist in the absence of a tariff. The degree of protection afforded by a tariff reflects the extent to which domestic prices can rise above foreign prices before the home producers are priced out of the market.

The nominal tariff rate published in a country's tariff schedule gives us a general idea of the level of protection afforded the home industry. But it may not always truly indicate the actual, or effective, protection given. For example, it is not necessarily true that a 25 percent import tariff on an automobile provides the domestic auto industry a protective margin of 25 percent against foreign producers. This is because the nominal tariff rates apply only to the total value of the final import product. But in the production process, the home import competing industry may use imported material inputs or intermediate products that are subject to a different tariff than that on the final product; in this case, the effective tariff rate will differ from the nominal tariff rate.

The **nominal tariff rate** is the extent to which the price of the good to domestic consumers is raised by the existence of the tariff. However, economists are concerned, when using the **effective rate of protection** (ERP), also called as **effective tariff rate**, about the extent to which "value added" in the domestic import-competing industry is altered by the existence of the whole tariff structure (that is, the tariff rate not only on the final good but also on the intermediate goods that go into making the final good). Indeed, the ERP is defined as the percentage change in the value added in an industry because of the imposition of a tariff structure by the country rather than the existence of free trade.

Consider a situation in which Good F is the final good and Goods A and B are intermediate inputs used in making F. Assume that A and B are the only intermediate inputs and that 1 unit each of A and B is used in producing 1 unit of final good F. Goods A and B can be imported goods or domestic goods that compete with imports and thus have their prices influenced by the tariffs on the competing imports. Suppose that, under free trade, the price of the final good (P_F) is $\$1,000$ and the prices of the inputs are $P_A = \$500$ and $P_B = \$200$. In this free-trade situation, the value added is $\$1,000 - (\$500 + \$200) = \$300$.

Now consider a situation where protective tariffs exist; a prime mark next to a price (P') indicates a tariff-protected price. Suppose that the tariff rate (t_F) on the final good is 10 percent and that the tariff on Input A (t_A) is 5 percent and on Input B (t_B) is 8 percent. If we assume that the country is a small nation (it takes world prices as given and cannot influence them), then the domestic prices of the goods with the tariffs in place are:

$$P_F' = \$1,000 + 10\% \times \$1,000 = \$1,100$$
$$P_A' = \$500 + 5\% \times \$500 = \$525$$
$$P_B' = \$200 + 8\% \times \$200 = \$216$$

The value added in Industry F under protection is $\$1,100 - (\$525 + \$216) = \$359$. The industry has experienced an increase in its value added because of the tariffs, and therefore the factors of production (land, labor, and capital) working in Industry F are able to receive higher returns than under free trade. There is thus an economic incentive for factors of production in other industries to move into Industry F. Since the effective rate of protection is the percentage change in the value added when moving from free trade to protection, the ERP in this example is:

$$\frac{\text{Value added under protection} - \text{Value added with free trade}}{\text{Value added with free trade}} = \frac{VA' - VA}{VA}$$

$$= \frac{\$359 - \$300}{\$300} = 19.7\%$$

Thus, the factors of production in Industry F have benefited from the tariffs, although consumers have lost. A more common formula for calculating the ERP for any industry j utilizing inputs designated as i is

$$ERP = \frac{t_j - \sum_i a_{ij} t_i}{1 - \sum_i a_{ij}}$$

where a_{ij} represents the free-trade value of input i as a percentage of the free-trade value of the final good j, t_j and t_i represent the tariff rates on the final good j and on any input i, respectively, and the $\sum_i$ sign means that we are summing over all the inputs. In the example, the a_{ij} for Input A is $\$500/\$1,000$ or 0.50, and the value of the a_{ij} for Input B is $\$200/\$1,000$ or 0.20. The ERP in the example is the same as in the calculation above:

$$ERP = \frac{10\% - (0.50 \times 5\% + 0.20 \times 8\%)}{1 - (0.50 + 0.20)} = 19.7\%$$

This second method of calculating the ERP has the advantage of illustrating three general rules about the relationship between nominal rates and effective rates of protection. These rules are (1) if the nominal tariff rate on the final good is higher than the weighted average nominal tariff rate on the inputs, then the ERP will be higher than the nominal rate on the final goods; (2) if the nominal tariff rate on the final good is lower than the weighted average nominal tariff rate on the inputs, then the ERP will be lower than the nominal rate on the final goods; (3) if the nominal tariff rate on the final good is equal to the weighted average nominal tariff rate on the inputs, then the ERP will be equal to the nominal rate on the final goods.

Two consequences of the effective rate calculation are worthy of mention. First, the degree of effective protection increases as the value added by domestic producers declines (the ratio of the value of the imported input to the value of the final product increases). In the formula, the higher the value of a_{ij} is, the greater the effective protection rate for any given nominal tariff rate on the final product will be. Second, a tariff on imports used in the production process reduces the level of effective protection. The higher the value of t_i, the lower the effective protection rate for any given nominal tariff on the final product. In the formula, as t_i rises, the numerator of the formula decreases and hence ERP decreases. Note that it is possible for the effective tariff rate to assume a negative value, depending on the values of the components in the formula for the calculation of the effective tariff rate.

Generalizing from this analysis, when material inputs or intermediate products enter a country at a very low duty while the final imported commodity is protected by a high duty, the result tends to be a high protection rate for the domestic producers. The nominal tariff rate on finished goods thus understates the effective rate of protection. But should a tariff be imposed on imported inputs that exceeds that on the finished good, the nominal tariff rate on the finished product would tend to overstate its protective effect. Such a situation might occur if the home government desires to protect suppliers of raw materials more than domestic manufacturers.

As illustrated in Table 4-2, in many industrialized countries the effective rate of protection is more than twice the nominal rate. An apparently low nominal tariff on a final import product may thus understate the effective rate of protection, which takes into account the effects of tariffs levied on raw materials and intermediate goods. In addition, the tariff structures of industrialized countries have generally been characterized by rising rates that give greater protection to intermediate and finished products than to primary commodities. This is commonly referred to as **tariff escalation**. Although raw materials are often imported at zero or low tariff rates, the nominal and effective protection increases at each stage of production. Tariffs often rise significantly with the level of processing in many industrialized countries. This is especially true for agricultural products.

Table 4-2　Nominal and Effective Tariff Rates

Product	The United States		Japan	
	Nominal rate (%)	Effective rate (%)	Nominal rate (%)	Effective rate (%)
Wearing apparel	27.8	50.6	13.8	27.1
Glass and glass products	10.7	16.9	7.5	11.5
Footwear	8.8	13.1	16.4	33.6
Furniture and fixtures	8.1	12.3	7.8	15.1
Metal products	7.5	12.7	6.9	12.0
Food, beverages, and tobacco	6.3	13.4	25.4	51.1
Electrical machinery	6.6	9.4	7.4	11.0
22-industry average	5.2	8.1	8.4	13.2

Source: Alan V. Deardorff and Robert M. Stern, *The Michigan Model of World Production and Trade: Theory and Applications*, Cambridge: MIT Press, 1986.

The tariff structures of the industrialized countries may indeed discourage the growth of processing, thus hampering diversification into higher value-added exports for the less developed countries. The industrialized countries' low tariffs on primary commodities encourage the developing countries to expand operations in these sectors, while the high protective rates levied on manufactured goods pose a significant entry barrier for any developing country wishing to compete in this area. From the point of view of the less developed countries, it may be in their best interest to discourage disproportionate tariff reductions on raw materials. The effect of these tariff reductions is to magnify the discrepancy between the nominal and effective tariffs of the industrialized countries, worsening the potential competitive position of the less developed countries in the manufacturing and processing sectors.

4.2.3   Tariff Welfare Effects

Consumer Surplus and Producer Surplus

To analyze the effect of trade policies on national welfare, it is useful to separate the effects on consumers from those on producers. For each group, a measure of welfare is needed; these measures are known as consumer surplus and producer surplus.

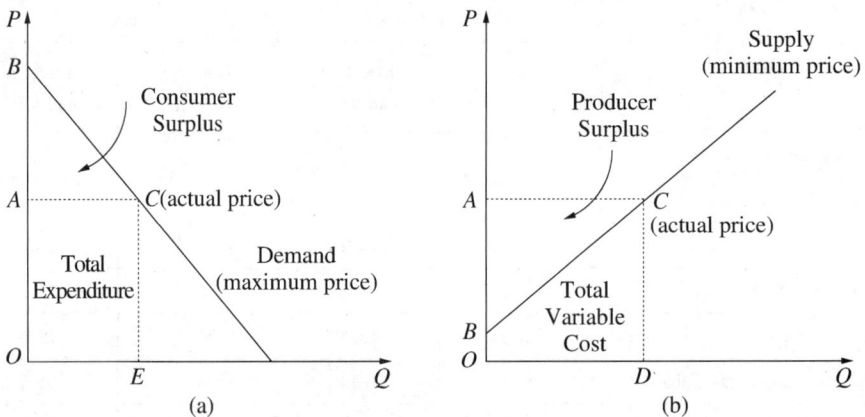

Figure 4-1   Consumer Surplus and Producer Surplus

Consumer surplus refers to the difference between the amount that buyers would be willing and able to pay for a good and the actual amount they do pay. Consumer surplus can be depicted graphically. Let us first remember that (1) the height of the market demand curve indicates the maximum price that buyers are willing and able to pay for each successive unit of the good, and (2) in a competitive market, buyers pay a single price (the equilibrium price) for all units purchased.

Referring now to Figure 4-1(a), assume the market price of cloth is *OA* per unit. If buyers purchase *OE* units at this price, total expenditure can be represented by Area *ACEO*. For those *OE* units of cloth, the amount buyers would have been willing and able to pay is shown by Area *OBCE*. The difference between what buyers actually spend and the amount they were willing and able to spend is consumer surplus; in this case, it is denoted by Area *ABC*.

The size of consumer surplus is affected by the market price. A decrease in the market price will lead to an increase in the quantity purchased and a larger consumer surplus. Conversely, a higher market price will reduce the amount purchased and shrink the consumer surplus.

Let us now consider the other side of the market: producers. **Producer surplus** is the revenue producers receive over and above the minimum amount required to induce them to supply the good. This minimum amount has to cover the producer's total variable costs. Recall that total variable cost equals the sum of the marginal cost of producing each successive unit of output.

In Figure 4-1 (b), producer surplus is represented by the area above the supply curve of cloth and below the good's market price. Recall that the height of the market supply curve indicates the lowest price at which producers are willing to supply cloth; this minimum price increases with the level of output because of rising marginal costs. Suppose that the market price of cloth is *OA* per unit, and *OD* units are supplied. The total revenue that producers receive is represented by Area *OACD*. The minimum revenue they must receive to produce *OD* units of cloth equals total variable cost, which is depicted by Area *OBCD*. Producer surplus is the difference, and is depicted by Area *ABC*.

If the market price of cloth rises, more cloth will be supplied, and producer surplus will rise. It is equally true that if the market price of cloth falls, producer surplus will fall.

In the following sections, we will use the concepts of consumer surplus and producer surplus to analyze the effects of import tariffs on the country's welfare.

Trade Welfare Effect of Tariff in a Partial Equilibrium Setting

A. The Small-Nation Case

To measure the effects of a tariff on a country's welfare, consider the case of a country whose imports constitute a very small portion of the world market supply. This **small nation** would be a price taker, facing a constant world price level for its import commodity. This is not a rare case; many countries are not important enough to influence the terms at which they trade.

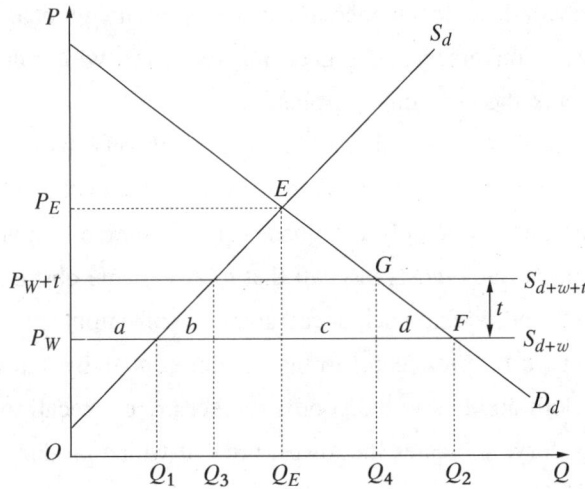

Figure 4-2   Tariff Trade and Welfare Effects: Small-Nation Model

In Figure 4-2, the small nation before trade produces at market equilibrium point E, as determined by the intersection of its domestic supply and demand curves. At equilibrium price P_E, the quantity supplied is Q_E units, and the quantity demanded is Q_E units. Now suppose that the economy is opened to foreign trade and that the world cloth price is P_W, less than the domestic price. Because the world market will supply an unlimited quantity of cloth at price P_W, the world supply schedule would appear as a horizontal (perfectly elastic) line. Line S_{d+w} shows the supply of cloth available to the small nation's consumers from domestic and foreign sources combined. This overall supply curve is the one that would prevail in free trade.

Free trade equilibrium is located at Point F in the figure. Here the quantity of cloth demanded is Q_2 units, whereas the quantity produced domestically is Q_1

units. The excess domestic cloth demand is fulfilled by imports of $Q_1 Q_2$ cloth. Compared with the situation before trade occurred, free trade results in a fall in the domestic cloth price from P_E to P_W. Consumers are better off because they can import more cloth at a lower price. However, domestic producers now sell less cloth at a lower price than they did before trade.

Under free trade, the domestic cloth industry is being injured by foreign competition. Industry sales and revenues are falling, and workers are losing their jobs. Suppose the management and workers unite and convince the government to levy a protective tariff on cloth imports. Assume the small nation imposes a tariff of t on cloth imports. Because this small nation is not important enough to influence world market conditions, the world supply price of cloth remains constant, unaffected by the tariff. This means that the small nation's terms of trade remain unchanged. The introduction of the tariff raises the home price of imports by the full amount of the duty, and the increase falls entirely on domestic consumers. The overall supply shifts upward by the amount of the tariff, from S_{d+w} to S_{d+w+t}.

The protective tariff results in a new equilibrium quantity at Point G, where the domestic cloth price is P_{W+t}. Domestic production increases by $Q_1 Q_3$ units, whereas domestic consumption falls by $Q_4 Q_2$ units. Imports decrease from their pre-tariff level of $Q_1 Q_2$ units to $Q_3 Q_4$ units. This reduction can be attributed to falling domestic consumption and rising domestic production. The effects of the tariff are to impede imports and protect domestic producers. But what are the tariff's effects on the national welfare?

Figure 4-2 shows that with the tariff, consumer surplus falls. An overall loss in consumer surplus equals to Areas $a + b + c + d$. This change affects the country's welfare in a number of ways. The welfare effects of a tariff include a revenue effect, a redistribution effect, a protective effect, and a consumption effect. As might be expected, the tariff provides the government with additional tax revenue and benefits domestic cloth producers; at the same time, however, it wastes resources and harms domestic consumers.

The tariff's **revenue effect** represents the government's collections of duty. Found by multiplying the quantity of imports ($Q_3 Q_4$ units) with the tariff (t), government revenue equals Area c. This represents the portion of the loss of consumer surplus, in monetary terms, which is transferred to the government. For the country as a whole, the revenue effect does not result in an overall welfare loss; consumer surplus is merely shifted from the private to the public sector.

The **redistributive effect** is the transfer of consumer surplus, in monetary terms, to domestic producers of the import-competing product. This is represented by Area a. Under the tariff, domestic consumers will buy from domestic firms Q_3 units of cloth at a price of P_{W+t}, for a total expenditure of $[(P_{W+t}) \times Q_3]$. At the free trade price of P_W, the same Q_3 units of cloths would have yielded $(P_W \times Q_3)$. The imposition of the tariff thus results in home producers' receiving additional revenues totaling Areas $a+b$ (the difference between $[(P_{W+t}) \times Q_3]$ and $(P_W \times Q_3)$. As the tariff encourages domestic production to rise from Q_1 to Q_3 units, however, producers must pay part of the increased revenue as higher costs of producing the increased output, depicted by Area b. The remaining revenue, Area a, is a net gain in producer income. The redistributive effect, therefore, is a transfer of income from consumers to producers. Like the revenue effect, it does not result in an overall loss of welfare for the economy.

Area b is referred to as the **protective effect** of the tariff. It illustrates the loss to the domestic economy resulting from wasted resources used to produce additional cloth at increasing unit costs. As the tariff-induced domestic output expands, resources that are less adaptable to cloth production are eventually used, increasing unit production costs. This means that resources are used less efficiently than they would have been with free trade, in which case cloth would have been purchased from low-cost foreign producers. A tariff's protective effect thus arises because less efficient domestic production is substituted for more efficient foreign production. Referring to Figure 4-2, as domestic output increases from Q_1 to Q_3 units, the domestic cost of producing cloths rises, as shown by supply curve S_d. But the same increase in cloths could have been obtained at a unit cost of P_W before the tariff was levied. Area b, which depicts the protective effect, represents a loss to the economy.

Most of the consumer surplus lost because of the tariff has been accounted for: Area c went to the government as revenue; Area a was transferred to home suppliers as income; and Area b was lost by the economy because of inefficient domestic production. The **consumption effect**, represented by Area d, is the residual not accounted for elsewhere. It arises from the decrease in consumption resulting from the tariff's artificially increasing the price of cloths from P_W to P_{W+t}. A loss of welfare occurs because of the increased price and lower consumption. Like the protective effect, the consumption effect represents a real cost to a community, not a transfer to other sectors of the economy. Together, these two effects equal the deadweight loss of the tariff (Areas $b + d$ in the figure).

Table 4-3 Welfare Cost of a Tariff Imposed by a Small Nation

Item	Welfare Change (Area)			
Change in consumer surplus	$-a$	$-b$	$-c$	$-d$
Change in producer surplus	a			
Change in government revenue			c	
Net welfare change		$-b$		$-d$

As long as it is assumed that a country accounts for a negligible portion of international trade, levying an import tariff necessarily lowers its national welfare. This is because there is no favorable welfare effect resulting from the tariff that would offset the deadweight loss of consumer surplus. If a country could impose a tariff that would improve its terms of trade vis-à-vis its trading partners, it would enjoy a larger share of the gains from trade. This would tend to increase its national welfare, offsetting the deadweight loss of consumer surplus. Because it is so insignificant relative to the world market, however, a small nation is unable to influence the terms of trade. Levying an import tariff, therefore, reduces a small nation's welfare.

B. The Large-Nation Case

Suppose that the country that imposes a tariff is a **large nation** in the sense that it is a significant importer (or exporter) of the product in question. In that case, as we are about to see, the imposition of a tariff may lead to a welfare improvement for the country, relative to free trade. In essence, because the country has market power, by imposing a tariff it is able to obtain goods it continues to purchase at a lower world price. By forcing down the world price, the tariff-imposing country, in effect, shifts some of the burden of the tariff onto the exporting country.

Assume Country A is an economically large nation. That is, Country A is an important world importer of a certain product, say, cloth. Let Country B export cloth to Country A. See Figure 4-3. In the left-hand panel we illustrate A's market for cloth. In the right-hand panel we present Country B's market for cloth. In the absence of trade, the price of cloth would be P_A in Country A and P_B in Country B. If trade were allowed to occur, then B would have comparative advantage in cloth and would export cloth to Country A. At any price below P_A, Country A would import cloth; at any price above P_B, Country B would export cloth.

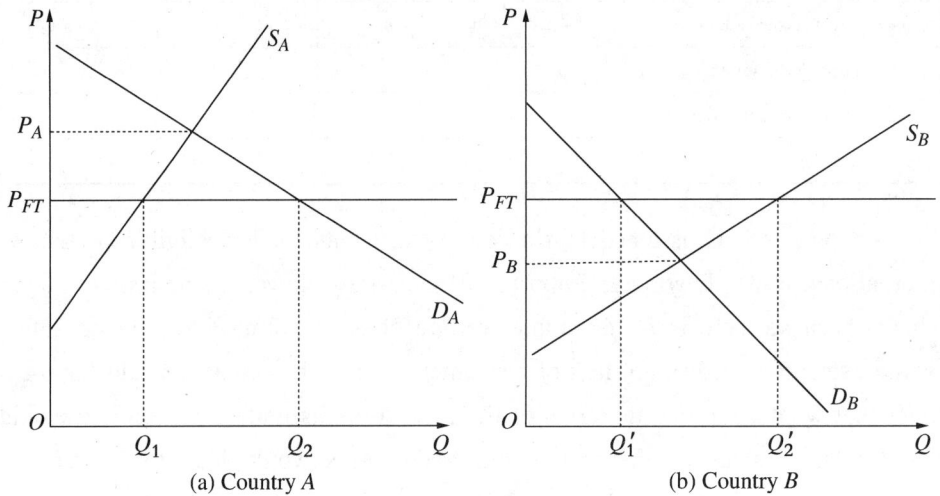

(a) Country A   (b) Country B

Figure 4-3   International Free-Trade Equilibrium

The equilibrium world price is defined as the price at which the quantity that consumers in Country A want to import is equal to the quantity that producers in Country B want to export. In the diagram, this price is denoted by P_{FT}. At that price, Country A's desired imports equal $Q_1 Q_2$ units, which exactly matches Country B's desired exports (denoted in the right-hand panel of the diagram as Q_1' Q_2' units). Note that P_{FT} is the only possible candidate for an equilibrium free trade price. At any price above P_{FT}, the demand for imports will fall in Country A, while the supply of exports from Country B will rise. In other words, at free-trade prices above P_{FT}, there will be an excess supply of cloth in the world market; excess supply will tend to force the price down. By identical reasoning, at any free trade price below P_{FT}, there will be international excess demand for cloth, and the market prices for the good will tend to rise.

The fact that the markets in Countries A and B interact in the way just described to determine the world price is the source of Country A's international market power. In particular, a change in Country A's demand for imports of cloth will have a direct effect on the world price. Increases in demand will drive the world price up; decreases in demand will drive it down.

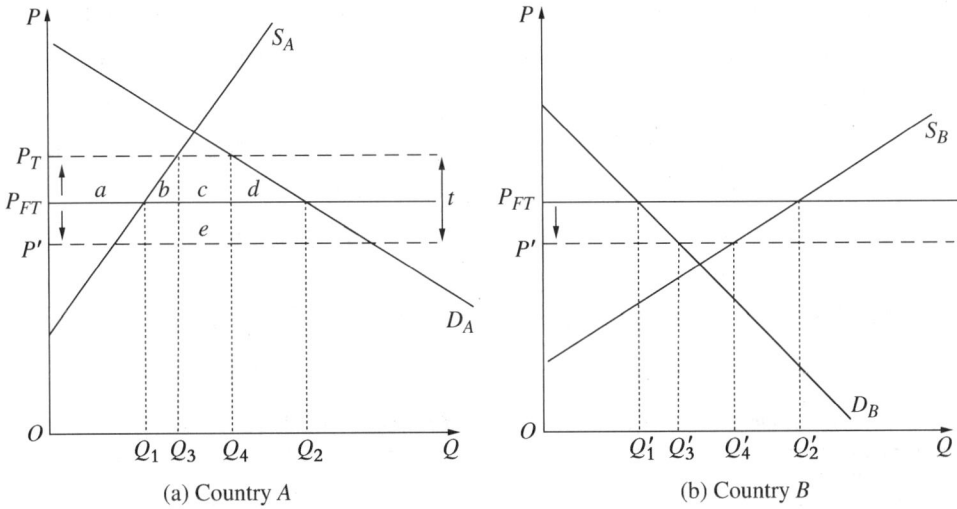

Figure 4-4 Tariff Trade and Welfare Effects: Large-Nation Model

Suppose that Country A imposes a tariff on imports of cloth, which causes imports to fall to $Q_3 Q_4$ units. This is illustrated in the left-hand panel of Figure 4-4 by the increase in price from P_{FT} to P_T. Note the effect of Country A's tariff has on Country B. Since Country A is an important customer of Country B's product, when Country A uses a tariff to reduce its demand, it causes the price in Country B to fall. As drawn, the price will fall until the world trade is balanced. This occurs at Price P', where Country B's exports equal $Q_3' Q_4'$ which exactly matches the $Q_3 Q_4$ units of cloth demanded by Country A after it imposes the tariff.

With the higher price, consumers in Country A lose Areas $a + b + c + d$ in consumer surplus. Producer surplus rises by Area a. The government revenue rises by Areas $c + e$. To see that, note first that by definition the size of the tariff equals the difference between the price consumers in Country A pay for the product (P_T) and the price producers in Country B receive (P'). That is, the per unit tariff of t equals $P_T - P'$. Thus, we see that in this case the price has gone up in Country A, but by less than the full amount of the tariff. What has happened is that Country A is such an important customer of Country B's product that producers in Country B attempt to maintain sales by absorbing some of the tariff in the form of price reductions. In the new equilibrium, the price received by producers in Country B falls from P_{FT} to P'.

This means that the cloth that Country A now imports comes into the country at a lower price. Then, once the tariff is imposed, the new price in Country A is $P_T(= P' + t)$. This leads to a convenient interpretation of Areas $c + e$. Here Area c represents the tariff proceeds paid by Country A's consumers to its government. We know this because the height of Rectangle c is equal to the increase in price to Country A's consumers, and the base equals the level of imports. Area e represents the amount to the tariff paid by Country B's producers. That is, the height of Rectangle e represents the amount that Country B's producers have cut their price, and the base is equal to the level of Country A's imports.

Table 4-4 Welfare Cost of a Tariff Imposed by a Large Nation

Item	Welfare Change (Area)				
Change in consumer surplus	$-a$	$-b$	$-c$	$-d$	
Change in producer surplus	a				
Change in government revenue			c		e
Net welfare change		$-b$		$-d$	e

What has been the impact on Country A's overall welfare due to the tariff? This is illustrated in Table 4-4. The change in welfare in Country A brought about by the imposition of a tariff equals $e - (b + d)$. This amount could be positive or negative, depending on the relative sizes of the two terms. Area e, referred to as

the terms of trade effect, represents the amount of the tariff revenue paid by foreigners because the world price of their exports has fallen. The larger Area e is, everything else held constant, the greater is the likelihood that Country A's welfare has increased because of the imposition of the tariff. Areas $b + d$ represent the usual deadweight costs of the tariff. The smaller this amount is, the greater the likelihood of welfare increases in Country A.

As Figure 4-4 clearly suggests, the amount b, d, and e all depend on the slopes of the various demand and supply curves and on the size of the tariff imposed by Country A. Thus, for a given set of demand and supply curves, it should be possible for the government of Country A to impose a tariff that raises Country A's welfare to the largest possible extent. That is, the tariff would be set to a level that maximizes the area $e - (b + d)$. Such a tariff is known as Country A's **optimal tariff**.

Trade Welfare Effect of Tariff in a General Equilibrium Setting

The discussion of the impact of trade restrictions has to this point focused largely on the market of the particular good that is the target of the restriction in question. While this is a useful exercise, as this market adjusts to the policy, other parts of the economy are also affected. Increased protection leads producers to reallocate resources to the protected industry and consumers to find substitutes for the present more expensive good. These reverberations need to be taken into account so as to assess fully the welfare impact of the trade restrictions.

A. The Small-Nation Case

To demonstrate the usefulness of the broader analysis of trade restrictions, let us return to the general equilibrium framework to demonstrate the gains from trade.

Assume that a small nation is engaged in free trade. See Figure 4-5. Initially, consumers are consuming at Point C_0, and producers are producing at Point B_0. The country is exporting X_0 of agricultural goods, and imports of textiles are equal to M_0.

Due to successful lobbying by the textile industry, an ad valorem import tariff is now imposed. In the small-nation case, this increases the domestic price of textiles by t percent, and the domestic price of textiles becomes $P_T(1 + t)$.

Domestic relative prices now become $P_A/[P_T(1+t)]$, which are strictly less than P_A/P_T, the international relative price. Producers see the increase in the relative price of textiles as a signal to produce more textiles (and consequently fewer agricultural goods) and adjust production until the marginal rate of transformation (MRT) of textiles into agricultural goods equals $P_A/[P_T(1+t)]$. This occurs when the flatter domestic price line is tangent to the production possibilities frontier (PPF) at Point B_1. This adjustment by producers represents a movement away from specialization and reduces the consumption possibilities frontier available to the country from Line $(P_A/P_T)_0$ to its parallel Line $(P_A/P_T)_1$. The adjustment in production thus leads to a reduction in real income and a consequent loss in welfare as consumers are forced to choose from a smaller consumption space along $(P_A/P_T)_1$ instead of $(P_A/P_T)_0$ and must therefore be on a lower indifference curve.

Consumers must make a new choice, given their lower level of real income. What point on the new consumption possibilities line $(P_A/P_T)_1$ will maximize their well-being in this tariff-distorted world? Since they face the same tariff-distorted price as producers, they will try to find a point on the new consumption possibilities line that represents an optimal consumption choice, given relative domestic price. This will occur at a combination of agricultural goods and textiles that lies on $(P_A/P_T)_1$ and what results in $MU_A/MU_T = P_A/[P_T(1+t)]$. This choice is indicated by Point C_1 in Figure 4-5. At C_1, the slope of lower indifference curve IC_1 is equal to the domestic price ratio that contains the tariff on textiles, $P_A/[P_T(1+t)]$. This is indicated by the tangent to IC_1 to the dashed line at Point C_1. The tariff in this case has a negative welfare impact on the country, represented by the shift from Point C_0 on the indifference curve IC_0 to Point C_1 on the community indifference curve IC_1.

The reduction in welfare comes from two effects. First, the economy no longer produces at a point that maximizes the value of income at world prices. The budget constraint that passes through B_1 lies inside the constraint passing through B_0. Second, consumers do not choose the welfare-maximizing point on the budget constraint; they do not move up to an indifference curve that is tangent to the economy's actual budget constraint. Both effects result from the fact that domestic consumers and producers face prices that are different from the world prices. The

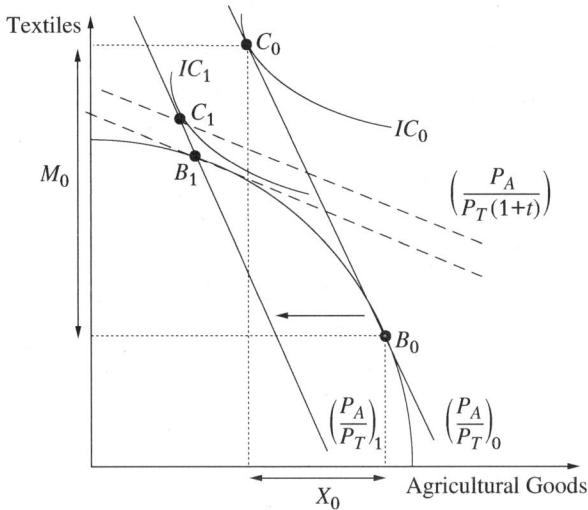

Figure 4-5   General Equilibrium Effects of Tariff in a Small Nation

loss in welfare due to inefficient production is the general equilibrium counterpart
of the production distortion loss we described in the partial equilibrium approach in
this chapter, and the loss in welfare due to inefficient consumption is the
counterpart of the consumption distortion loss.

Trade is reduced by the tariff. Both exports and imports are less than before
the tariff is imposed. These are the effects of a tariff imposed by a small nation.
We next turn to the effects of a tariff imposed by a large nation.

B. The Large-Nation Case

In the large-nation case, the welfare impact of protection is less clear and
concise. Because the large nation can influence international prices, the impact of
a tariff is felt not only domestically but also internationally. With its tariff, the
tariff-imposing country reduces both its import demand and export supply; that is,
it is less willing to trade. Consequently, both the international demand for the
imported good and the world supply of the exported good are reduced. Both
effects cause the international terms of trade to change, increasing the price of the
exported good relative to the imported good and improving the terms of trade of
tariff-imposing country. The overall reduction of welfare in the tariff-imposing

country resulting from the smaller amount of trade is thus offset, at least in part, by improved terms of trade. It is possible that the effects of the improved terms of trade could more than offset the effect of the reduction in trade and leave the tariff-imposing country better off, assuming, of course, that its trading partners do not retaliate.

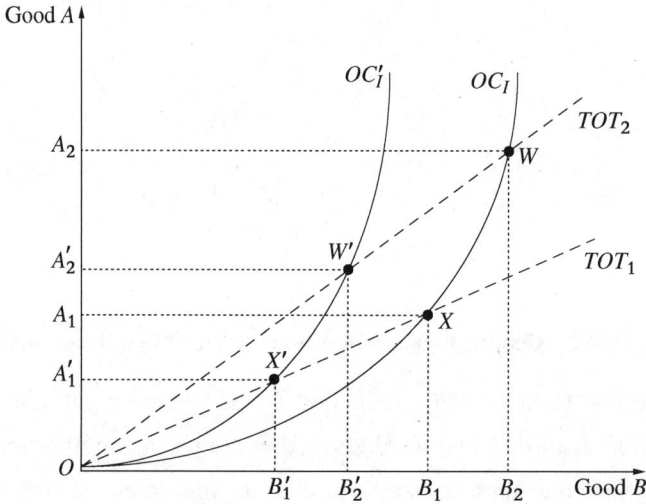

Figure 4-6   the Imposition of a Tariff in the Offer Curve Diagram

The general equilibrium effects of trade restrictions in the large-nation case can be examined by offer curves. To illustrate the impact of a tariff in such a framework, consider first the manner in which the curve shifts when a tariff is imposed. Figure 4-6 illustrates the offer curve for Country I which is exporting Good B and importing Good A. As you remember, the curve is derived by plotting the willingness of the country to trade at alternative terms of trade. Curve OC_I shows that Country I is willing to export quantity OB_1 of Good B and to import quantity OA_1 of Good A at TOT_1. Similarly, at TOT_2, the country is willing to export OB_2 and import OA_2.

When a tariff is imposed, the country is less willing to trade at each terms of trade. At TOT_1, on new offer curve OI', the country is only willing to export OB_1' and to import OA_1'. The willingness to trade at TOT_2 can be indicated similarly. Thus, the offer curve shifts inward with the imposition of a tariff.

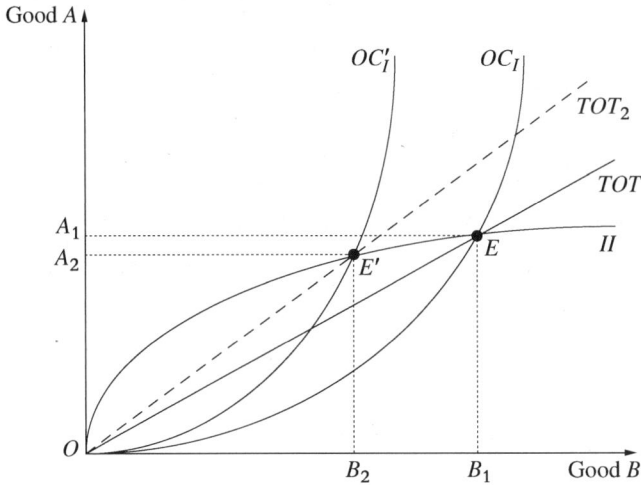

Figure 4-7   the Impact of a Tariff

With the imposition of a tariff, Country I's offer curve OC_I shifts inward to OC_I'. The equilibrium quantity of exports falls from OB_1 to OB_2, and the quantity of imports falls from OA_1 to OA_2. Country I's terms of trade improve from TOT_1 to TOT_2.

Figure 4-7 portrays the imposition of an import tariff with the foreign offer curve. Prior to the tariff, the free trade equilibrium is at Point E with quantity OB_1 of Good B exported from Country I and quantity OA_1 imported by Country I. With the imposition of the tariff, the offer curve OC_I' rather than OC_I becomes the relevant curve. The quantity of exports of Country I falls to OB_2, which exchanges for OA_2 of imports. Note also that the terms of trade improve for the tariff-imposing country, since TOT_2 is steeper than TOT_1.

4.3   Nontariff Trade Barriers

4.3.1   An Introduction to Nontariff Trade Barriers

Besides the use of tariffs which distort the free-trade allocation of resources, policy makers have become very adept at using other, less visible, forms of trade barriers. These are usually called **nontariff trade barriers** (NTBs), and they have become more prominent in recent years. Economists have noted that as tariffs have been reduced through multilateral tariff negotiations during the last decades, the impact of this reduction may haven been largely offset by the proliferation of NTBs. Our purpose now is to introduce some of these NTBs.

NTBs encompass a variety of measures. Some have unimportant trade consequences; for example, labeling and packaging requirements can restrict trade, but generally only marginally. Other NTBs significantly affect trade patterns; examples include import quotas, voluntary export restraints, subsidies, and domestic content requirements. These NTBs are intended to reduce imports and thus benefit domestic producers.

Import Quota

An import quota is a physical restriction on the quantity of goods that may be imported during a specific period; the quota generally limits imports to a level below which imports would occur under free-trade conditions. For example, a quota might state that no more than 1 million kilograms of cheese or 20 million kilograms of wheat can be imported during a certain specific period. Table 4-5 gives examples of import quotas that have been used by the United States.

Table 4-5　Examples of the U.S. Import Quotas

Imported Article	Quota Quantity (yearly)
Condensed milk (Australia)	91,625kg
Condensed milk (Denmark)	605,092kg
Evaporated milk (Germany)	9,997kg
Evaporated milk (Netherlands)	548,393kg
Blue-mold cheese (Argentina)	2,000kg
Blue-mold cheese (Chile)	80,000kg
Cheddar cheese (New Zealand)	8,200,000kg
Italian cheese (Poland)	1,325,000kg
Italian cheese (Romania)	500,000kg
Swiss cheese (Switzerland)	1,850,000kg

Source: U.S. International Trade Commission, *Tariff Schedule of the United States*, Washington, D.C., Government Printing Office, 2000.

A common practice to administer an import quota is for the government to require an import license. Each license specifies the volume of imports allowed, and the total volume allowed should not exceed the quota. These licenses require importers to spend time filling out forms and waiting for official permission. Licenses can be sold to importing companies at a competitive price, or simply a fee. Instead, government may just give away licenses to preferred importers. However, this allocation method provides incentives for political lobbying and bribery.

Import quotas on manufactured goods have been outlawed by the World Trade Organization. Import quotas used by developed countries such as Japan and the United States are desired to protect agricultural producers. However, recent trade negotiations have called for countries to convert their quotas to equivalent tariffs.

Tariff-Rate Quota: A Two-Tier Tariff

Another restriction used to insulate a domestic industry from foreign competition is the tariff-rate quota. The U. S. government has imposed this restriction on imports such as steel, brooms, cattle, fish, sugar, milk, and other agricultural products.

As its name suggests, a tariff-rate quota displays both tariff-like and quota-like characteristics. This device allows a specified number of goods to be imported at one tariff rate (the **within-quota tariff rate**), whereas any imports above this level face a higher tariff rate (the **over-quota tariff rate**). A tariff-rate quota thus has three components: (1) a quota that defines the maximum volume of imports charged the within-quota tariff, (2) a within-quota tariff, and (3) an over-quota tariff. To put it simply, a tariff rate quota is a two-tier tariff. Tariff-rate quotas are applied for each trade year and if not filled during a particular year, the market access under the quota is lost. Table 4-6 provides examples of tariff-rate quotas applied to U.S. imports.

Table 4-6   Examples of the U.S. Tariff-Rate Quotas

Product	Within-Quota Tariff Rate	Import-Quota Threshold	Over-Quota Tariff Rate
Peanuts	9. 35 cents/kg	30,393 tons	187. 9 percent ad valorem
Beef	4. 4 cents/kg	634,621 tons	31. 3 percent ad valorem

continued

Product	Within-Quota Tariff Rate	Import-Quota Threshold	Over-Quota Tariff Rate
Milk	3. 2 cents/L	5. 7 million L	88. 5 cents/L
Blue Cheese	10 cents/kg	2. 6 million kg	$ 2. 60/kg
Cotton	4. 4 cents/kg	2. 1 million kg	36 cents/kg

Source: U. S. International Trade Commission, *Harmonized Tariff Schedule of the United States*, Washington, D.C., Government Printing Office, 2000.

The tariff-rate quota appears to differ little from the import quota discussed earlier in this chapter. The distinction is that under an import quota it is legally impossible to import more than a specified amount. Under a tariff-rate quota, however, imports can exceed this specified amount, but a higher, over-quota tariff is applied on the excess.

In principle, a tariff-rate quota provides more access to imports than an import quota. In practice, many over-quota tariffs are prohibitively high and effectively exclude imports in excess of the quota. It is possible to design a tariff-rate quota so that it reproduces the trade volume limit of an import quota. Concerning the administration of tariff-rate quotas, license on demand allocation is the most common technique for the quotas that are enforced. Under this system, licenses are required to import at the within-quota tariff. Before the quota period begins, potential importers are invited to apply for import licenses. If the demand for license is less than the quota, the system operates like a first-come, first-served system. Usually, if demand exceeds the quota, the import volume requested is reduced proportionally among all applicants. Other techniques for allocating quota licenses are historical market share and auctions.

Orderly Marketing Agreements

An orderly marketing agreement (OMA) is a market-sharing pact negotiated by trading partners. Its main purpose is to moderate the intensity of international competition, allowing less efficient domestic producers to participate in markets that would otherwise have been lost to foreign producers who sell a superior product at a lower price. OMAs involve trade negotiations between importing and exporting countries, generally for a variety of labor-intensive manufactured goods.

A typical OMA consists of voluntary quotas applied to exports. These controls are known as **voluntary export restraints** (VERs) ; they are sometimes supplemented by backup import controls to ensure that the restraints are effective. For example, Japan may impose limits on steel exports to Europe, or Taiwan may agree to cutbacks on shoe exports to the United States. Because OMAs are reached through negotiations, on the surface they appear to be less one-sided than unilateral protectionist devices such as import tariffs and quotas.

In practice, the distinction between negotiated versus unilateral trade curbs becomes blurred. Trade negotiations are often carried out with the realization that the importing countries may adopt more stringent protectionist devices should the negotiators be unable to reach an acceptable settlement. An exporting country's motivation to negotiate OMAs may thus stem from its desire to avoid a more costly alternative, that is, a full-fledged trade war.

Domestic Content Requirements

Today, many products, such as autos and aircrafts, are produced globally. Domestic manufacturers of these products purchase resources or perform assembly functions outside the home country, a practice known as outsourcing or production sharing. For example, General Motors has obtained engines from its subsidiaries in Mexico, Chrysler has purchased ball joints from Japanese producers, and Ford has acquired cylinder heads from European companies. Firms have used outsourcing to take advantage of lower production costs overseas, including lower wage rates. Domestic workers often challenge this practice, maintaining that outsourcing means that cheap foreign labor takes away their jobs and imposes downward pressure on their wages. To limit the practice of outsourcing, organized labor has lobbied for the use of domestic content requirements. These requirements stipulate the minimum percentage of a product's total value that must be produced domestically. The effect of content requirements is to pressure both domestic and foreign firms who sell products in the home country to use domestic inputs (workers) in the production of those products. The demand for domestic inputs thus increases, contributing to higher input prices. Manufacturers generally lobby against domestic content requirements, because they prevent manufacturers from obtaining inputs at the lowest cost, thus contributing to higher product prices and loss of competitiveness.

Subsidies

National governments sometimes grant subsidies to their producers to help improve their trade position. By providing domestic firms with a cost advantage, a subsidy allows them to market their products at prices lower than warranted by their actual cost or profit considerations. Governmental subsidies assume a variety of forms, including outright cash disbursements, tax concessions, insurance arrangements, and loans at below-market interest rates. Table 4-7 provides examples of governmental subsidies for several countries. For purposes of our discussion, two types of subsidies can be distinguished: a domestic subsidy which is sometimes granted to producers of import-competing goods, and an export subsidy which goes to producers of the goods that are to be sold overseas. In both cases, the government adds an amount to the price purchasers pay rather than subtracts from it. The net price actually received by the producers equals the price paid by purchasers plus the subsidy. The subsidized producers are thus able to supply a greater quantity at each price consumers pay.

Table 4-7   Examples of Governmental Subsidies

Country	Subsidy Policy
Australia	Export market development grants: extended to Australia exporters to seek out and develop overseas markets
Canada	Rail transportation subsidies: granted to Canadian exporters of wheat, barley, oats, and alfalfa
European Union	Export subsidies: provided to many agricultural products such wheat, beef, poultry, fruits, and dairy products; financial assistance: extended to airbus
Japan	Financial assistance: extended to Japanese aerospace producers, including loans at low interest rates and assistance with R&D costs
The United States	Export subsidies: provided to U. S. producers of agricultural and manufactured goods through the Commodity Credit Corporation and the Export-Import bank

Source: Office of the U. S. Trade Representative, *Foreign Trade Barriers*, Washington, D. C., U. S. Government Printing Office, various issues.

Dumping

The case for protecting import-competing producers from foreign competition is bolstered by the antidumping argument. Dumping is recognized as a form of international price discrimination. It occurs when foreign buyers are charged lower prices than domestic buyers for an identical product, after allowing for transportation costs and tariff duties. Selling in foreign markets at a price below the cost of production is also considered dumping.

Commercial dumping is generally viewed as sporadic, predatory, or persistent in nature. Each type is practiced under different circumstances.

Sporadic dumping (distress dumping) occurs when a firm disposes of excess inventories on foreign markets by selling abroad at lower prices than at home. Although sporadic dumping may be beneficial to importing consumers, it can be quite disruptive to import-competing producers, who face falling sales and short-run losses. Temporary tariff duties can be levied to protect home producers, but because sporadic dumping has minor effects on international trade, governments are reluctant to grant tariff protection under these circumstances.

Predatory dumping occurs when a producer temporarily reduces the prices charged abroad to drive foreign competitors out of business. When the producer succeeds in acquiring a monopoly position, prices are then raised commensurate with its market power. Home governments are generally concerned about predatory pricing for monopolizing purposes and may retaliate with antidumping duties that eliminate the price differential. Although predatory dumping is a theoretical possibility, economists have not found empirical evidence that supports its existence.

Persistent dumping, as its name suggests, goes on indefinitely. In an effort to maximize economic profits, a producer may consistently sell abroad at lower prices than at home.

Despite the benefits that dumping may offer to importing consumers, governments have often levied penalty duties against commodities they believe are being dumped into their markets from abroad.

4.3.2　Effects of Import Quota

To illustrate the welfare effect of a quota, we employ a supply and demand model to show that the economic effects of a quota are very similar to the effects of a tariff. Figure 4-8 illustrates the effects of a quota on the domestic market for cloth of a small importing nation. The domestic demand and supply curves of cloth are shown as D and S, respectively. In the absence of trade, equilibrium would occur at Point E with the domestic price of cloth equaling P.

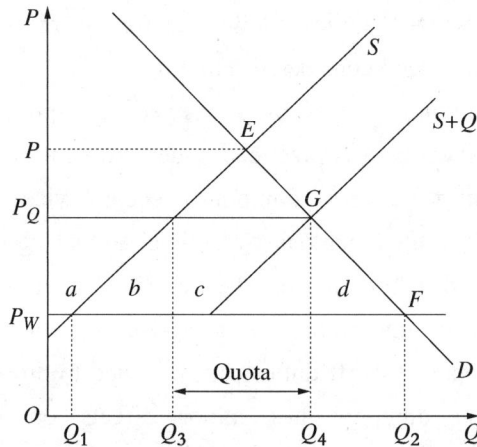

Figure 4-8   the Effects of an Import Quota

Now, assume that this country has a comparative disadvantage in the production of cloth and decides to open its borders to trade. In this case, the country will import cloth at price P_W and the free trade equilibrium is located at Point F. Under conditions of free trade, the domestic price of cloth would fall to the world price P_W, with Q_1 cloth being produced domestically and Q_2Q_1 being imported. If a tariff were imposed in this market, the domestic price of cloth would rise. As a result, domestic production of cloth would expand and import would decline. Identical effects on the domestic price, domestic production, and the amount imported would occur if the government imposed an import quota.

Assume the government imposes an import quota that restricts the supply of imported cloth to Q units. The imposition of the quota changes the amount of cloth supplied to the importing country. For all prices above the world price P_W, the total supply of cloth in the importing country would equal the domestic supply S, plus the quota Q. This total supply of cloth in the importing country is illustrated by the supply curve of $S + Q$. Because the supply of imported cloth is reduced at the world price of P_W, the price of cloth will begin to rise until a new equilibrium is reached at G. In this case, domestic consumers are harmed as consumer surplus declined by Areas $a + b + c + d$. Like our analysis of a tariff, domestic producers benefit as they produce more of the product and sell at higher price. The increase in producer welfare (surplus) by imposing a quota is represented by Area a. In addition, there are efficiency losses of Areas b and d. Remember that, the small triangle b is the cost of resources transferred from their best use to the production of more cloth. In a free market, this represents a loss to society, as these resources would have been used to produce a product in which the importing country has a comparative advantage. Transferring resources to the quota-restricted industry necessarily entails a loss of resources to some other more productive industry. Finally, Area d is a consumption effect caused by a quota as consumers purchase less cloth.

Who receives Area c is the only difference between a tariff and a quota. In the case of a tariff, Area c is the amount of tariff revenue the domestic government collects. In the case of a quota, Area c accrues to the foreign producers and makes them more profitable. The net welfare loss to the quota-imposing country is larger under a quota. The country loses Areas $b + c + d$ under a quota but only Areas $b + d$ under a tariff. With a tariff, the domestic government gains revenue, Area c which can be spent on the provision of public goods. With a quota, Area c is lost to the foreign producers.

There are two methods available for a government or community to capture Area c from foreign producers under a quota. First, the domestic government could auction quotas to importers in a free market. The advantage to this auction method is that the domestic government would gain Area c. The limited quota supply would go to those importers most in need of the product who would pay the higher prices.

The other method available to a government to capture Area c is to convert the quota into an equivalent tariff. The conversion of a quota into a tariff has several advantages. First, tariffs are legal under the World Trade Organization (WTO) and quotas are not. If foreign firms find the quota sufficiently restrictive, they can perhaps petition their government to complain to the WTO for relief or an alternative relief remedy. Second, calculating a tariff equivalent for an existing quota is relatively easy to do. To calculate an equivalent tariff, one would take the difference between the good's world market price and the quota-constrained domestic price and divide that difference by the world market price. Calculating these tariff equivalents has become an important process in world trade.

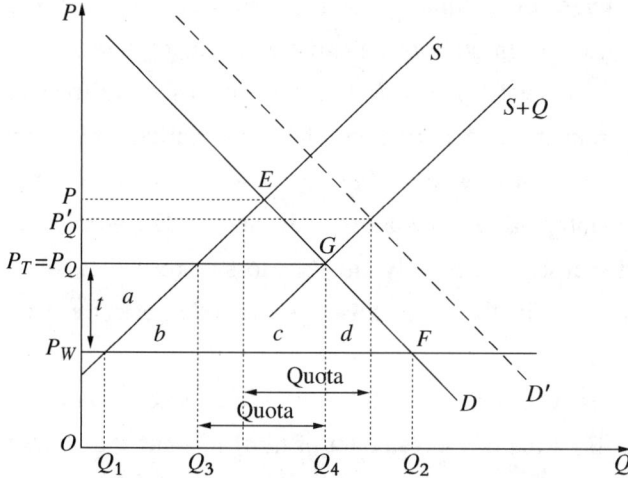

Figure 4-9　Domestic Effects of a Quota When Demand Increases

A tariff is much less restrictive in the domestic market when the domestic demand for the product increases. This is illustrated in Figure 4-9, where we have assumed that the demand for cloth increases from D to D' after a quota has been imposed. As a result of the quota, the quantity imported, Q_4Q_3, cannot increase when there is an increase in demand and the price of cloth rises from P_Q to P_Q'. In the case of a tariff, the price would remain constant at P_T and the additional demand for cloth would cause additional imports. However, in the presence of a quota, the domestic producers supply the increase in demand. In this case, the foreign producers of cloth also gain as the price they receive for their product increases. The important point is that the losses for consumers and community are much larger in the case of a quota than in the case of a tariff when demand increases. These losses are shown by Areas $b + c + d$. As the figure indicates, these losses to the community increase as the demand for the product increases.

Although quotas reduce foreign competition in the short run, the long-run anticompetitive effects may be greatly diminished for two reasons. First, quotas may entice foreign firms that are exporting to the domestic market to engage in foreign direct investment in the quota-constrained market. If the market in the importing country is large enough and the barriers to exporting are sufficiently high, foreign firms may find it profitable to build production facilities in the importing country. This effect is analogous to firms building plants to jump over high tariffs. Second, when an importing country enforces a quota, the quota is stated as a specific number of units without regard to their price. In this case, the exporters have a clear incentive to export the highest quality and most expensive products.

4.3.3 Effects of Export Subsidy

In a small nation, the imposition of subsidy directly raises the price received by producers for exported units of the product. For every unit exported, producers receive the international price plus the subsidy. Producers are thus given the incentive to shift sales from domestic market to foreign markets to receive the government subsidy. The end result is that the export subsidy reduces the quantity sold in the domestic market, increases the price in the domestic market to where it equals the international price plus the subsidy, and increases the quantity supplied by producers as they respond to the higher price, leading finally to increased exports.

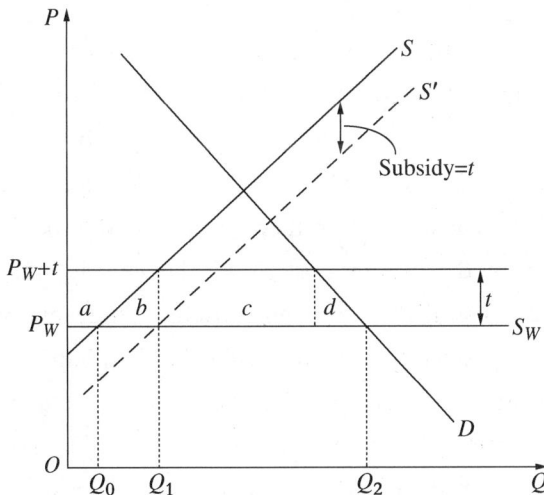

Figure 4-10   Welfare Effects of a Domestic Production Subsidy

Consider Figure 4-10. The demand and supply responses are evident in the partial equilibrium analysis for a small nation. Consider a per unit production subsidy of t paid by the government to domestic cloth manufactures coupled with free trade. The effect of the subsidy would be to shift the domestic supply downward by the amount of the subsidy — reflecting the lower costs the industry now faces. This is illustrated by the supply curve labeled S'. Because of the subsidy, domestic producers would expand their output to the point where their subsidy-augmented supply curve crosses the world price line. That is, they would choose to produce Q_1 units.

What is the economic cost of a subsidy program? First, there is the subsidy itself. From the figure, we can easily see that producers receive $a + b$. That is, they receive t times every unit produced domestically (Q_1 units). Where does the government get the money needed to finance the subsidy? The answer must be that it is paid by taxpayers, who are assumed to be in the consumer sector.

What do producers gain under the subsidy? The answer is that domestic profits rise by Area a. The remainder of the money they receive goes to pay for the additional cost of resources required to expand production from Q_0 to Q_1 units. Thus, just as with tariffs, we can think of Area b as a deadweight cost of the government policy, in this case the cost of the subsidy program. Putting it all together, consumers lose Areas $a + b$ in the form of higher taxes, while producers gain Area a in profits. The cost to the community is Area b, the production deadweight cost of the subsidy. This compares favorably with a tariff of t that would produce deadweight cost Areas $b + d$. That is, the difference between a tariff and a subsidy is that with the former, there is both a production deadweight cost and a consumption deadweight cost. With the subsidy and free trade, goods sell at the world price, so that there is no consumption deadweight cost.

Finally, it is important to note that subsidies are superior to protection in another way: they are more visible. If governments are making payments on a regular basis to domestic industry, it becomes a part of the public record. Unlike with trade barriers, it becomes easy to understand subsidies are the costs to community for supporting any given industry.

Chapter 5

Regional Trading Arrangements

Key Concepts and Terms

Regional Trading Arrangement	区域贸易安排
Free Trade Area (FTA)	自由贸易区
Customs Union (CU)	关税同盟
Common Market	共同市场
Economic Union	经济联盟
Monetary Union	货币联盟
Static Effect	静态效应
Dynamic Effect	动态效应
Trade Diversion	贸易转移
Trade Creation	贸易创造
Tariff Factory	保税工厂
Value-added Tax(VAT)	增值税
European Union (EU)	欧盟
North American Free Trade Area (NAFTA)	北美自由贸易区
Association of Southeast Asian Nations (ASEAN)	东盟

Since World War Ⅱ, developed countries have significantly lowered their trade restrictions. Such trade liberalization has stemmed from two approaches. The first is a reciprocal reduction of trade barriers on a nondiscriminatory basis. The second approach to trade liberalization occurs when a small group of countries, typically on a regional basis, forms a **regional trading arrangement**. Under this system, member countries agree to impose lower barriers to trade within the group than to trade with nonmember countries. In this chapter, we discuss several different types of regional trading arrangements, present a framework for analyzing the welfare impacts of these special relationships, and examine recent effort of regional trading arrangement in the world.

5.1　Types of Regional Trading Arrangements

Regional trading arrangements can be generally classified as free trade area, customs union, common market and economic union.

Free Trade Area

The most common scheme is referred to as a **free trade area** (FTA), in which all members of the group remove tariffs on each other's product, while at the same time each member retains its independence in establishing trading policies with nonmembers. In other words, the members of a FTA can maintain individual tariffs and other trade barriers on the "outside world". This scheme is usually assumed to apply to all products between member countries, but it can clearly involve a mix of free trade in some products and preferential, but still protected, treatment in others. It needs to be noted that when each member country sets its own external tariff, nonmember countries may find it profitable to export a product to the member country with the lowest level of outside protection and sell them through it to other member countries whose protection levels against the outside world are higher. An example of this stage of integration is the *North American Free Trade Agreement* (*NAFTA*), consisting of Canada, Mexico, and the United States.

Customs Union

Like a free trade association, a **customs union** (CU) is an agreement among two or more trading partners to remove all tariff and nontariff trade barriers among themselves. In this stage, all tariffs are removed between members and the group adopts a common external commercial policy toward nonmembers. Furthermore, the group acts as one body in the negotiation of all trade agreements with nonmembers. The existence of the common external tariff takes away the possibility of transshipment by nonmembers. The customs union is thus a step closer toward economic integration than the FTA. An example of a customs union is that of Belgium, the Netherlands and Luxembourg (Benelux), which was formed in 1947 and absorbed into the European Community in 1958.

Common Market

A **common market** is a group of trading countries that permits the free movement of goods and services among member countries, the initiation of common external trade restrictions against nonmembers, and the free movement of factors of production across national borders within the economic bloc. The common market thus represents a more complete stage of integration than a free trade area or a customs union. The Treaties of Rome in 1957 established a common market within the European Community (EC), which officially began on January 1, 1958 and became the European Union (EU) on November 1, 1993.

Economic Union

Beyond these stages, economic integration could evolve to the stage of **economic union**, which includes all features of a common market but also implies the unification of economic institutions and the coordination of economic policy throughout all member countries. While separate political entities are still present, an economic union generally establishes several supranational institutions whose decisions are binding upon all members. In fact, the task of creating an economic union is much more ambitious than achieving the other forms of integration. This is because a free-trade area, customs union, or common market results primarily from the abolition of existing trade barriers, but an economic union requires an agreement to transfer economic sovereignty to a supranational authority. The ultimate degree of economic union would be the unification of national monetary policies and the acceptance of a common currency administered by a supranational monetary authority. The economic union would thus include the dimension of a **monetary union**.

Table 5-1   Some Regional Trading Arrangements in the World Economy

Organization	Included Countries
Association of Southeast Asian Nations (ASEAN)	Brunei, Cambodia, Indonesia, Laos, Malaysia, Myanmar, Philippines, Singapore, Thailand, Vietnam
Economic Community of West African States (ECOWAS)	Benin, Burkina Faso, Cabo Verde, Côte d'Ivoire, Gambia, Ghana, Guinea, Guinea-Bissau, Liberia, Mali, Niger, Nigeria, Senegal, Sierra Leone, Togo

continued

Organization	Included Countries
European Union (EU)	Austria, Belgium, Bulgaria, Cyprus, Croatia, Czechia, Denmark, Estonia, Finland, France, Germany, Greece, Hungary, Ireland, Italy, Latvia, Lithuania, Luxembourg, Malta, Netherlands, Poland, Portugal, Romania, Slovakia, Slovenia, Spain, Sweden
Latin American Integration Association (LAIA)	Argentina, Bolivia, Brazil, Chile, Colombia, Cuba, Ecuador, Mexico, Paraguay, Peru, Uruguay, Venezuela
North American Free Trade Agreement (NAFTA)	Canada, Mexico, the United States
South African Customs Union (SACU)	Botswana, Lesotho, Namibia, South Africa, Swaziland

Source: Appleyad, D., Fied, Jr. A. J., 1992, *International Economics*, 4th Edition, McGraw-Hill Companies, Inc.

5.2 Effects of Customs Union

What are the possible welfare implications of a customs union? We can delineate the theoretical benefits and costs of such devices from two perspectives. First are the static effects of a customs union on productive efficiency and consumer welfare. Second are the dynamic effects of a customs union, which relate to its member countries' long-run rates of growth. Because a small change in the growth rate can lead to substantial cumulative effect on national output, the dynamic effects of trade policy changes can yield substantially larger magnitudes than those based on static models. These static and dynamic effects determine the overall welfare gains or losses associated with the formation of a regional trading arrangement.

5.2.1 Static Effects

The static welfare effects of lowering tariff barriers among members of a trade bloc are illustrated in the following example. We suppose that there exist three countries in the world: *A*, *B* and *C*, and begin by assuming that *A* is the world high-cost producer of a product, say, beer, and that initially *A* protects its producers with an ad valorem tariff of 100 percent against all foreign producers. Suppose that, in autarky, beer would cost $5 per bottle in *A*, and *B* would be willing to export beer to A for $2 per bottle, while C, the low-cost world producer, is willing to export beer at a price of $1.5 per bottle.

Figure 5-1 illustrates the market for beer in Country A. The lines S_B and S_C denote the export supply curves to A's market from Countries B and C, respectively. Under free trade, A would import IJ bottles of beer from C, at a price of $1.5 each. Since A can buy beer from C at $1.5, there is no demand for beer from B, which is priced at $2.

Now, recall that we have assumed that A has a 100 percent tariff in place. The effect of this tariff is to double the price of imported beer. Thus, the price of beer imported from C rises to $3 per bottle. This is lower than the $4 price ($2 plus $2 tariff) of beer that could be imported from B. So A continues to import beer only from C, EF bottles at $3 each.

Suppose that A were to negotiate a customs union (CU) with Country B. Under such an arrangement, goods coming to A from Country B would not be charged a tariff. The tariff would remain on any goods coming from Country C. Suppose the tariff on beer from B were dropped—what would happen? Clearly, consumers in A could buy beer from B at a price of $2. If they were to buy from C instead, the price would be $3. Thus, there would be a natural tendency for A to switch its beer purchases from C to B. In the process, imports would expand from EF bottles to GH bottles. All of these would come, however, from Country B rather than Country C.

As this example shows, the formation of a CU can have two effects on international trade. First, there is the shift in the source of trade from C, the lowest-cost world producer, to B, the lowest-cost CU member country. This shift in the source of trade is known as **trade diversion**. In general, trade diversion is viewed as welfare reducing for the world. The intuition for thinking this is that A no longer imports from the country that has a natural comparative advantage (i.e., Country C). Instead, it has agreed to discriminate in favor of its fellow CU partner, Country B. In the process, resources are directed away from beer production in the low-cost world producer, Country C, to beer production in the higher-cost partner, Country B.

The second effect of the formation of the CU is that trade expands for Country A. Imports rise from EF to GH. This comes about because consumers are able to pay a lower price for imports. The expansion of trade that results from CU formation is known as **trade creation**. From a world welfare perspective, trade creation is good. This is because the highest-cost producer is availing itself to a greater extent of the benefits available from international trade.

Whether or not the creation of a CU is beneficial to the member countries depends on the relative strengths of the forces of trade creation and trade diversion. Consider again Figure 5-1. Let us calculate the welfare impact on Country A of the creation of a CU between A and B. If A forms a CU with Country B, consumers in A's benefit. The price they pay falls from \$3 to \$2. Consumer surplus rises by $a + b + c + d$. Producer surplus falls by a, while tariff revenue falls by $c + e$. Netting out these changes in surpluses yields a welfare impact on A of $(b + d) - e$ (See Table 5-2).

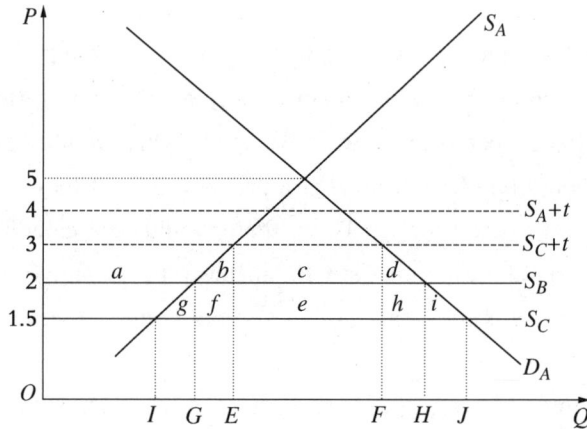

Figure 5-1 Static Effects of Customs Union

Because of the trade diversion, A no longer trades with Country C. The impact of this is for tariff revenues to fall. Part of this loss of tariff revenues, c, accrues to domestic residents in the form of lower prices. The remainder, e, represents a loss to A. This loss occurs because the CU between A and B means consumers in A must pay a higher price to producers in B than otherwise pay for the same goods purchased from C. The size of Area e represents the amount that the price has increased and the base of Area e is the quantity of trade diverted away from C by the CU. Thus, e is the increased amount that B's producers receive relative to what C's producers had received prior to the CU. This is the cost of trade diversion to A.

Because trade expands, however, there is an offsetting gain. Consumers in A pay a lower price to purchase the good, and hence, trade expands. The benefits of international trade are the familiar triangles equal in value to $b + d$. To interpret these areas in the context of this example, note that the height of these triangles represents the amount that the retail price of imports has fallen because the CU was formed. The lengths of the bases of the two triangles sum to equal the amount that trade has increased because of the CU. Thus, the sum of these two triangles represents the gain to A from trade creation. Thus, Areas $b + d$ measure the amount of the effect of trade creation. Overall, A is better off if the benefits of trade creation exceed the costs of trade diversion (measured by Area e), but there is nothing in the diagram to guarantee that this will occur.

Table 5-2   The Welfare Effects of a CU on Country A

Item	Welfare Changes (Area)				
Change in consumer surplus	a	b	c	d	
Change in producer surplus	$-a$		$-c$		
Change in government revenue					$-e$
Net welfare change (for Country A)		b		d	$-e$

What about the other countries? Clearly, B gains on the export side from this arrangement. It obtains export markets in A that it had previously been unable to penetrate. On the other hand, if A is a higher-cost producer than C, then when B lowers its tariffs on goods from A, it faces ambiguous welfare prospects. Meanwhile, Country C loses because its producers have lost markets. Clearly, since the effect on A and B is ambiguous and C loses, the worldwide welfare effect of the formation of CU or other preferential trading relationships is anything but certain. The world could gain, or it could lose. What will make the difference?

In general, preferential trading arrangements that maximize trade creation will

have the greatest positive world welfare effect. Let us return to Figure 5-1 and
consider a CU between Country A and Country C. In this case, A would eliminate
its tariff with respect to Country C. The price of beer would fall to $\$1.5$, and
imports from C would expand to IJ. The increase in imports represents pure trade
creation. That is, in this example, trade diversion would be zero, since, both
before and after the agreement, A trades with C. For A, the welfare gains of the
formation of a CU relative to tariff are $b + f + g + d + h + i$. Country C gains as
well, because its exports rise. B neither gains nor loses in this case, because its
trade has not been affected.

5.2.2 Dynamic Effects

Besides the static effects discussed above, the countries forming a CU are
likely to receive several important dynamic benefits. Theses are due to increased
competition, economies of scale, stimulus to investment, and better utilization of
economic resources. These will be examined in turn.

The greatest dynamic benefit from the formation of a customs union is the
increased competition that is likely to result. That is, in the absence of a CU,
producers are likely to grow sluggish and complacent behind trade barriers. But
when a CU is formed and trade barriers among member countries are eliminated,
producers in each country become more efficient to meet the competition of other
producers within the union. The increased level of competition is also likely to
stimulate the development and utilization of new technology. All of these efforts
will cut costs of production to the benefit of consumers. A CU must, of course,
be careful that such oligopolistic practices as collusion and market-sharing
agreements, which earlier might have restricted competition nationally, are not
replaced by similar union-wide practices after the formation of the CU. The EU
has attempted to do just that.

A second possible benefit from the formation of a CU is that economies of
scale are likely to result from the enlarged market. However, it must be pointed
out that even a small country that is not a member of any CU can overcome the
smallness of its domestic market and achieve substantial economies of scale in
production by exporting to the rest of the world. For example, it was found that
plants in many major industries in such relatively small countries as Belgium and

the Netherlands were already of comparable size to U.S. plants before they joined the EU and thus already enjoyed substantial economies of scale by producing for the domestic market and for export. Nevertheless, significant economies were achieved after the formation of the EU by reducing the range of differentiated products manufactured in each plant and increasing "production runs".

Another possible benefit is the stimulus to investment to take advantage of the enlarged market and to meet the increased competition. Furthermore, the formation of a CU is likely to spur outsiders to set up production facilities within the CU to avoid the trade barriers imposed on non-union products. These are the so-called tariff factories. The massive investments that U.S. firms made in Europe after 1955 and again after 1986 can be explained by their desire not to be excluded from this rapidly growing market.

Finally, in a CU that has nearly developed into a common market, the free community-wide movement of labor and capital is likely to result in better utilization of the economic resources of entire community.

These dynamic gains resulting from the formation of a CU are presumed to be much greater than the static gains discussed above and to be very significant. Indeed, the United Kingdom joined the EU in 1973 primarily because of these dynamic considertations. Recent empirical studies seem to indicate that these dynamic gains are about five to six times larger than the static gains.

What needs to be pointed out, however, is that joining a CU because of the static and dynamic benefits that it provides is only a second-best solution. The best policy may be for a country to unilaterally eliminate all trade barriers. For a country such as the U. S. that is large enough to affect its terms of trade, however, the efficiency benefits resulting from unilaterally eliminating its trade barriers must be weighed against the worsening of its terms of trade. The unilateral elimination of all trade barriers would also be difficult politically because of strong opposition from the very vocal and influential minorities who would be hurt in the process. A related question is whether regional blocs are building blocks or stumbling blocks to free multilateral trade. There is a great deal of disagreement here. Some economists believe that regional blocs permit more rapid trade liberalization. Others, such as Bhagwati, feel that they retard multilateral trade liberalization and lead to potential inter-bloc conflicts. Perhaps we can have the best if trading blocs strive to reduce external as well as internal trade barriers and easily admit new members.

5.3   Practice of Regional Integration

In this section, we briefly survey some attempts at economic integration, starting with the formation of the European Union (EU), then the North American Free Trade Area (NAFTA), and finally the Association of Southeast Asian Nations (ASEAN).

5.3.1 European Union

In the years immediately after World War Ⅱ, the countries of Western Europe suffered balance-of-payments deficits in response to reconstruction efforts. To shield its firms and workers from external competitive pressures, they initiated an elaborate network of tariff and exchange restrictions, quantitative controls, and state trading. In the 1950s, however, these trade barriers were generally viewed to be counterproductive. Therefore, Western Europe began to dismantle its trade barriers in response to successful tariff negotiations under the auspices of the General Agreement on Tariffs and Trade (GATT).

It was against this background of trade liberalization that the European Union (EU), first known as the European Community, was created by the Treaty of Rome in 1957. The EU initially consisted of six countries: Belgium, France, Italy, Luxembourg, the United Kingdom and Ireland, and then Denmark joined the trade bloc. Greece became the tenth member in 1981, and the entry of Spain and Portugal in 1987 raised the membership to 12 countries. In 1995, Austria, Finland, and Sweden were admitted into the EU. Table 5-3 gives an economic profile of the union's member.

Table 5-3   European Union: Economic Profile, 2000

Country	Population (Millions)	Area (Thousands of Sq. km)	Per Capita GNP (Dollars)
Austria	8.1	84	26,310
Belgium	10.3	31	27,500

continued

Country	Population (Millions)	Area (Thousands of Sq. km)	Per Capita GNP (Dollars)
Denmark	5.3	43	27,120
Finland	5.2	338	24,610
France	58.9	552	24,470
Germany	82.2	357	25,010
Greece	10.6	132	16,940
Ireland	3.8	70	25,470
Italy	57.7	301	23,370
Luxembourg	0.5	3	41,058
Netherlands	15.9	37	26,170
Portugal	10.0	92	16,180
Spain	39.4	505	19,180
Sweden	8.9	450	23,770
United Kingdom	59.7	245	23,550

Source: Carbaugh., R. J., *International Economics*, ninth edition, Thomson Learning, 2005.

According to the Treaty of Rome of 1957, the EU agreed in principle to follow the path of economic integration and eventually become an economic union. In pursuing this goal, members of the EU first dismantled tariffs and established a free trade area by 1968. This liberalization of trade was accompanied by a fivefold increase in the value of industrial trade — higher than the world trade, in general. The success of the free trade area inspired the EU to continue its process of economic integration. In 1970, the EU became a full-fledged customs union when it adopted a common external tariff system for its members. On January 1, 1993, the EU removed all remaining restrictions on the free flow of goods, services, and resources among its members, thus becoming a single unified market. The expanded Union represents the largest trading bloc in the world. Intra-EU trade has been estimated to be double what it would have been in the absence of integration.

The formation of the EU significantly expanded trade in industrial goods with nonmembers. This was due to (1) the rapid growth of the EU, which increased its demand for imports of industrial products from outside the union, and (2) the reduction to very low levels of the average tariff on imports of industrial products as a result of the Kennedy and Tokyo Rounds of GATT. On the other hand, the formation of the EU resulted in trade diversion in agricultural commodities, particularly in temperate products such as grain from the United States.

At the Lome Convention in 1975, the EU eliminated most trade barriers on imports from 46 developing countries in Africa, the Caribbean, and the Pacific region that were former colonies of EU countries. This treaty was renewed every five years. Earlier in 1971, the EU had granted generalized tariff preferences to imports of manufactured and semimanufactured products from developing countries. But textiles, steel, consumer electronics, shoes, and many other products of great importance to developing countries were excluded. Preferences were extended to trade in tropical products in the Tokyo Round in 1979. However, since these preferences fell short of the complete elimination of trade barriers granted to former colonies, a bitter controversy arose because of the alleged trade diversion. Quotas and tariffs on developing countries' exports are now scheduled to be gradually reduced as a result of the Uruguay Round of GATT completed in December 1993. In February 2000, Lome Ⅳ expired and was replaced by a new agreement has the same general purpose as the Lome Convention and is to remain in force for 20 years, subject to revisions every five years.

Several studies have been conducted on the overall impact of the EU on its members' welfare during the 1960s and 1970s. In terms of static welfare benefits, one study concluded that trade creation was pronounced in machinery, transportation equipment, chemicals, and fuels; whereas trade diversion was apparent in agricultural commodities and raw materials. The broad conclusion can be drawn that trade creation in the manufactured goods sector during the 1960s and 1970s was significant: 10 percent to 30 percent of total EU imports of manufactured goods. Moreover, trade creation exceeded trade diversion by a wide margin, estimated at 2 percent to 15 percent. In addition, analysts also noted that the EU realized dynamic benefits from integration in the form of additional competition and investment and also economies of scale. For instance, it has been determined that many firms in small countries, such as the Netherlands and

Belgium, realized economies of scale by producing both for the domestic market and for export. However, after becoming members of EU, sizable additional economies of scale were gained by individual firms, reducing the range of products manufactured and increasing the output of the remaining products.

Other highlights in the operation of the EU are as follows: (1) Member countries have adopted a common *value-added tax system*, under which a tax is levied on the value added to the product at each stage of its production and passed on to consumers; (2) The *Commission* (the executive body of the EU headquartered in Brussels) proposes laws, monitors compliance with treaties, and administers common policies such as antitrust policies; (3) The *Council of Ministers* (whose members represent their own national governments) makes final decisions but only on the recommendation of the *Commission*. There is also a *European Parliament* (with 626 members elected by direct vote in the member countries every five years but without much power at present) and a *Court of Justice* (with power to rule on the constitutionality of the decision of the *Commission* and the *Council*); (4) Plans have also been drawn for harmonization of monetary and fiscal policies, and eventual full political union.

In 2004, 10 countries, mostly from the former communist bloc in Central and Eastern Europe, became members of the EU. The 10 countries are Poland, Hungary, Czech Republic, Slovakia, Slovenia, Estonia, Lithuania, Latvia, Malta, and Cyprus. Bulgaria and Romania joined in 2007.

5.3.2   North American Free Trade Agreement

The success of Europe in forming the European Union has inspired the United States with discussions for a free trade agreement with Canada, which became effective in 1989. This paved the way for Mexico, Canada, and the United States to form the North American Free Trade Agreement (NAFTA) that went into effect in 1994.

The establishment of NAFTA was expected to provide each member country better access to the other's markets, technology, labor and expertise. In many respects, there were remarkable fits between the countries: The United States would benefit from Mexico's pool of cheap and increasingly skilled labor, while Mexico would benefit from the U.S. investment and expertise. NAFTA eliminates tariffs among the three member countries over a 15-year period and at the same time substantially reduces nontariff barriers. Several of the more important sector agreements involved automobiles, textiles and apparel, apparel, agriculture, energy and petrochemicals, and financial services.

In the case of automobiles, Mexican tariffs were immediately reduced from 20 to 10 percent and were scheduled to decline to zero over the next 10 years. In addition, tariffs on auto parts were to be reduced to zero, and rules of origin specified that to qualify for preferential tariff treatment, vehicles must contain 62.5 percent North American content. Further, the requirement that autos supplying the Mexican market be produced in Mexico was to be gradually eliminated over a 10-year period.

In the textile and apparel industry, trade barriers were eliminated on 20 percent of U.S.-Mexican trade and barriers on an additional 60 percent are to be removed over a 6-year period. In addition, rules of origin required that to receive NAFTA tariff preferences, apparel must be manufactured in North America from the yarn-spinning stage forward. In agriculture, tariffs were immediately reduced from initial levels of 10 to 20 percent to zero for one-half of U.S. exports to Mexico, with the understanding that the tariffs on the remaining agricultural products would be reduced to zero over the 15-year adjustment period.

With respect to foreign investment and financial services in general, all barriers to the movement of capital were immediately dropped. In addition, Mexico's restrictions on Canadian and U. S. ownership and provision of commercial banking, insurance, securities trading, and other financial service were to be removed. Finally, U. S. and Canadian financial firms are now permitted to establish wholly owned subsidiaries in Mexico and to operate them in the same manner as Mexico firms operate. In like manner, Canada, Mexico, and the United States are to extend "national treatment" in service to each other, meaning that foreign-owned service firms are treated exactly like domestic firms, and to guarantee most favored nation treatment in services.

Table 5-4   Estimated Effects of NAFTA on Trade Flows (thousands of U.S. dollars)

Trade Flow	Trade Expansion	Trade Creation	Trade Diversion
U.S. imports from Canada	1,074,186	689,997	384,189
U.S. imports from Mexico	334,912	284,774	50,138
Canadian import from U.S.	63,656	38,444	25,212
Canadian imports from Mexico	167,264	3,321	163,943
Mexico imports from U.S.	77,687	50,036	27,651
Mexico imports from Canada	28,001	902	27,099

Source: Appleyard, D. R., Field, Jr. A. J., *International Economics*, fourth Edition, the McGraw-Hill Companies, Inc., 2001.

NAFTA was the first regional agreement among countries with such diverse income levels, and an important aspect of the agreement was the anticipated reinforcement that it would give to the strong growth that Mexico had achieved at the time of NAFTA formation since adopting structural, market-oriented reforms in the mid-1980s. Table 5-4 presents the results of the estimations by some researchers of what might be expected from NAFTA.

5.3.3   Association of Southeast Asian Nations

The Association of Southeast Asian Nations (ASEAN) now comprises 10 members: Brunei, Indonesia, Malaysia, Philippines, Singapore, Thailand, Vietnam, Laos, Myanmar and Cambodia. Among them, the last four are known as CMLV (Cambodia, Myanmar, Laos and Vietnam) who are latecomers to ASEAN. In 1992, ASEAN signed ASEAN Free Trade Area (AFTA) agreement supporting local manufacturing in all members.

The primary goals of AFTA seek to (1) increase ASEAN's competitive edge as a production base in the world market through the elimination of tariffs and non-tariff barriers within ASEAN and (2) attract more foreign direct investment to ASEAN. ASEAN members are to apply a tariff rate of 0 to 5 percent (the four latecomers were given additional time to implement the reduced tariff rates) for goods originating within ASEAN.

ASEAN Plus Three is a forum that functions as a coordinator of cooperation between ASEAN and the three East Asian countries of China, Japan, and South Korea. The first leaders' meeting was held in 1997 and the group's significance was strengthened by the Asian financial crisis. The grouping was institutionalized by 1999. ASEAN Plus Three has been credited as forming the basis for financial stability in Asia.

The ASEAN-China Free Trade Area (ACFTA) is a free trade area among the ten members of ASEAN and China. The initial framework agreement was signed in 2002 with the intent on establishing a free trade area among the eleven countries by 2010. The free trade area came into effect on 1 January 2010. ACFTA is the largest free trade area in terms of population and the third largest in terms of nominal GDP. By July 2010, ASEAN had become China's third largest trade partner and China had been ASEAN's largest trade partner. Closer regional cooperation is the general trend in an age of economic globalization and the surest way to build up risk resistance capacity. ACFTA has served as a driving force for regional economic cooperation.

Chapter 6

Balance of Payments and Foreign Exchange

Key Concepts and Terms

Balance of Payments	国际收支
Credit Transaction	贷方交易
Debit Transaction	借方交易
Current Account	经常账户
Capital and Financial Account	资本金融账户
Balance of Trade	贸易差额
Trade Surplus	贸易盈余
Trade Deficit	贸易赤字
Factor Income	要素收入
Unilateral Transfers	单边转移支付
Foreign Direct Investment（FDI）	对外直接投资
Portfolio Investment	证券组合投资
Reserve Assets	储备资产
Special Drawing Rights（SDRs）	特别提款权
Price-specie Flow Mechanism	价格—现金流动机制
Quantity Theory of Money	货币数量说
Sterilization	冲销
Foreign Exchange Market	外汇市场
Carry Trade	利差交易
Hedge Fund	对冲基金
Exchange Rate	汇率
Direct Quotation	直接标价法
Appreciation	升值

Depreciation	贬值
Spot Transaction	即期交易
Forward Transaction	远期交易
Currency Swap	货币互换
Exchange Rate System	汇率体系
Floating Exchange Rate	浮动汇率
Fixed Exchange Rate	固定汇率
Managed Floating Exchange Rate	有管理的浮动汇率
Pegged Exchange Rate	钉住汇率
Currency Board	货币局
Anchor Currency	锚货币

Hitherto, we have dealt with the "real" economy, as opposed to the monetary side of the economy. From now on, we begin to discuss the monetary aspects of international economics, or international finance by examining the balance of payments. In this chapter, we concern some fundamental concepts on which our further study is based.

6.1 Balance of Payments

A **balance of payments** (**BP**) sheet is an accounting record of all monetary transactions between a country and the rest of the world. These transactions include payments for the country's exports (X) and imports (M) of goods, services, and financial capital, as well as financial transfers. The BP summarizes international transactions for a specific period, usually a year. Some countries also keep such a record on a quarterly basis.

The arrangement of international transactions into a balance of payments account requires that each transaction be entered as a credit or a debit. A **credit transaction** is one that results in a receipt of a payment from foreigners and a **debit transaction** is one that leads to a payment to foreigners. Since every international transaction involves an exchange of assets, it has both a credit and a debit side. Thus, each credit entry is balanced by a debit entry, and vice versa. So the recording of any international transaction leads to two offsetting entries.

This is called as double entry accounting system. Thus, the total balance of payments account must always be in balance. There is no such thing as an overall balance of payments surplus or deficit. But subaccounts of the statement need not necessarily be in balance.

The balance of payments consists of two primary subaccounts: the current account (CA) and the capital and financial account (KA).

6.1.1　Current Account

The **current account** refers to the monetary value of international flows associated with transactions in goods and services, factor income, and unilateral transfers. It is the sum of the balance of trade, net factor income and net unilateral transfer.

The **balance of trade**, or **trade balance**, is the difference between a country's exports of goods and services and its imports of goods and services. A positive or favorable balance of trade is known as a **trade surplus** if exports exceed imports; a negative or unfavorable balance is referred to as a **trade deficit**. Because exports generate positive net sales, and the trade balance is typically the largest component of the current account, a current account surplus is usually associated with positive net exports.

The trade balance is identical to the difference between a country's output and its domestic demand. If the current account is in surplus, the country's net international asset position increases correspondingly. Equally, a deficit decreases the net international asset position.

The **net factor income**, or **income account**, is usually presented under the headings income payments as outflows, and income receipts as inflows. Income refers not only to the money received from investments made abroad (note: investments are recorded in the capital account but income from investments is recorded in the current account) but also to the money sent by individuals working abroad, known as remittances, to their families back home. If the income account is negative, the country is paying more than it is taking in interest and dividends.

Finally, the balance of payment summary is expanded to include **unilateral transfers.** Private transfer payment corresponds to gifts from foreigners, or pension payments to foreign residents who once worked in the host country.

Government transfers refer to gifts or grants made by one government to foreign residents or foreign governments. Examples of certain transfer payments include financial aid, social security, and government subsidies for certain businesses.

6.1.2 Capital and Financial Account

The current account is one of two primary components of the balance of payments, the other being the capital and financial account. Whereas the current account reflects a country's net income, the **capital and financial account** reflects net change in national ownership of assets. It can be further divided into capital account and financial account.

Capital Account

The capital account involves (1) capital transfers and (2) the acquisition or disposal of non-financial (for example, a physical asset such as land) and non-produced assets, which are needed for production but have not been produced (for example, a mine used for the extraction of diamonds). Capital transfers are monetary flows branching from the transfer of ownership on fixed assets (such as equipment used in the production process to generate income), the transfer of funds received to the sale or acquisition of fixed assets, the transfer of goods and financial assets by migrants leaving or entering a country, and debt forgiveness.

Financial Account

The financial account involves foreign direct investment, portfolio investment, other investment and reserve assets.

- *Foreign direct investment* (FDI). FDI occurs when residents of one country acquire a controlling interest in a business enterprise in another country. It often involves long-term capital investment such as the purchase or construction of machinery, buildings or even whole manufacturing plants. If foreigners are investing in a country, that is an inbound flow and counts as a surplus item on the capital and financial account. If a country's residents are investing in foreign countries, that's an outbound flow that will count as a deficit. After the initial investment, any yearly profits not re-invested will flow in the opposite direction, but will be recorded in the current account.

- *Portfolio investment.* Portfolio investment refers to the purchase of shares and bonds. As with FDI, the income derived from these assets is recorded in the current account — the capital and financial account entry will just be for any international buying and selling of the portfolio assets.

- *Other investment.* It refers to capital flows into bank accounts or provided as loans. Large short-term capital flows between accounts in different countries are commonly seen when the market is able to take advantage of fluctuations in interest rates and the exchange rate between currencies.

- *Reserve assets.* The reserve assets account is operated by a country's central bank, and can be a source of large capital flows to counteract those originating from the market. Reserve assets include gold reserves, convertible currencies that are readily acceptable as payment for international transactions and can be easily exchanged for one another, the special drawing rights (SDRs), and the reserve position that a country maintains in the International Monetary Fund (IMF).

Except reserve assets which are public-sector transactions, all other components of the capital and financial account are categorized into private-sector transactions.

When all components of the BP sheet are included, it must balance — that is, it must sum to zero — there can be no overall surplus or deficit. For example, if a country is importing more than it exports, its trade balance will be in deficit, but the shortfall will have to be counter-balanced in other ways — such as by funds earned from its foreign investments, by running down reserves or by receiving loans from other countries.

While the overall BP sheet will always balance when all types of payments are included, imbalances are possible on individual components of the BP, which can be trade balance (exports of goods and services minus imports of goods and services), current account balance, capital and financial account balance or overall BP balance (the current account plus the capital and financial account except for reserve assets). Most frequently, when we mention an imbalance in the BP, we actually refer to the current account balance.

6.1.3 Automatic Adjustment of the Balance of Payments

When the initial equilibrium has been disrupted, an adjustment mechanism works for the return to equilibrium. The process of BP adjustment takes two different forms. First, automatic adjustment can be expected under certain conditions through such factors as price, interest rate and income. Second, if automatic adjustments can not work, the government may adopt discretionary policies to achieve BP equilibrium. Actually, the balance of payments might be restored automatically under floating exchange rates rather than under fixed exchange rates. We leave the discretionary adjustments to Chapter 8 and only show an example of automatic adjustment called as price-specie flow mechanism here.

Price-Specie Flow Mechanism

The price-specie flow mechanism initially was a logical argument by David Hume against the Mercantilist idea that a country should strive for a positive balance of trade, or net exports. Hume argues that under a gold standard, when a country has a positive balance of trade, gold would flow into the country in the amount that the value of exports exceeds the value of imports. Conversely, when such a country has a negative balance of trade, gold would flow out of the country in the amount that the value of imports exceeds the value of exports. Consequently, in the absence of any offsetting actions by the central bank on the quantity of money in circulation (called sterilization), the money supply would rise in a country with a positive balance of trade and fall in a country with a negative balance of trade. According to **the quantity theory of money**, in countries where the quantity of money increases, inflation would set in and the prices of goods and services would tend to rise while in countries where the money supply decreases, deflation would occur as the prices of goods and services fall.

The higher prices would, in the countries with a positive balance of trade, cause exports to decrease and imports to increase, which will alter the balance of trade downwards towards a neutral balance. Inversely, in countries with a negative balance of trade, the lower prices would cause exports to increase and imports to decrease, which will improve the balance of trade towards a neutral balance. These adjustments in the balance of trade will continue until it equals zero in all countries involved in the exchange.

But the price-specie flow mechanism has incurred vehement criticisms. First, the classical linkage between changes in a country's gold supply and changes in its money supply no longer exists. Second, the full employment on which the quantity theory of money holds is not common. Thus, changes in money supply will do affect national output and may have little influence on prices — prices will no longer adjust to the change in money supply. Third, in a modern industrial world, prices and wages sticky in a downward direction — people are reluctant to see their income to fall, causing prices and wages unable to adjust downward.

These criticisms against the price-specie flow mechanism imply that the automatic adjustments may not be dependable and sometimes we need resort to discretionary policies.

6.2   Foreign Exchange Market and Exchange Rates

6.2.1   Foreign Exchange Market

International transactions are settled by means of foreign bills of exchange which are bought in the foreign exchange market. The **foreign exchange market** is a worldwide decentralized over-the-counter financial market for the trading of currencies. Financial centers around the world function as anchors of foreign exchange trading between a wide range of different types of buyers and sellers around the clock, with the exception of weekends. The foreign exchange market determines the relative values of different currencies. It is the largest and most liquid financial market in the world.

The primary purpose of the foreign exchange market is to assist international trade and investment, by allowing businesses to convert one currency to another. For example, it permits a Chinese business to import European goods and pay Euros, even though the business income is in RMB. It also supports speculation, and facilitates the carry trade, in which investors borrow low-yielding currencies and lend (invest in) high-yielding currencies.

Unlike a stock market, the foreign exchange market is divided into levels of access which are determined by the amount of money with which they are trading. At the top is the inter-bank market, which is made up of the largest commercial banks and securities dealers. The top-tier inter-bank market accounts for more than a half of all transactions. After that there are usually smaller banks, followed by large multi-national corporations (which need to hedge risk and pay employees in different countries), large hedge funds, and some other financial institutions. National central banks also participate in the foreign exchange market to align currencies to their economic needs.

6.2.2 Exchange Rate

The **exchange rate** between two currencies specifies how much one currency is worth in terms of the other. It is either directly quoted or indirectly quoted. In **direct quotation** which China adopts, the exchange rate is the value of a foreign country's currency in terms of the home country's currency. For example, an exchange rate of 6.82 ¥/$ means that CNY 6.82 is worth the same as USD 1.

The appreciation of a country's currency refers to an increase in the value of that country's currency. The **depreciation** of a country's currency refers to a decrease in the value of that country's currency. For instance, if RMB appreciates relative to the dollar, the exchange rate falls — it takes fewer RMB to purchase 1 dollar. While if RMB depreciates relative to the dollar, the exchange rate rises — it takes more RMB to purchase 1 dollar.

Types of Foreign Exchange Transactions

When buying or selling foreign currencies, banks promise to pay a stipulated amount of currency to another bank or customer on an agreed date. There are generally three types of foreign exchange transactions: spot, forward and swap.

A **spot transaction** is an outright purchase and sale of foreign currency for cash settlement no more than two business days after the date the transaction is recorded as a spot deal. Usually, the settlement date is the second business day after the date on which the transaction is agreed to by the two traders.

Sometimes, a business or financial institution knows it will receive or pay an amount of foreign currency on a specific date in the future. For example, a Chinese exporter will receive an amount of dollar in 3 months. In order to guard against the possibility of dollar depreciation, the exporter might contract with a bank to sell that amount of dollar at a stipulated exchange rate 3 months later. When the contract matures, the exporter sells the dollar at the stipulated exchange rate. This is known as a **forward transaction**. In a forward transaction, the exchange rate is fixed when the contract is initially made.

A **currency swap** is the conversion of one currency to another at one point in time, with an agreement to reconvert it back to the original currency at a specified time in the future. The rates of both exchanges are agreed to in advance. Swaps provide an efficient mechanism through which banks can meet their foreign exchange needs over a period of time.

Supply of and Demand for Foreign Exchange

Many macroeconomic factors affect exchange rates and in the end, currency prices are a result of dual forces of demand and supply. Therefore, before taking up the mechanism of foreign exchange, it may be well to examine briefly the sources of supply and demand which give rise to foreign bills. The principal sources of foreign exchange supply are exports of merchandise, sales of securities abroad, transfers of foreign banking capital to this side, and the sale of financial bills to foreigners. The principal sources of foreign exchange demand are imports of merchandise, purchases of foreign securities, remittances of dividends and interest on foreign capital invested here, expenditures of tourists, and remittances for freight and insurance.

The export and import of goods and services are the largest factor in the supply of and demand for foreign exchange. For example, the supply of dollars is generated by China's exporting goods and services to the U.S., borrowing funds from the U.S., attracting U.S. FDI, drawing back U.S. debts, and receiving U.S. transfer payments. In each of these cases, the U.S. offers dollars in the foreign exchange market. And China's demand for dollars may stem form its desire to import U.S. goods and services, make FDI in the U.S., or make transfer payments to the U.S.. The determination of exchange rates by supply of and demand for foreign exchange is depicted by lines in Figure 6-1 where the horizontal axis depicts the quantity of foreign exchange f and the vertical axis depicts the exchange rate e. As RMB depreciates against the dollar, U.S. goods and services become more expensive to Chinese importers and China's goods and services become cheaper in the U.S.. Higher exchange rate reduces the quantity imported and increases the quantity exported, and vice versa.

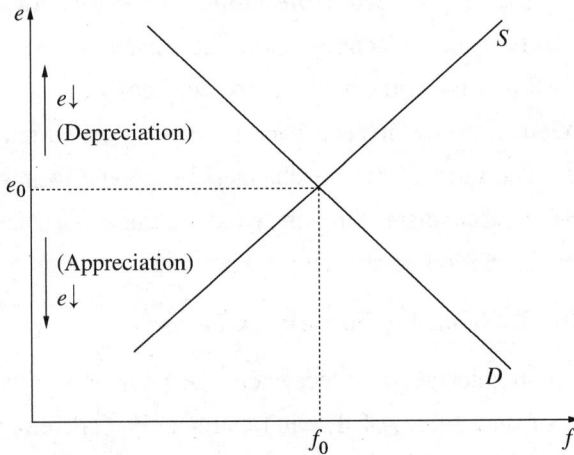

Figure 6-1   The Determination of Exchange Rates

6.2.3   Determinants of Exchange Rates

The supply of and demand for any given currency, and thus its value, are not influenced by any single element, but rather by several. These elements generally fall into two categories: economic factors and market psychologies.

Economic Factors

These factors include economic policies implemented by government agencies and central banks, and economic conditions which are generally revealed through economic reports and other economic indicators.

- *Economic policies*. They comprise the government's fiscal policy and the central bank's monetary policy.
- *Government budget deficit or surplus*. The market usually reacts negatively to widening government budget deficit, and positively to government budget surplus. The impact is reflected in the value of a country's currency.
- *Balance of trade levels and trends*. The trade flow between countries illustrates the demand for goods and services, which in turn indicates demand for a country's currency to conduct trade. Surpluses and deficits in trade of goods and services reflect the competitiveness of a country's economy. For example, trade deficits may have a negative impact on a country's currency.
- *Inflation levels and trends*. Typically a currency will lose value if there is

a high level of inflation in the country or if inflation levels are perceived to rise. This is because inflation erodes purchasing power, thus demand for that particular currency.

- *Economic growth and health.* Reports such as GDP, employment levels, retail sales, capacity utilization and others, detail the levels of a country's economic growth and health. Generally, the more healthy and robust a country's economy is, the better its currency will perform, and the more demand for it there will be.

- *Productivity of an economy.* Increasing productivity in an economy should positively influence the value of its currency. Its effects are more prominent if the increase is in the traded sector.

Market Psychologies

Market psychology and trader perceptions influence the foreign exchange market in a variety of ways:

- *Flights to quality.* Unsettling international events can lead to a "flight to quality", with investors seeking a "safe haven". There will be a greater demand, thus a higher price, for currencies perceived as stronger over their relatively weaker counterparts. The U.S. dollar, Swiss franc and gold have been traditional safe havens during times of political or economic uncertainty.

- *Long-term trends.* Currency markets often move in visible long-term trends. Although currencies do not have an annual growing season like physical commodities, business cycles do make themselves felt. Cycle analysis looks at longer-term price trends that may rise from economic or political trends.

- *"Buy the rumor, sell the fact".* This market truism can apply to many currency situations. It is the tendency for the price of a currency to reflect the impact of a particular action before it occurs and, when the anticipated event comes to pass, react in exactly the opposite direction. This may also be referred to as a market being "oversold" or "overbought". To buy the rumor or sell the fact can also be an example of the cognitive bias known as anchoring, when investors focus too much on the relevance of outside events to currency prices.

- *Economic figures.* While economic figures can certainly reflect economic policy, some reports and numbers take on a talisman-like effect: the figures itself becomes important to market psychology and may have an immediate impact on short-term market moves. "What to watch" can change over time. In recent years, for example, money supply, employment, trade balance figures and inflation rates have all taken turns in the spotlight.

- *Technical trading considerations*. As in other markets, the accumulated price movements in a currency pair such as EUR/USD can form apparent patterns that traders may attempt to use. Many traders study price charts in order to identify such patterns.

6.3 Exchange Rate System

The **exchange rate system** is the way a country manages its currency in respect to foreign currencies and the foreign exchange market. It is closely related to monetary policy and the two are generally dependent on many of the same factors.

The basic types are the floating exchange rate where the market dictates the movements of exchange rates and the fixed exchange rate which ties the currency to another currency, mostly more widespread currencies such as the U.S. dollar or Euro.

Floating Exchange Rate

A **floating exchange rate** is a type of exchange rate system wherein a currency's value is allowed to fluctuate according to the foreign exchange market. A currency that uses a floating exchange rate is known as a floating currency.

The floating exchange rate is the most common exchange rate system today. For example, the dollar, euro, yen, and British pound all float. In cases of extreme appreciation or depreciation, a central bank will normally intervene to stabilize the currency. Thus, the exchange rate system of floating currencies may more technically be known as **managed floating**.

Fixed Exchange Rate

A **fixed exchange rate**, sometimes called as a **pegged exchange rate**, matches a currency's value to the value of another single currency or to a basket of other currencies, or to another measure of value, such as gold.

A fixed exchange rate is usually used to stabilize the value of a currency relative to the currency it is pegged to. It makes trade and investments between the two countries easier and more predictable, and is especially useful for small economies where external trade forms a large part of their GDP.

Currency Board

A **currency board** is a monetary authority which is required to maintain a fixed exchange rate with a foreign currency. This policy objective requires the conventional objectives of a central bank to be subordinated to the exchange rate target.

The currency board's foreign currency reserves must be sufficient to ensure that all holders of its notes and coins (and all banks creditor of a reserve account at the currency board) can convert them into the reserve currency.

The currency board maintains absolute, unlimited convertibility between its notes and coins and the currency against which they are pegged (the anchor currency) at a fixed rate of exchange with no restrictions on the current account or the capital and financial account transactions.

A currency board only earns profit from interests on foreign reserves, and does not engage in forward-exchange transactions. These foreign reserves exist because local notes have been issued in exchange, or because commercial banks must by regulation deposit a minimum reserve at the Currency Board.

A currency board has no discretionary powers to affect monetary policy and does not lend to the government. Governments cannot print money, and can only tax or borrow to meet their spending commitments.

Chapter 7

Theories of Exchange Rate Determination

Key Concepts and Terms

International Monetary System	国际货币体系
Gold Standard	金本位
Gold Coin Standard	金币本位
Gold Bullion Standard	金块本位
Gold Exchange Standard	金汇兑本位
Paper Standard	纸币本位
Gold Content	含金量
Bank Note	银行券
Mint Parity	铸币平价
Purchasing Power Parity（PPP）	购买力平价
Absolute Purchasing Power Parity	绝对购买力平价
Relative Purchasing Power Parity	相对购买力平价
Law of One Price	一价定律
Transportation Cost	运输成本
Trade Barrier	贸易壁垒
Real Exchange Rate	实际汇率
Tradable Goods	可贸易商品
Nontradable Goods	不可贸易商品
Commodity Arbitrage	商品套利
Base Period	基期
Interest Rate Parity	利率平价
Covered Interest Rate Parity（CIP）	有抛补的利率平价
Uncovered Interest Rate Parity（UIP）	无抛补的利率平价

Balance of Payments Approach to Exchange Rates	汇率决定的国际收支说
Asset Market Approach to Exchange Rates	汇率决定的资产市场说
Monetary Approach to Exchange Rates	汇率决定的货币分析法
Portfolio Approach to Exchange Rates	汇率决定的资产组合说
Flexible-price Monetary Approach	弹性价格货币分析法
Sticky-price Monetary Approach	粘性价格货币分析法
Exchange Rate Overshooting	汇率超调

Determination of exchange rates is closely related to international monetary system. Monetary systems in general have experienced the stage of gold standard which can be further divided into gold coin standard, gold bullion standard and gold exchange standard and the stage of paper standard. Under gold coin standard, gold coins of each country have their gold contents and the exchange rates can be calculated by their gold contents with a small fluctuating range caused by gold transportation costs. With the development of the world economy, the production of gold could no longer keep up with the demand of economic growth and the gold coin standard was then replaced by gold bullion standard and gold exchange standard. Under the gold bullion standard, bank notes were issued with denominated gold contents but note holders could not exchange their notes for gold except for in a large amount. Under the gold exchange standard, only when bank notes were used for international payments could they be exchanged for gold in the central bank of the country. The exchange rates of bank notes fluctuated around mint parities which were determined by the denominated gold contents in the bank notes exchanged.

When paper currencies no longer had gold contents and could not be exchanged for gold, the international monetary system evolved into the paper standard. Under the paper standard, the determination of exchange rates becomes complicated and thus many theories have been advanced.

7.1 Theory of Purchasing Power Parity

The theory of purchasing power parity (PPP) believes that the value of money lies in its purchasing power, so the exchange rates of different currencies are determined by the ratios of their purchasing powers which are inversely related to the price levels of the countries. The theory of purchasing power parity can be further divided into absolute purchasing power parity and relative purchasing power parity.

7.1.1   Absolute Purchasing Power Parity

The foundation of purchasing power parity is the **law of one price**. It asserts that identical goods should cost the same in all countries, assuming that there are neither transportation costs nor trade barriers. It can be expressed as

$$P = e \cdot P^*$$ (7-1)

where P, e *and* P^* stand for home price, the exchange rate and foreign price respectively. The superscript $*$ indicates it is the variable of a foreign country. The right side of Equation 7-1 indicates the price of a good sold in the foreign country in terms of home currency. In July 2010, for example, iPad was sold in the United States for \$499, and the exchange rate was 6.78 ¥ / \$, so the RMB price of iPad sold in the United States was ¥3,383. If iPad was sold in China at ¥3,383, the law of one price then proved to be true. If the prices do not equal, in theory, commodity arbitrage will equalize the price of identical products in different countries.

Absolute purchasing power parity is derived when we rewrite Equation 7-1 as

$$e = \frac{P}{P^*}$$ (7-2)

Equation 7-2 indicates the equilibrium exchange rate between two currencies is equal to the ratio of the price levels in the two countries.

According to the theory of absolute purchasing power parity, ideal exchange rates should keep the law of one price tenable. When absolute purchasing power parity holds, the real exchange rate $e \cdot \dfrac{P^*}{P}$ will always equal to 1 since the nominal exchange rate e adjusts to the changes of P and P^*.

Though the theory of absolute purchasing power parity seems quite reasonable, several factors prevent it from being realistic. First, not all products made by a country can be traded internationally. We call those can be traded internationally as **tradable goods** and those cannot be traded internationally as **nontradable goods**. The prices of tradable goods may be equalized by commodity arbitrage but nontradable goods vary from a country to another in price. Second, the actually-existing transportation costs and trade barriers make the law of one price unrealistic. Third, it ignores the influence of international capital flow on exchange rates. In fact, capital inflows can improve the capital and financial account and appreciate the domestic currency while capital outflows depreciate the domestic currency.

7.1.2   Relative Purchasing Power Parity

The theory of **relative purchasing power parity** acknowledges the defects of absolute purchasing power parity, and claims that the changes of exchange rates are proportional to the relative changes of two countries' prices in a certain period. It can be expressed as

$$e_1 = \frac{P_1/P_0}{P_1^*/P_0^*} \cdot e_0 \qquad (7\text{-}3)$$

where subscripts 1 and 0 refer to Period 1 and the base period respectively. For instance, e_1 and e_0 stand for the exchange rates in Period 1 and in the base period respectively.

When used with the technique of logarithm, Equation 7-3 can be approximately rewritten as

$$\dot{e} = \pi - \pi^* \qquad (7\text{-}4)$$

where $\dot{e}$, π and π^* stand for the percentage of the exchange rate change, home inflation rate and foreign inflation rate respectively. Equation 7-4 is used more frequently since it can provide a quick judgment on the change of exchange rates once a country's inflation rate has been known.

Compared with absolute purchasing power parity, the theory of relative purchasing power parity averts itself from the strict preconditions of the former and is then closer to the real world. But relative purchasing power parity also bears flaws. First, it tends to overvalue the exchange rates of developed countries and to undervalue the exchange rates of developing countries because the prices of nontradable goods in developed countries are usually higher than those in developing countries. Second, it is hard to choose the base period in which the existing exchange rates should be in equilibrium.

In general, the theory of purchasing power parity holds true in the long run rather than in the short run.

7.2　Theory of Interest Rate Parity

In the real world, the links of capital and financial markets between countries are even closer than those of goods market. International capital flows are closely linked to interest rates. The theory of interest rate parity explores the relations between exchange rates and interest rates. Compared with the theory of purchasing power parity, it is a short-run analysis. The theory of interest rate parity can be further divided into covered interest rate parity (CIP) and uncovered interest rate parity (UIP).

7.2.1　Covered Interest Rate Parity

Suppose an investor would invest a sum of money in either the home country or a foreign country for 1 year. For simplicity, we postulate the sum of money is 1. See Figure 7-1. Assume there is no restriction on or transaction costs of capital flows. The interest rate in the home country is r and in the foreign country r^*. The spot exchange rate now is e and the spot exchange rate one year later is e_f. If he deposits the money in a bank in the home country, the return will be $1 + r$ one year later. But if he exchanges the money for the foreign currency ($1/e$) and deposits it in a bank in the foreign country for one year ($1/e \cdot (1 + r^*)$), after exchanging it back to the home currency, his return becomes $e_f/e \cdot (1 + r^*)$.

Actually, the spot exchange rate one year later is uncertain. To cover losses arising from exchange rate fluctuations, he sells a 1-year forward contract in a forward exchange rate f. Thus he earns a certain return $f/e \cdot (1 + r^*)$ from his foreign investment.

Obviously, whether he invests in the home country or the foreign country depends on their returns. If the home return is higher than the foreign return, i.e. $1 + r > f/e \cdot (1 + r^*)$, he will invest in the home country. If the home return is lower than the foreign return, i.e. $1 + r < f/e \cdot (1 + r^*)$, he will invest in the foreign country. Since there are numerous investors in the market, the final result

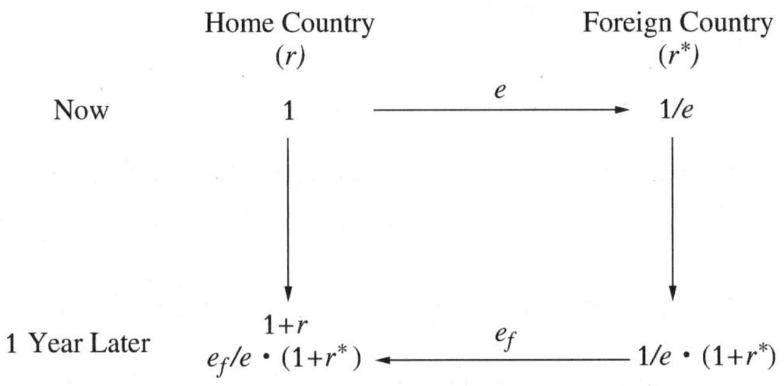

Home Country
(r)

Foreign Country
(r^*)

Now   1 $\xrightarrow{\quad e \quad}$ $1/e$

1 Year Later $\dfrac{1+r}{e_f/e \cdot (1+r^*)}$ $\xleftarrow{\quad e_f \quad}$ $1/e \cdot (1+r^*)$

Figure 7-1   Interest Rate Arbitrage

of this arbitrage will be the equal returns in the two countries, i. e. $1 + r = f/e \cdot (1 + r^*)$. It can be rewritten as

$$\frac{f}{e} = \frac{1+r}{1+r^*} \tag{7-5}$$

We use ρ to denote the premium or discount between the spot exchange rate and the forward exchange rate, that is,

$$\rho = \frac{f-e}{e} \tag{7-6}$$

Combine Equation 7-5 with 7-6, we have $\rho + \rho r^* = r - r^*$. Since ρr^* is a tiny value, it then can be approximately depicted as

$$\rho = r - r^* \tag{7-7}$$

The above equation is the **covered interest rate parity**. It indicates that the premium or discount ratio of the forward exchange rate equals the difference between two countries' interest rates. If home interest rates are higher than foreign interest rates, there will be a premium in the forward exchange rate, i. e. a depreciation of future currency in the future. If home interest rates are lower than foreign interest rates, there will be a discount in the forward exchange rate, i. e. an appreciation of the domestic currency in the future. Changes of exchange rates will offset the difference between interest rates to keep financial markets in equilibrium.

7.2.2   Uncovered Interest Rate Parity

In the above analysis, if the investor chooses to invest on his expectation of future exchange rate Ee_f and leave the risks of loss uncovered rather than sell a forward contract, then Equation 7-5 turns to be

$$\frac{Ee_f}{e} = \frac{1+r}{1+r^*} \qquad (7\text{-}8)$$

In the similar way, Equation 7-8 can be approximately depicted as

$$E\rho = r - r^* \qquad (7\text{-}9)$$

where $E\rho = \dfrac{Ee_f - e}{e}$ stands for the expected changing ratio of future exchange rates.

Equation 7-9 is the **uncovered interest rate parity**. It indicates that the expected changing ratio of future exchange rates equals to the difference between two countries' interest rates. If home interest rates are higher than foreign interest rates, the market will expect the domestic currency to depreciate in the future.

To sum up, the theory of interest rate parity applies in the short run. It explains the relations between exchange rates and interest rates from the perspective of capital flows.

7.3   Balance of Payments Approach to Exchange Rates

This theory assumes exchange rates are floating and the government does not intervene in foreign exchange markets. It maintains exchange rates are determined by the supply of and demand for foreign exchange and any transactions of foreign exchange are reflected in the balance of payments.

The balance of payments consists of a current account and a capital and financial account whose sum is 0. It can be depicted as

$$BP = CA + KA = 0 \qquad (7\text{-}10)$$

where CA stands for the current account and KA stands for the capital and financial account.

The current account is mainly determined by exports and imports. Exports are decided by foreign national income Y^* and real exchange rate $e \cdot \dfrac{P^*}{P}$ while imports are decided by home national income Y and the real exchange rate. Thus we have

$$CA = CA(Y, Y^*, P, P^*, e) \qquad (7\text{-}11)$$

The capital and financial account is mainly determined by home interest rate r, foreign interest rate r^* and the expectation of future exchange rate Ee_f. Thus we have

$$KA = KA(r, r^*, Ee_f) \qquad (7\text{-}12)$$

Combining Equations 7-10 with 7-11 and 7-12, we can find the factors affecting the balance of payments as shown in the below equation

$$BP = BP(Y, Y^*, P, P^*, r, r^*, e, Ee_f) \qquad (7\text{-}13)$$

When $CA = -KA$, the balance of payments is in equilibrium, i.e. $BP = 0$. The exchange rate then is in equilibrium. So the equilibrium exchange rate can be depicted as

$$e = f(Y, Y^*, P, P^*, r, r^*, Ee_f) \qquad (7\text{-}14)$$

Equation 7-14 demonstrates the factors affecting the equilibrium exchange rate include the national incomes of the home and the foreign countries, the price levels of the two countries, the interest rates of the two countries, and the expectation of future exchange rate.

Given other factors constant, an increase in home national income Y will cause more imports, increase the demand for foreign exchange and worsen the balance of payments, leading to a depreciation of the domestic currency (See Figure 7-2(a)). An increase in foreign national income Y^* will result in more exports of the home country and an increase in the supply of foreign exchange, leading to an appreciation of the domestic currency.

A rise in home price level will cause an appreciation of the real exchange rate, reduce the competitiveness of home products, decrease exports and the supply of foreign exchange, increase imports and the demand for foreign exchange, and worsen the balance of payments, resulting in a depreciation of the domestic currency (See Figure 7-2(b)). On the contrary, a rise in foreign price level will lead to an appreciation of the domestic currency.

A rise in home interest rate will attract capital to flow in, increase the supply of foreign exchange, reduce the desire to invest in foreign financial assets and the demand for foreign exchange, and cause a surplus in the balance of payments, leading to an appreciation of the domestic currency (See Figure 7-2(c)). In contrast, a rise in foreign interest rate will cause capital outflows and a depreciation of the domestic currency.

If domestic currency is expected to depreciate in the future, people will buy foreign exchange and sell domestic currency in markets, causing more demand for

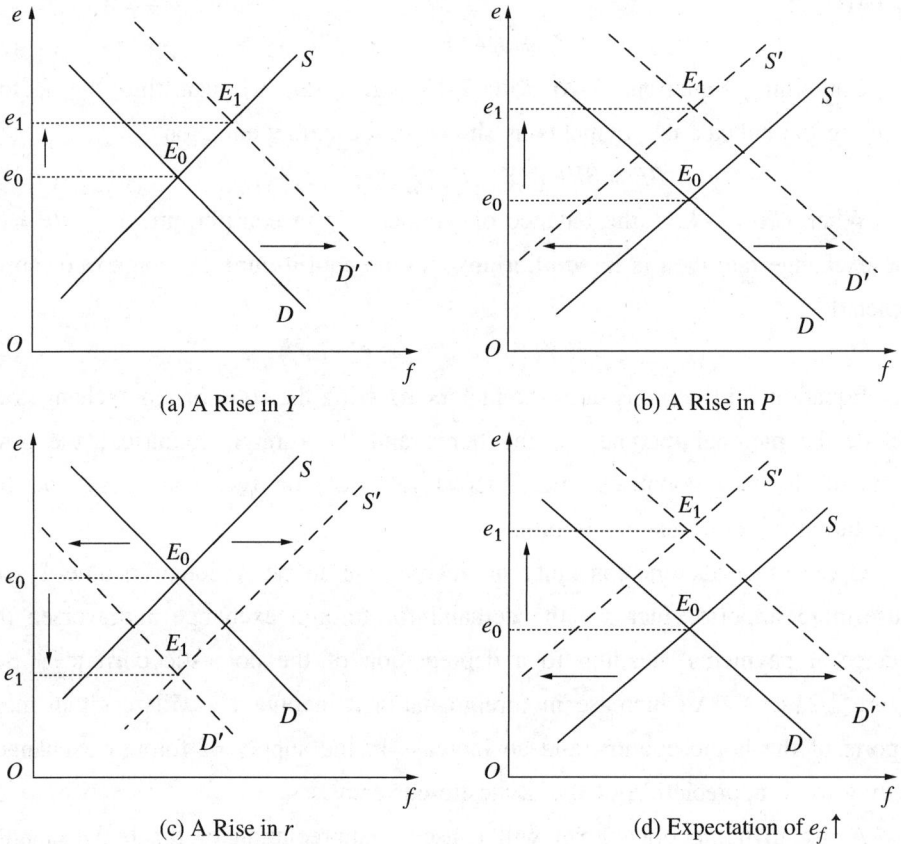

(a) A Rise in Y

(b) A Rise in P

(c) A Rise in r

(d) Expectation of $e_f \uparrow$

Figure 7-2   Balance of Payments Approach to Exchange Rate

and less supply of foreign exchange and leading to an immediate depreciation of the domestic currency (See Figure 7-2 (d)). In contrast, an expectation of domestic currency appreciation will cause an immediate appreciation of the domestic currency.

In conclusion, the balance of payments approach takes all important factors affecting exchange rates into consideration. It is helpful for analyzing the determination and changes of exchange rates in the short run.

7.4   Asset Market Approach to Exchange Rates

Since 1970s, international capital flows have become increasingly frequent.

Factors other than foreign trade have played more prominent roles in exchange rate determination. The exchange rate is regarded as a kind of asset price and the asset market approach has become dominant for the exchange rate analysis.

The asset market approach to exchange rates can be divided into monetary approach and portfolio approach. The monetary approach further consists of flexible-price monetary approach and sticky-price monetary approach.

7.4.1 Flexible-Price Monetary Approach

There are three assumptions for flexible-price monetary approach. First, purchasing power parity holds. Second, outputs are at the full-employment level and prices can adjust flexibly. Thus, changes of money supply will only influence price levels rather than interest rates and outputs. Third, uncovered interest rate parity (UIP) holds.

According to Keynesian theory of money demand, people demand for money for three motives: transaction motive, precautionary motive and speculative motive. The first two motives are positively influenced by prices and income, and the third is inversely influenced by interest rates. Thus we can depict home money demand function as

$$\ln M_d = \ln P + \alpha \ln Y - \beta r \qquad (7\text{-}15)$$

where M_d, P, Y and r stand for home country's money demand, price, national income and interest rate respectively, and α and β are positive parameters. Here we use the logarithm form for the consideration of simplicity in the following process.

Similarly, foreign money demand function can be depicted as

$$\ln M_d^* = \ln P^* + \alpha \ln Y^* - \beta r^* \qquad (7\text{-}16)$$

Here, we assume foreign money demand function has the same parameters to those of the home country for simplicity.

When the money market is in equilibrium, the money demand is equal to the money supply. Thus

$$M_s = M_d \qquad (7\text{-}17)$$

and

$$M_s^* = M_d^* \qquad (7\text{-}18)$$

where M_s and M_s^* stand for the money supplies of the home country and of the foreign country respectively.

Substitute Equations 7-15 and 7-16 with 7-17 and 7-18, and rearrange them as

$$\ln P = \ln M_s - \alpha \ln Y + \beta r \qquad (7-19)$$

and

$$\ln P^* = \ln M_s^* - \alpha \ln Y^* + \beta r^* \qquad (7-20)$$

From the purchasing power parity we have

$$e = \frac{P}{P^*} \qquad (7-21)$$

Its logarithm form is

$$\ln e = \ln P - \ln P^* \qquad (7-22)$$

Substitute $\ln P$ and $\ln P^*$ in Equation 7-22 with Equations 7-19 and 7-20, and we get

$$\ln e = (\ln M_s - \ln M_s^*) + \alpha(\ln Y^* - \ln Y) + \beta(r - r^*) \qquad (7-23)$$

Equation 7-23 is the basic model of **flexible-price monetary approach**. In the model, money supply, national income and interest rates of either the home country or the foreign country affect exchange rates via the price level of each country.

Given other factors constant, the effect of a once-for-all increase in home money supply is shown in Figure 7-3 where the horizontal axis refers to time. The increase in home money supply causes an excess money supply and results in a price increase in the home country and a depreciation of the domestic currency. Since the economy is at the full employment level, its output keeps constant. And an increase in money demand resulting from the higher price offsets the excess money supply and keeps the interest rate constant.

An increase in home national income brings about more money demand. With a fixed money supply which is controlled by the central bank, the price level falls. When absolute purchasing power parity holds, the exchange rate falls or in other words, the domestic currency appreciates.

A rise in home interest rate reduces money demand and causes the price level to increase. The exchange rate then rises according to absolute purchasing power parity.

Finally, Let us analyze the effect of a rise in the expectation of future exchange rates. Since the uncovered interest rate parity is assumed tenable, we

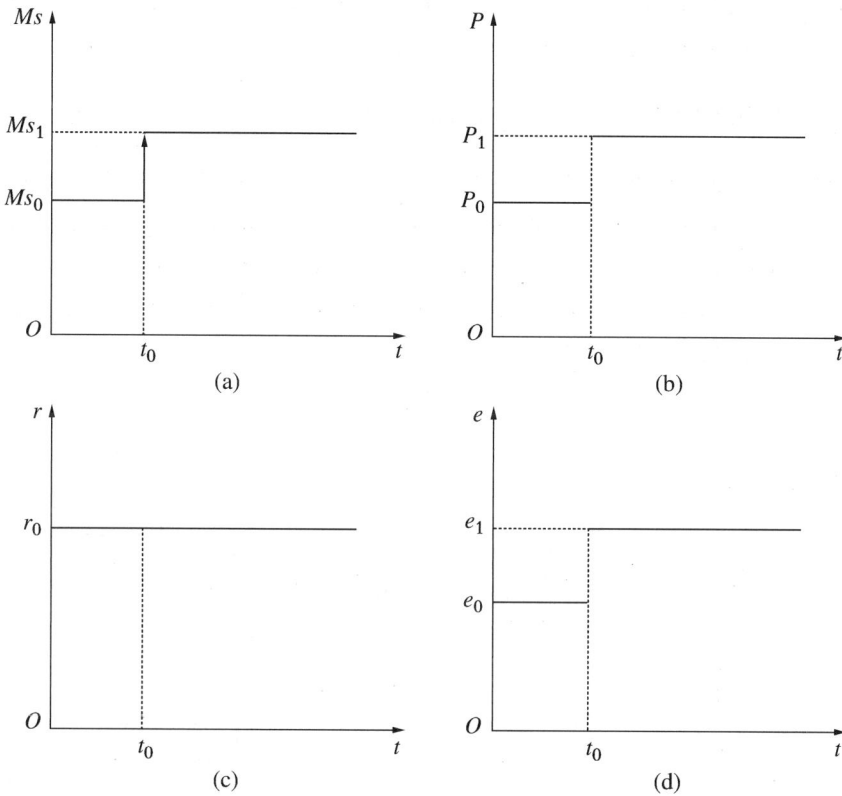

Figure 7-3   Effects of Home Money Supply in Flexible-Price Monetary Approach

have the logarithm form of Equation 7-8 as

$$\ln Ee_f - \ln e = \ln(1 + r) - \ln(1 + r^*) \qquad (7\text{-}24)$$

Remember, when r and r^* are small values, $\ln(1 + r)$ and $\ln(1 + r^*)$ are approximately equal to r and r^* respectively. Thus we have

$$\ln Ee_f - \ln e = r - r^* \qquad (7\text{-}25)$$

Substitute $r - r^*$ in Equation 7-23 with Equation 7-25 and rearrange it. Then we get

$$\ln e = \frac{1}{1 + \beta}[(\ln M_s - \ln M_s^*) + \alpha(\ln Y^* - \ln Y) + \beta \ln Ee_f] \qquad (7\text{-}26)$$

Equation 7-26 indicates the spot exchange rate will change in the same direction to the expectation of future exchange rates. Thus a rise in the expectation of future exchange rates will result in an immediate depreciation of the domestic currency.

To summarize, the flexible-price monetary approach is based on purchasing power parity and flexible price and is helpful for analyzing the long-run trend of exchange rates. It is the simplest one among the asset market approaches.

7.4.2 Sticky-Price Monetary Approach

The sticky-price monetary approach maintains absolute purchasing power parity holds in the long run rather than in the short run. In the short run, the price level is sticky and money supply can influence national output and interest rates.

Given other factors constant, let us analyze the effect of a once-for-all money supply increase (See Figure 7-4).

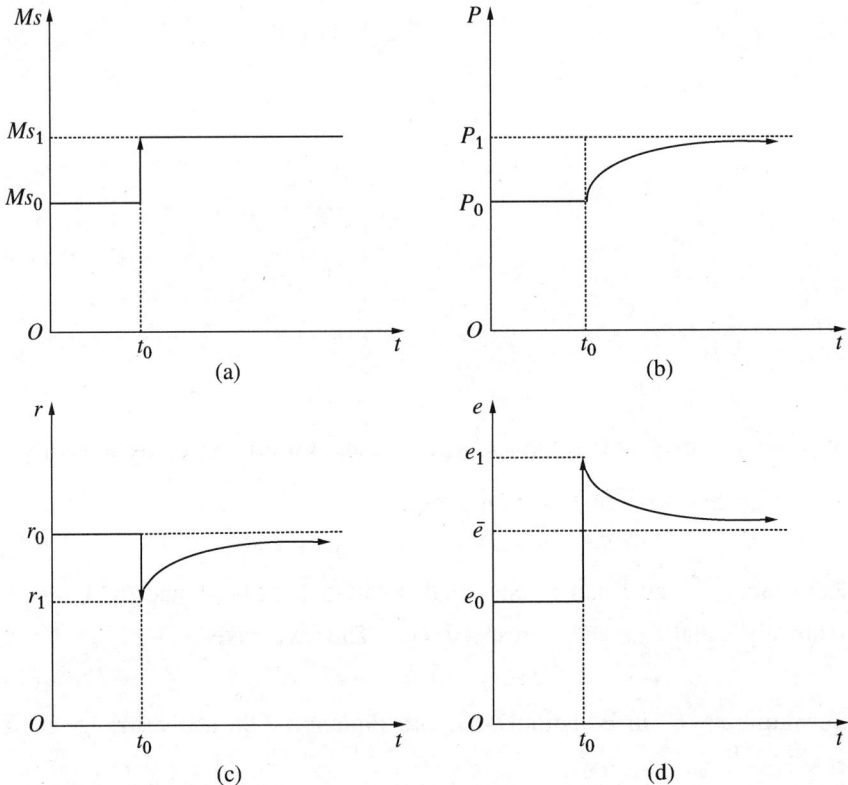

Figure 7-4 **Effects of Home Money Supply in Sticky-Price Monetary Approach**

In the long run, since the purchasing power parity is tenable, the result should be the same to that of the flexible-price monetary approach. That is, while the output and the interest rate keep constant, the price level rises (P_1 in Figure 7-4(b)) and the long-run exchange rate increases ($\bar{e}$ in Figure 7-4(d)).

But in the short run, due to the more realistic assumption of price stickiness, the consequence becomes quite different. First, since the price is sticky, it is not able to change (P_0 in Figure 7-4 (b)) at the time when the money supply is increased. Second, excess money supply causes the interest rate to fall (r_1 in Figure 7-4 (c)) because the money market can adjust rapidly. Third, the spot exchange rate rises (e_1 in Figure 7-4 (d)) even higher than the long-run exchange rate $\bar{e}$, which we need to explain in detail.

Remember uncovered interest rate parity. Based on it, we educe Equation 7-25. Rearrange it as

$$\ln e = \ln Ee_f - (r - r^*) \qquad (7\text{-}27)$$

where Ee_f is the expectation of future exchange rates. Since people are rational, they expect the future exchange rate will stay at the level of the long-run exchange rate, that is, $Ee_f = \bar{e}$. Thus Equation 7-27 turns to be

$$\ln e = \ln \bar{e} - (r - r^*) \qquad (7\text{-}28)$$

We have worked out that home interest rate falls to r_1 in the short run because of the excess money supply. From Equation 7-28, we learn that the spot exchange rate e will be even higher than the long-run exchange rate $\bar{e}$. That means, the exchange rate responds to a change in the money supply or other factor shocks greater in the short run than in the long run. This phenomenon is called as **exchange rate overshooting**. In this sense, the sticky-price monetary approach is also called as **overshooting model**.

As time goes by, the price becomes no longer sticky and is rising due to the excess money supply. Higher price results in more money demand and the interest rate is caused to be increasing. According to the theory of interest rate parity, the exchange rate is falling with an increasing interest rate. The process continues until the long-run equilibrium is reached.

The sticky-price monetary approach explains the determination and changes of exchange rates in a more realistic way. It also provides governments with the ground for intervening the economy since otherwise the over-fluctuation of exchange rates will do greater damage to the economy.

7.4.3 Portfolio Approach to Exchange Rates

The portfolio approach maintains exchange rates are affected by different portfolios of financial assets. It assumes that the home country is a small nation. In other words, it cannot affect foreign interest rate r^*. The wealth of home residents is made up of three financial assets: home money, home bonds and foreign bonds. It can be expressed as

$$W = M + B + e \cdot F \qquad (7\text{-}29)$$

where W refers to the wealth of home residents; M, B and F stand for home money, home bonds and foreign bonds respectively; and e refers to exchange rate. Since foreign bonds are denominated in foreign currency, they should multiply the exchange rate to be converted into a value in terms of the home currency. Here home bonds and foreign bonds are assumed to be imperfect substitutes.

In home money market, money supply is controlled by the central bank and money demand is inversely affected by home interest rate r and foreign interest rate r^* and positively affected by the total wealth W. When either home interest rate or foreign interest rate rises, residents tend to invest their money in bonds rather than hold it at hand and thus the money demand falls. More wealth allows residents to invest more in each asset, including home money.

In home bonds market, the supply of home bonds is controlled by the government while the demand for home bonds is inversely affected by foreign interest rate and positively affected by home interest rate and the total wealth. Higher home interest rate attracts residents to buy more home bonds. However, higher foreign interest rate makes foreign bonds more attractable and lessens the demand for home bonds.

In foreign bonds market, the supply of foreign bonds is acquired by the surplus of the current account. The demand for foreign bonds is inversely affected by home interest rate and positively affected by foreign interest rate and the total wealth.

In Figure 7-5, the horizontal axis refers to home interest rate and the vertical axis refers to the exchange rate.

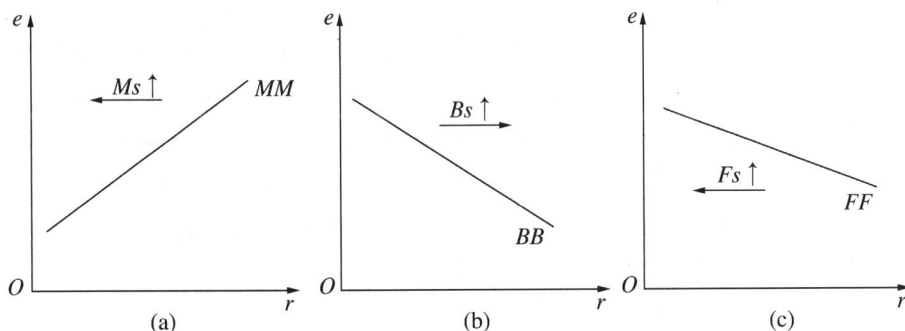

Figure 7-5   *MM* Curve, *BB* Curve and *FF* Curve

MM curve shows the combinations of exchange rates and home interest rates when home money market is in equilibrium (See Figure 7-5 (a)). *MM* curve slopes upward. A rise in the exchange rate increases the value of foreign bonds in terms of the home currency and the total wealth. Increased total wealth brings about more money demand, causing higher interest rate. Thus, the exchange rate changes in the same direction to the interest rate in a balanced home money market. If money supply is increased, *MM* curve shifts leftward because a fall in the interest rate is then required so as to increase money demand to match the expanded money supply and keep the home money market in equilibrium.

BB curve shows the combinations of exchange rates and home interest rates when home bonds market is in equilibrium (See Figure 7-5 (b)). *BB* curve slopes downward. A rise in the exchange rate increases the value of foreign bonds in terms of home currency and the total wealth. Increased total wealth brings about more demand for home bonds, causing the price of home bonds to rise and the interest rate to fall. So, the exchange rate changes in the opposite direction to the interest rate in a balanced home bonds market. If the supply of home bonds is increased, *BB* curve shifts rightward because a rise in the interest rate is then required so as to reduce the price of home bonds and increase their demand. Thus the added supply of home bonds is matched and the equilibrium of home bonds market is restored.

FF curve shows the combinations of exchange rates and home interest rates when foreign bond market is in equilibrium (See Figure 7-5 (c)). *FF* curve slopes downward. A rise in the exchange rate increases the value of foreign bonds in terms of home currency and the demand for foreign bonds increases. More demand for foreign bonds in turn raises their price and causes the interest rate to fall. Thus, the exchange rate changes in the opposite direction to the interest rate in a balanced foreign bonds market. If the supply of foreign bonds is increased, FF curve shifts leftward because a fall in the interest rate is then required so as to increase the demand for foreign bonds. Thus the added supply of foreign bonds is matched and the equilibrium of foreign bonds market is restored. FF curve is flatter than BB curve because the home bonds market is more sensible to the change of home interest rate. That is, when the exchange rate changes, a smaller change of home interest rate is needed to restore the equilibrium of home bonds market than to restore the equilibrium of foreign bonds market.

When we put MM curve, BB curve and FF curve together in one coordinate plane, a basic model for portfolio balance approach is completed.

See Figure 7-6. Suppose for some reason, the central bank of the home country expands its money supply. Increased money supply pulls MM curve leftward to MM' and augments the total wealth. With the supply of home bonds controlled by the government and the supply of foreign bonds restricted by the current account, augmented total wealth causes excess demands for both home bonds and foreign bonds. The excess demand for home bonds brings about higher price of home bonds and lower the interest rate, pulling BB curve leftward to BB'. And the excess demand for foreign bonds results in an appreciation of the foreign currency and a depreciation of the domestic currency, pushing FF curve rightward to FF'. New overall equilibrium reaches at E_1, where the exchange rate rises and home interest rate falls.

Now suppose an increase in foreign bond supply resulting from a surplus current account. See Figure 7-7. Increased supply of foreign bonds pulls FF curve leftward to FF' and augments the total wealth. With the home money supply controlled by the central bank and the supply of home bonds restricted by the government, augmented total wealth causes excess demands for both home money and home bonds. The excess demand for home money brings about higher home interest rate, pushing MM curve rightward to MM'. And the excess demand for home bonds results in higher price of home bonds and lower home interest rate, pulling BB curve leftward to BB'. New overall equilibrium reaches at E_1, where the exchange rate falls.

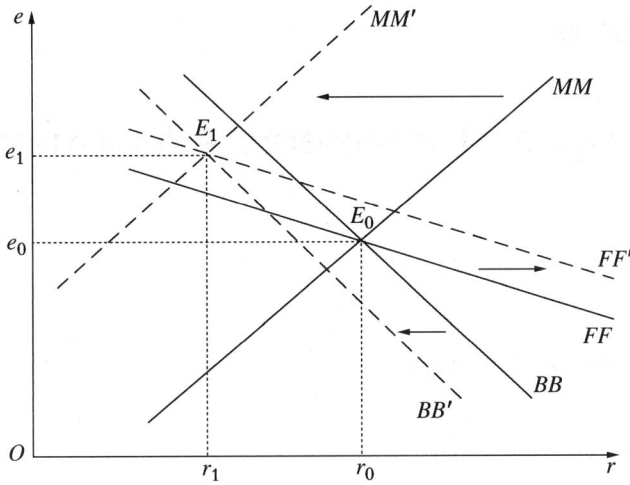

Figure 7-6   Effect of Money Supply Increase

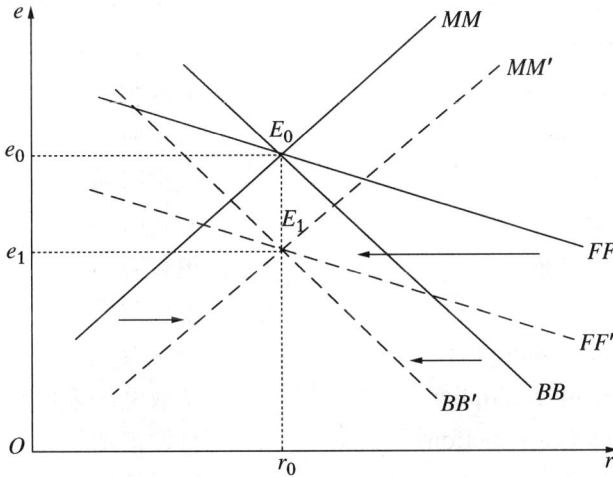

Figure 7-7   Effect of Foreign Bond Supply Increase

In summary, the portfolio balance approach points out the imperfect substitution between home assets and foreign assets and takes the current account into consideration. These make the approach more realistic and helpful for decision making.

Chapter 8

Balance of Payments Adjustments

Key Concepts and Terms

Elasticities Approach	弹性方法
Multiplier Approach	乘数方法
Absorption Approach	吸收方法
Monetary Approach	货币方法
Marshall-Lerner Condition	马歇尔—勒纳条件
J-Curve Effect	J曲线效应
Demand Elasticity	需求弹性
Recognition Lag	认识时滞
Decision Lag	决策时滞
Delivery Lag	交货时滞
Replacement Lag	更替时滞
Production Lag	生产时滞
Foreign Trade Multiplier	外贸乘数
Open Economy Multiplier	开放经济乘数
Autonomous Consumption	自发消费
Marginal Propensity to Consume	边际消费倾向
Marginal Propensity to Absorb	边际吸收倾向
Progressive Tax	累进税
Idle Resources Effect	闲置资源效应
Real Cash Balance Effect	实际现金余额效应
Income Redistribution Effect	收入再分配效应
Taxation Effect	税收效应
Bretton Woods System	布雷顿森林体系

| Cambridge Equation | 剑桥方程式 |

In Chapter 6, we have learned the balance of payments could be restored automatically. But the automatic restoration occurs only on some strict conditions and requires quite a long time. Sometimes, the automatically restoring process brings about intolerable damages to economy. Thus, interventions are needed to help restore the balance of payments. In this chapter, we will consider four approaches to balance of payments adjustments.

8.1   Elasticities Approach to the Balance of Payments

The traditional approaches to the balance of payments assume that capital flows occur only as a means of financing current account transactions. Hence, the quantity of foreign exchange demanded and the quantity of foreign exchange supplied depend only on international transactions of goods and services.

Derivation of the Demand for Foreign Exchange

We know that the quantity of a currency demanded in the foreign exchange market is derived from the country's demand for imports. In this chapter we provide a more complete derivation of the demand for foreign exchange.

Suppose that Chinese residents export toys to the U.S. and import iPod from the U.S. For simplicity, we assume that the world price of an iPod is $100 and that the world price of a toy is $10. Furthermore, we shall assume that the dollar prices of these two goods are given. Panel (a) of Figure 8-1 illustrates an import demand curve for iPod in China. Point A of Panel (a) indicates that at a price of ¥700 for each iPod, the quantity of iPod demanded is 10 million, while Point B indicates that at a price of ¥800 the quantity of iPod demanded is 8 million. The hypothetical import demand curve containing Points A and B and denoted D_I illustrates all of the various combinations of import prices and quantities demanded.

This import demand curve determines Chinese residents' demand for foreign exchange, or dollars. At a spot exchange rate of 7.00 ¥/$, the world price of iPod in RMB is 700 ($100 × 7.00 ¥/$ = ¥700). Hence, at a spot exchange rate of 7.00 ¥ / $, China imports 10 million iPods. The dollar value of Chinese imports at this spot exchange rate and, therefore, the quantity of dollars demanded, is $1,000 million ($100 × 10 million = $1,000 million). Point A of Panel (b) shows this combination of the spot exchange rate and the quantity of dollars demanded.

At a spot exchange rate of 8.00 ¥ / $, the price of an iPod in RMB is 800 ($100 × 8.00 ¥ / $ = ¥800). Point B of Panel (a) indicates that at this price, China imports 8 million iPods. The dollar value of Chinese imports at this spot exchange rate and, therefore, the quantity of dollars demanded is $800 million ($100 × 8 million = $800 million). Point B of Panel (b) shows this combination of the spot exchange rate and quantity of dollars demanded. The demand curve formed by connecting Points A and B and denoted $D_\$$ in Panel (b) illustrates all of the various combinations of spot exchange rates and quantities of dollars demanded.

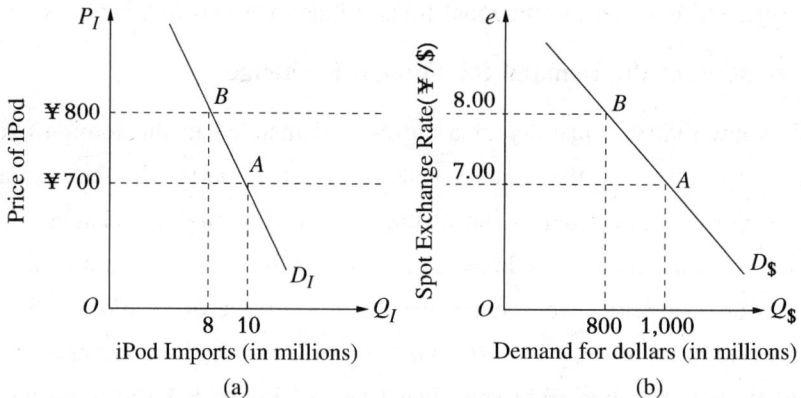

Figure 8-1   China's Import Demand Curve and the Demand for dollar

Figure 8-1 shows that if the price of iPod increases from ¥700 to ¥800, the quantity of iPod demanded falls from 10 million to 8 million. Suppose that for the same increase in price, the quantity of iPod demanded falls to 6 million, as denoted by Point B' in Figure 8-2(a). We would say that in this second case, the quantity of iPod demanded is more responsive to the change in price. In this second case, therefore, the demand for iPod is more elastic. As shown in Figure 8-2(a), the new demand curve formed by Points A and B' and denoted $D_I{}'$ is more elastic over the same price range as compared with the previous demand *curve D_I.*

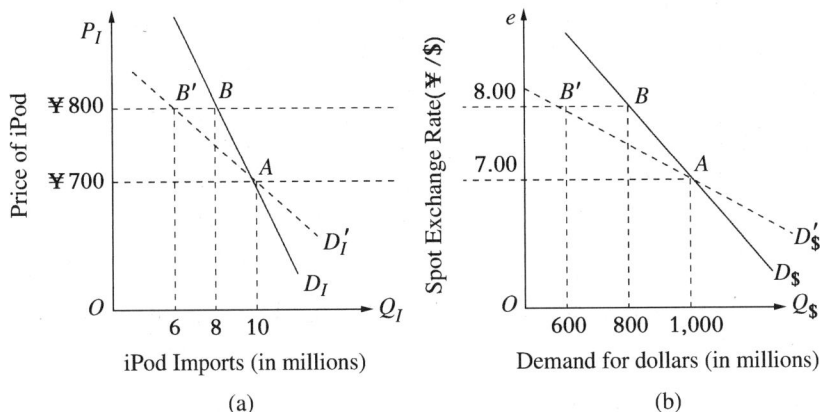

Figure 8-2   **Elasticity of Import Demand and the Elasticity of Foreign Exchange Demand**

As explained earlier, at a spot exchange rate of 8 ¥ / $, the RMB price of iPod is 800. Using the import demand curve D_I', at a price of ¥800 China imports 6 million iPods. The dollar value of Chinese imports at this spot exchange rate, which is the quantity of dollars demanded at Point B' on the dollar demand curve $D_\$'$, is equal to $600 million ($100 ×6 million = $600 million). The new foreign exchange demand curve formed by Points A and B' and denoted $D_\$'$ is more elastic over the same range of exchange rates than the previous demand curve $D_\$$. Consequently, the elasticity of the import demand curve influences the elasticity of the foreign exchange demand curve. A more elastic import demand curve yields a more elastic demand for foreign exchange. A less elastic import demand curve yields a less elastic demand for foreign exchange.

Derivation of the Supply of Foreign Exchange

In the traditional, trade-based theories of exchange rates, the supply of foreign exchange to a country results from its exports of goods and services.

Figure 8-3(a) illustrates a hypothetical export supply curve for China. Point A shows that at a price of ¥70, the quantity of toys supplied by China's producers for export is 60 million, while Point B shows that at a price of ¥80, the quantity of toys supplied is 80 million.

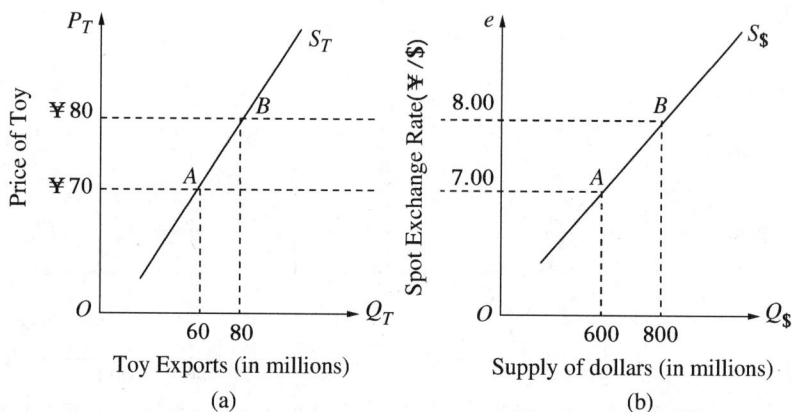

Figure 8-3   China's Export Supply Curve and the Supply of Dollar

Recall that the world price of toys is $10 per toy. At an exchange rate of 7.00 ¥/$, the RMB price of toys is ¥70 per toy ($10 × 7.00 ¥/$ = ¥70), at which China exports 60 million toys. The value of China's exports at this exchange rate is $600 million ($10 × 60 million = $600 million). Thus, at an exchange rate of 7.00 ¥/$, the quantity of foreign exchange supplied is $600 million. Point A in Panel (b) of Figure 8-3 illustrates this combination of the spot exchange rate and the quantity of dollars supplied in the foreign exchange market.

If the RMB depreciates relative to the dollar, from 7.00 ¥/$ to 8.00 ¥/$, the RMB price of toys rises to ¥80 per toy ($10 × 8.00 ¥/$ = ¥80). Figure 8-3(a) indicates that at this price China's producers are willing to export 80 million toys. The value of China's exports at this new exchange rate, therefore, is $800 million ($10 × 80 million = $800 million). Thus, at this exchange rate the quantity of dollars supplied in the foreign exchange market is $800 million. Point B in Figure 8-3 (b) shows this combination of the quantity of foreign exchange supplied and the spot exchange rate. Figure 8-3(b) depicts the dollar supply curve $S_{\$}$, containing Points A and B.

Just as the demand elasticity of imports determines the supply elasticity of the demand for foreign exchange demand, the supply elasticity of exports also determines the elasticity of the supply of foreign exchange. Along the toy supply curve S_T in Figure 8-3(a), if the price of toys rises from ¥70 at Point A to ¥80 at Point B, the quantity of toys supplied by China's producers increases from 60 million to 80 million. Suppose that, for the same price change, the quantity of toys supplied instead increases to 100 million, shown at Point B' on the toy supply curve S_T' in Figure 8-4(a). In this second case, the quantity of toys supplied is more responsive to the price increase, so the proportional change in quantity supplied in response to the same proportional change in price is greater for the supply curve S_T' than for the toy supply curve S_T. Hence, over this price range, the supply curve S_T' is more elastic than the supply curve S_T.

Because the supply of exports determines the supply of foreign exchange, the elasticity of the supply of exports determines the elasticity of the supply of foreign exchange. At an exchange rate of 8.00 ¥ / $ and a world price for toys of $10, the RMB price of a toy is ¥80. If China' producers export 100 million toys at this exchange rate, then the value of China's exports to U.S., and thus the quantity of dollars supplied by the U.S. residents, is $1,000 million ($10 × 100 million = $1,000 million).

Point B' in Figure 8-4(b) shows this new combination of the spot exchange rate and the quantity of dollars supplied. As the figure shows, the foreign exchange supply curve containing Points A and B' and denoted $S_{\$}'$, is more elastic over this range of exchange rates than the original supply curve $S_{\$}$. Thus, the elasticity of the export supply curve determines the elasticity of the foreign exchange supply curve. If the supply of exports is more elastic, the supply of foreign exchange is also more elastic. Likewise, if the supply of exports is less elastic, the supply of foreign exchange is also less elastic.

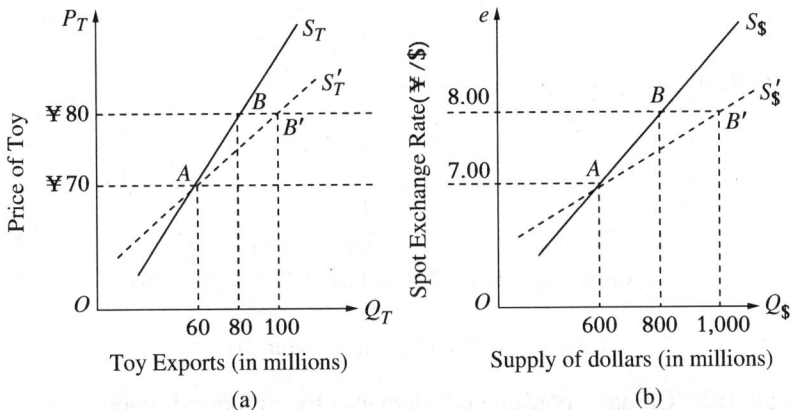

Figure 8-4   Supply Elasticities of Exports and Foreign Exchange

Elasticities Approach

The elasticities approach centers on changes in the prices of goods and services as the determinant of a country's balance of payments and the exchange value of its currency. As already explained, elasticity is a measure of the responsiveness of quantity to a change in price.

The previous section also showed that a change in the exchange rate affects the domestic currency price of goods and services.

To understand the effects of a currency devaluation or depreciation and the roles of the elasticities of import demand and export supply, Let us consider a country that currently experiences a current account deficit. Figure 8-5 illustrates the two foreign exchange demand curves $D_\$$ and $D_\$'$ from Figure 8-2 and the two foreign exchange supply curves $S_\$$ and $S_\$'$ from Figure 8-4. Suppose that the spot exchange rate between RMB and dollar is 7.00 ¥/$. As Figure 8-5 shows, at this spot exchange rate, the quantity of foreign exchange demanded exceeds the quantity of foreign exchange supplied by $400 million.

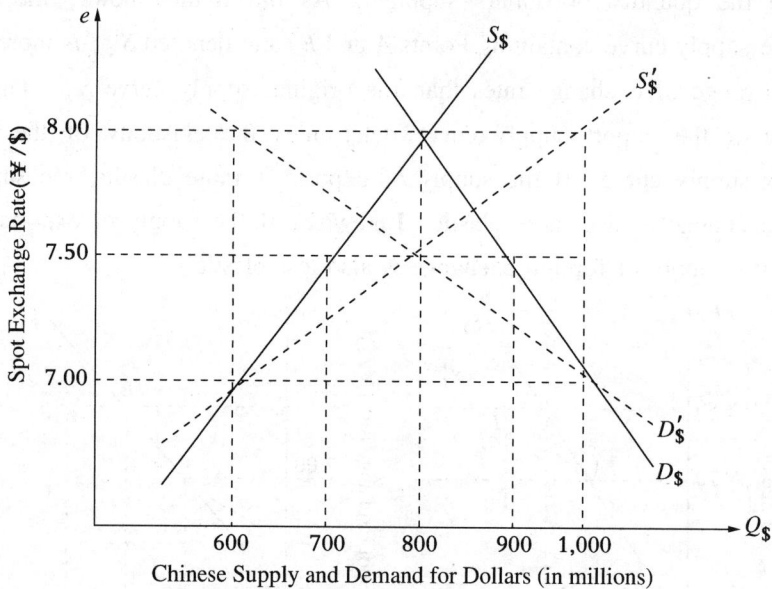

Figure 8-5   The Current Account Deficit

Recall that China's consumers' demand for imported goods and services generates their demand for foreign exchange and that China's producers' supply of exports yields the supply of foreign exchange. Hence, when the quantity of foreign exchange demanded by China's consumers exceeds the quantity of foreign exchange supplied by China's producers to the U.S., China experiences a current account deficit. The difference, $400 million in this example, or its RMB equivalent amount of ¥2,800 million ($400 × 7.00 ¥/$ = ¥2,800 million), is the amount of China's current account deficit.

Let us suppose Chinese government is willing to allow the value of RMB to depreciate relative to dollar. As Figure 8-5 illustrates, when the number of RMB required to purchase each dollar increases, the quantity of foreign exchange demanded decreases, and the quantity of foreign exchange supplied increases. In other words, China's producers' exports of goods and services rise, and China's consumers' imports of goods and services fall.

The Role of Elasticity

How much of a depreciation of RMB is required to completely eliminate the current account deficit? As Figure 8-5 also illustrates, the answer to this question depends on which set of supply and demand curves we consider. Take a look at foreign exchange demand curve $D_\$'$ and foreign exchange supply curve $S_\$'$. The difference between the quantity of foreign exchange demanded and the quantity supplied and, therefore, the current account deficit, is eliminated at an exchange rate of 7.5 ¥/$.

In contrast, if we consider foreign exchange demand curve $D_\$$, and foreign exchange supply curve $S_\$$ in Figure 8-5, a depreciation to 7.5 ¥/$ is not enough to eliminate the current account deficit. A deficit of $200 million remains. The spot exchange rate would have to rise to 8.00 ¥/$ in order to completely eliminate the deficit.

Because the demand curve $D_\$'$ is more elastic relative to the demand curve $D_\$$, a depreciation to 7.5 ¥/$ generates a larger change in the quantity of foreign exchange demanded along curve $D_\$'$ than it does along the less elastic demand curve $D_\$$. Likewise, a depreciation to 7.5 ¥/$ generates a larger change in the quantity of foreign exchange supplied along the relatively more elastic supply curve $S_\$'$ than it does along the supply curve $S_\$$. Thus, the elasticities of the supply of and demand for foreign exchange are fundamental determinants of adjustment to a balance-of-payments deficit.

The Marshall-Lerner Condition

Based on the previous example, it appears that depreciation will always improve a balance-of-payments deficit to some extent. This is not necessarily the case. It is theoretically possible that depreciation can increase the difference between the quantity of foreign exchange supplied and the quantity of foreign exchange demanded. Likewise, appreciation may increase the difference between the quantity of foreign exchange demanded and the quantity of foreign exchange supplied.

The Marshall-Lerner condition specifies the necessary condition for a positive effect of depreciation of domestic currency on the balance of payments. Here again, assume that capital flows occur only as a means of financing current account (CA) transactions, that is, the status of the balance of payments is reflected by that of the current account. Still, we assume trade balance exclusively represents the current account, ignoring other components of the current account for simplicity. Though the current account is commonly denominated in foreign currencies, usually in dollar, we'd like to evaluate it in domestic currency in consideration that it is convenient to convert the domestic currency value of CA into its foreign currency value while this trick can make the following work much simpler. Then the current account in terms of domestic currency can be expressed as

$$CA = PX - eP^* M \tag{8-1}$$

where CA is the current account denominated in domestic currency, P and P^* stand for the price level of the home country and the foreign country respectively, X and M stand for the quantity of the home country's exports and imports respectively, and e stands for the exchange rate in direct quotation. The first part of the right side of Equation 8-1 is the domestic currency value of exports and the second part is the domestic currency value of imports.

Derivate Equation 8-1 with the exchange rate e, remembering e has the impact on both exports X and import M:

$$\frac{dCA}{de} = P\frac{dX}{de} - P^* M - eP^* \frac{dM}{de} \tag{8-2}$$

Suppose the initial CA is in equilibrium, i.e. the export value (PX) equals the import value (eP^*M). Thus

$$\frac{eP^*M}{PX} = 1 \qquad (8\text{-}3)$$

Multiply the first part of the right side of Equation 8-2 with the left side of Equation 8-3, then we get

$$\frac{dCA}{de} = P\frac{eP^*M}{PX}\frac{dX}{de} - P^*M - eP^*\frac{dM}{de} \qquad (8\text{-}4)$$

Rearrange Equation 8-4 and we get

$$\frac{dCA}{de} = P^*M(\frac{dX}{de}\frac{e}{X} - \frac{dM}{de}\frac{e}{M} - 1) \qquad (8\text{-}5)$$

Define the demand elasticity of exports (η_x) and the demand elasticity of imports (η_m) respectively as $\eta_x = \frac{dX}{de}\frac{e}{X}$ and $\eta_m = -\frac{dM}{de}\frac{e}{M}$. Note the minus "$-$" in η_m is for keeping the value positive since a rise in the exchange rate e reduces imports M and makes M change in opposite direction to e. Thus Equation 8-5 changes into

$$\frac{dCA}{de} = P^*M(\eta_x + \eta_m - 1) \qquad (8\text{-}6)$$

If a depreciation of domestic currency (i. e. a rise in e) is expected to improve the current account, then

$$\frac{dCA}{de} > 0 \qquad (8\text{-}7)$$

Since P^* and M are positive values, Inequality 8-7 then requires

$$\eta_x + \eta_m > 1 \qquad (8\text{-}8)$$

Inequality 8-8 is the **Marshall-Lerner condition**. It states that a depreciation of domestic currency can improve a country's balance of payments only when the sum of the demand elasticity of exports and the demand elasticity of imports exceeds unity.

The Marshall-Lerner condition is met in most situations. It is possible, however, that if we consider a very short time horizon, the Marshall-Lerner condition may not be met.

J-Curve Effect

The Marshall-Lerner condition implies that the demand for exports (in foreign countries) and for imports (in the home country) must be sufficiently elastic for a depreciation to reduce the country's balance-of-payments deficit. Elasticity measures generally differ over the time horizon that is considered. Because a longer time interval provides households and businesses the time needed to adjust to price changes, supply and demand tend to be relatively more price elastic over longer time intervals and relatively less elastic over shorter time intervals. For example, in the short run, households and businesses may be obligated by contracts to complete a purchase of an imported good. Further, households and businesses might not have the opportunity to find domestic suppliers of imported goods and services, and thus might alter their planned expenditures on imports.

Over longer time horizons, however, if the prices of imported goods and services rise, households and businesses can adjust their planned expenditures. They can seek alternatives to imported goods and services and reduce their reliance on imports. Hence, over longer time intervals, households and businesses are more responsive to price changes, and over shorter time intervals they are less responsive to price changes. We can conclude, therefore, that import demand and export demand tend to be relatively more elastic over long time intervals and relatively less elastic over short time intervals.

Import demand and export demand are less elastic in the short run. Consequently, a depreciation of the domestic currency is unlikely to immediately improve a country's balance-of-payments deficit. It is even possible that depreciation could cause a country's balance of payments to worsen before it improves, a phenomenon known as the **J-curve effect**.

Figure 8-6 illustrates the J-curve effect graphically. At time t_0, the economy suffers BP deficit (Point A). Suppose the Marshall-Lerner condition could be satisfied, so the government decides to depreciate its currency in the hope of eliminating its BP deficit. But the existence of several lags leads its balance of payments to deterioration rather than to improvement. These lags include:

- *Recognition lags* of changing competitive conditions;
- *Decision lags* in forming new business connections and placing new orders;
- *Delivery lags* between the time new orders are placed and their impact on

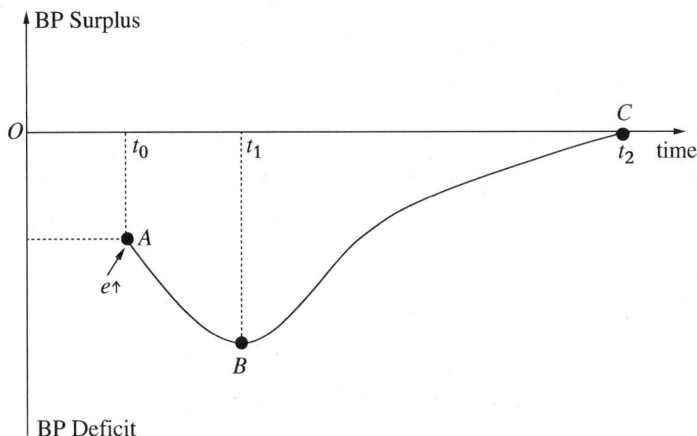

Figure 8-6   The J-curve Effect

trade and payment flows is felt;

  ● *Replacement lags* in using up inventories and wearing out existing machinery before placing new orders;

  ● *Production lags* involved in increasing the output of commodities for which demand has increased.

Due to these lags, during the short time interval, net exports could not rise in time and the balance of payments keeps deteriorating until time t_1. From then on, the positive effect of currency depreciation on the balance of payments works. The economy restores its balance of payments finally at time t_2. The graph shows the initially worsening of the current account deficit before it improves, resulting in a J-shaped curve.

8.2   Multiplier Approach to the Balance of Payments

The multiplier approach is a modified and extended version of the elasticity analysis in the sense that it sees about the limitations of the latter. It constitutes another flow approach to the balance-of-payments whereby exchange rates is assumed fixed, in addition to prices. That is why the multiplier theory is suitable to analyze the adjustment process under a peg regime. With all prices (including exchange rates and interest rates) constant, the only possibility for balance-of-payments adjustment in this model is by changes in (national) income. In this sense, the foreign trade multiplier approach complements the elasticities approach to the balance of payments, since in the latter income is assumed unchanged.

The key assumptions, common to similar models, are (1) underemployed resources; (2) rigidity of all prices, including exchange rates and interest rates; (3) absence of capital mobility, so that the balance of payments is synonymous with the balance on goods and services or the current account; and (4) all exports are made out of current output.

Linear functions are assumed in what follows, for simplicity of the exposition. With this in mind, the foreign trade multiplier model is the standard Keynesian textbook model with an appended external sector:

$$Y = C + I + G + (X - M) \qquad (8\text{-}9)$$

$$C = C_0 + cY \qquad (8\text{-}10)$$

$$I = I_0 \qquad (8\text{-}11)$$

$$G = G_0 \qquad (8\text{-}12)$$

$$X = X_0 \qquad (8\text{-}13)$$

$$M = M_0 + mY \qquad (8\text{-}14)$$

where Y is national income, C, I, G, X and M stand for domestic consumption, investment, government purchases, exports and imports respectively, C_0, I_0, G_0, X_0, M_0 are the autonomous parts of respective variables, and c and m are marginal propensity to consume and to import respectively with $0 < c < 1$, $0 < m < 1$ and $c > m$ (domestic residents usually spend more of their added income on domestic consumption than on imports).

Replace the relevant variables in Equation 8-9 with Equations 8-10, 8-11, 8-12, 8-13, and 8-14, and we get

$$Y = C_0 + cY + I_0 + G_0 + (X_0 - M_0 - mY) \qquad (8\text{-}15)$$

Rearrange it as

$$Y = \frac{1}{1 - c + m}(C_0 + I_0 + G_0 + X_0 - M_0) \qquad (8\text{-}16)$$

where the coefficient $\dfrac{1}{1 - c + m}$ is **foreign trade multiplier** or **open economy multiplier** for a small-nation open economy. Since $0 < c < 1$, $0 < m < 1$ and $c > m$, it is safe to conclude $\dfrac{1}{1 - c + m} > 1$. The multiplier indicates the multiples of the change in national income resulting from a change in effective demand.

Derivate Equation 8-16 with G_0, I_0 and X_0 respectively, then

$$\frac{dY}{dG_0} = \frac{dY}{dI_0} = \frac{dY}{dX_0} = \frac{1}{1 - c + m} > 0 \qquad (8\text{-}17)$$

Equation 8-17 indicates that an expansionary fiscal policy (a rise in G_0), an expansionary monetary policy (a rise in I_0 resulting from lower interest rate), or added exports can increase national income, while a contractionary fiscal policy, a contractionary monetary policy or reduced exports will decrease national income.

Now let us examine the current account. It can be depicted as

$$CA = X - M = X_0 - (M_0 + mY) \qquad (8\text{-}18)$$

Replace Y in Equation 8-18 with Equation 8-16 and rearrange it, then we get

$$CA = X_0 - M_0 - \frac{m}{1 - c + m}(C_0 + I_0 + G_0 + X_0 - M_0) \qquad (8\text{-}19)$$

Derivate Equation 8-19 with G_0 and I_0 respectively, and we get

$$\frac{dCA}{dG_0} = \frac{dCA}{dI_0} = -\frac{m}{1 - c + m} < 0 \qquad (8\text{-}20)$$

Equation 8-20 indicates that an expansionary fiscal policy or an expansionary monetary policy will worsen a country's current account (and then its balance of payments), while a contractionary fiscal policy or monetary policy will improve its balance of payments.

Derivate Equation 8-19 with X_0, then

$$\frac{dCA}{dX_0} = \frac{1 - c}{1 - c + m} > 0 \qquad (8\text{-}21)$$

Equation 8-21 indicates that added exports will improve a country's current account (then its balance of payments) while reduced exports will worsen its balance of payments.

In conclusion, the multiplier approach maintains that when an economy has underemployed resources, fiscal policy, monetary policy and trade policies can be used for adjusting its balance of payments. Contractionary fiscal or monetary policy can improve the balance of payments but at the cost of a decrease in national output. Added exports resulting from export-encouraging policies will improve the balance of payments and meanwhile, increase national income.

8.3   Absorption Approach to the Balance of Payments

The absorption approach assumes that prices remain constant and emphasizes changes in real domestic income. Hence, the absorption approach is a real income theory of the balance of payments. Because of the assumption of constant prices, economists view the absorption approach as a short-run approach to the balance of payments.

The absorption approach separates the market values of a country's expenditures on domestic final goods and services into three basic categories: consumption expenditures (C), investment expenditures (I) and government expenditures (G). Exports (X) and Imports (M) are not included, because exports represent foreign expenditures on domestic final goods and services and imports represent domestic expenditures on foreign final goods and services.

Economists refer to the total of these three categories of expenditures as domestic absorption. That is, a country absorbs goods and services for consumption, investment, and public sector purposes. Hence, absorption is a country's total expenditures on domestic final goods and services. We shall express the identity representing a country's absorption as

$$A = C + I + G \qquad (8\text{-}22)$$

where A denotes absorption, C, I and G denote consumption expenditures, investment expenditures and government expenditures respectively.

A country's income, on the other hand, is equivalent to the expenditures on its output of final goods and services. Hence, national income is equal to consumption expenditures (C), investment expenditures (I), government expenditures (G), and exports minus imports ($X - M$). We shall depict a country's income as

$$Y = C + I + G + (X - M) \qquad (8\text{-}23)$$

In the absorption approach, the current account balance, ignoring any unilateral transfers, is represented by the difference between foreign expenditures on exports and domestic expenditures on imports. This is represented as

$$CA = X - M \qquad (8\text{-}24)$$

where CA denotes the current account balance. If exports exceed imports, more foreign assets flow in to buy the domestic goods and services, and the country is running a current account surplus. If exports are equal to imports, the country's current account is balanced. If exports are less than imports, more domestic financial assets flow out to buy foreign goods and services, and the country is running a current account deficit.

Combine Equations 8-24 with 8-22 and 8-23, and we obtain

$$CA = Y - A \tag{8-25}$$

Hence, a country's current account balance is determined by the difference between its national income and its absorption. A current account surplus means national income exceeds domestic absorption while a current account deficit means domestic absorption exceeds national income. Therefore, changing national income or domestic absorption can be used to adjust a country's current account (and then balance of payments).

The differential of both sides of Equation 8-25 shows

$$dCA = dY - dA \tag{8-26}$$

Equation 8-26 shows whether a currency depreciation can improve the current account (then the balance of payments) depends on its effect on national income and on domestic absorption.

The effect of depreciation on absorption can be divided into two parts: (1) the induced effect of income changes resulting from depreciation on absorption which is denoted by $a \cdot dY$ where a is called as marginal propensity to absorb; and (2) the direct effect of depreciation on absorption which is denoted by dA_d. Thus the overall effects of depreciation on absorption can be depicted as

$$dA = a \cdot dY + dA_d \tag{8-27}$$

Combine Equation 8-26 with Equation 8-27 and we get

$$dCA = (1 - a) \cdot dY - dA_d \tag{8-28}$$

Equation 8-28 indicates that the effects of depreciation on the current account consist of two parts: (1) the income effect $(1 - a) \cdot dY$ and (2) the absorption effect dA_d. Only when the income effect exceeds the absorption effect, i. e. $(1 - a) \cdot dY > dA_d$, can the current account be improved by depreciation. Let us discuss them in detail.

Effects of Depreciation on National Income

We can examine the effects of depreciation on national income from aspects as follows.

On the supply side, a depreciation would increase national income only when there are idle resources in the economy. It is called as **idle resources effect**. In this case, the depreciation causes a rise in exports which in turn expands national output. But keep in your mind that the rise in national income will also increase domestic consumption and investment, augmenting absorption and worsening the balance of payments. Whether the depreciation can eventually improve the current account relies on the marginal propensity to absorption a: if $a < 1$, then $(1 - a) \cdot dY > 0$, the rise in domestic absorption is less than that in national income and the current account improves; if $a > 1$, then $(1 - a) \cdot dY < 0$, the rise in domestic absorption exceeds that in national income and the current account becomes worse.

On the demand side, if a country meets the Marshall-Lerner condition, the depreciation can increase national income and thus the balance of payments improves.

From the perspective of government's macroeconomic regulation, if a country can loosen those protective or restrictive trade policies at the time a depreciation policy is taken, the distorting allocation of resources will be lessened and the depreciation will increase national income and further improve the balance of payments.

Direct Effects of Depreciation on Absorption

Depreciation affects absorption in the following respects.

• *Real cash balance effect*. Given money supply keeps constant, the depreciation of domestic currency will bring about a rise in domestic price level and reduce cash balance held by residents. Thus, they have either to decrease their expenditures on goods and services, resulting in a drop in consumption and absorption; or to withdraw their financial assets, causing a drop in prices of financial assets and a rise in interest rates which in turn discourages consumption and investment and finally reduces absorption. Hence, the effect of real cash balance requires the government to take tight monetary policy along with depreciation so as to guarantee the reduction in absorption and thus the improvement of the current account.

• *Income redistribution effect*. The depreciation of domestic currency drives the price level up but there are lags for wages to adjust. The rise in the price level redistributes income from fixed income earners (who depend on wages) to flexible income earners (who depend on profits). Since flexible income earners have relatively lower marginal propensity to consume (because they are much richer), the income redistribution reduces consumption and then absorption.

• *Taxation effect.* In a country with progressive tax rates, the depreciation leads to a rise in nominal income, pushing residents to higher taxation levels and reducing their disposable income. If the government can fulfill contractionary fiscal policy along with depreciation, the total absorption will drop down and the balance of payments improves.

In conclusion, the absorption approach proposes that a depreciation can be effective in improving the balance of payments when the economy has idle resources and meets the Marshall-Lerner condition and the government fulfills contractionary fiscal or monetary policy along with depreciation. But the approach has encountered many criticisms for its ignorance of capital flow and for its expenses of tax increase and income reduction.

8.4   Monetary Approach to the Balance of Payments

Before studying the monetary approach, we should know what the central banks do to attain their objectives.

Leaning With or Against the Wind

A central bank intervenes either on its own account or on behalf of its national government in an effort to influence the value of its country's currency in the foreign exchange market. If a central bank intervenes to support or speed along the current trend in the value of its country's currency in the foreign exchange market, then economists say that its interventions lean with the wind.

In contrast, economists say that a central bank's interventions intended to halt or reverse a recent trend in the value of its country's currency are leaning against the wind. Most often, central banks lean against the wind solely to halt, at least temporarily, sharp swings in market exchange rates. Consequently, a key rationale for many instances of leaning against the wind is simply to reduce volatility in exchange rates. A central bank does not necessarily lean against the wind with an aim to bring about long-term reversals in the trend value of their currencies, although in some instances this might be an ultimate goal of a central bank or finance ministry upon whose behalf the central bank conducts a policy of leaning against the wind.

Foreign Exchange Interventions

Whatever central banks seek to attain international objectives or focus on domestic policy objectives, they typically do so in part through foreign exchange interventions, buying or selling financial assets denominated in foreign currencies in an effort to influence exchange rates. To show how central banks conduct their interventions through the private banking system, changing the monetary base and thereby altering the money stock, we consider only the purchase or sale of foreign-currency-denominated bank deposits. These deposits are assets of domestic individuals, firms, brokers, and banks, which they hold at foreign banks. Hence, foreign exchange transactions of the central bank affect the balance sheets of domestic private banks and the balance sheets of foreign private banks. Indirectly, therefore, foreign exchange interventions influence the domestic money stock and potentially the foreign country's money stock.

Sterilization of Interventions

A central bank sterilizes foreign exchange interventions when it buys or sells domestic assets in sufficient quantities to prevent the interventions from influencing the domestic money stock. A key money measure is the monetary base, which we can view as either the sum of domestic credit plus foreign exchange reserves or as the sum of domestic currency and bank reserves. Thus, sterilization of the sale of foreign exchange reserves requires an equal-sized expansion of domestic credit, perhaps via a central bank open-market purchase, that would maintain an unchanged monetary base.

After the collapse of the Bretton Woods system, economists sought to develop approaches to understand the balance of payments adjustment that allowed for floating exchange rates and greater integration of goods and financial markets across economies. Their efforts yielded the monetary approach, which quickly became popular among many economists.

The monetary approach to the balance of payments postulates that changes in a country's balance of payments are a monetary phenomenon. That is, the balance of payments deficits or surpluses result from differences between the quantity of money supplied and the quantity of money demanded.

Money Demand

The famous theory of the demand for money is **Cambridge Equation**

$$M_d = kPy \tag{8-29}$$

where M_d denotes the total quantity of nominal money balances that all households desire to hold, k is a fraction between zero and one, P is the aggregate price level in the economy, and y is total real income. Because P is the aggregate price level and y is real income, multiplying the two together yields nominal income. Hence, the Cambridge equation constitutes a hypothesis that people hold a fraction of their nominal incomes as money.

Money Supply

A country's quantity of money is equal to a money multiplier times the monetary base

$$M_s = m(D + F) \tag{8-30}$$

where M_s denotes the total quantity of nominal money supply, m is the money multiplier, and D and F stand for domestic credit and foreign exchange reserves respectively. Here, we express the monetary base as the sum of domestic credit (D) and foreign exchange reserves (F).

The Relationship between Money Stock and the Balance of Payments

Recall that the current account balance plus the capital and financial account balance is equal to the official settlements balance. The official settlements balance consists mainly of changes in the central bank's foreign exchange reserves. To simplify our discussion, we will assume the country's foreign exchange reserves are equivalent to its official settlements balance.

Using this accounting identity, we can relate a country's money stock to its balance of payments. An increase in the official settlements balance is equivalent to a balance-of-payments surplus. If foreign exchange reserves are unchanged, the country's overall balance of payments continues to be zero. Hence, we can relate changes in the country's money stock to changes in its balance of payments.

The Monetary Equilibrium Condition

Economists who use the monetary approach assume that purchasing power parity holds in the long run. Remember, absolute purchasing power parity can be expressed as

$$e = \frac{P}{P^*} \tag{8-31}$$

where e, P and P^* are the spot exchange rate, the domestic price level and the foreign price level respectively.

Substitute P in Equation 8-29 with that in Equation 8-31 and we get

$$M_d = keP^* y \tag{8-32}$$

The relationship among the Cambridge equation of money demand, the money stock (and, therefore, the balance of payments), the foreign price level, and the spot exchange rate can be determined through an equilibrium condition in which the quantity of money demanded equals the money stock:

$$M_d = M_s \tag{8-33}$$

Substitute Equation 8-33 with Equations 8-32 and 8-30 so that

$$m(D + F) = keP^* y \tag{8-34}$$

In words, in equilibrium the actual money stock equals the quantity of money demanded. Proponents of the monetary approach, however, use this relationship to explain how key variables affect the country's balance of payments.

Next, we will analyze four situations: a change in domestic credit under fixed exchange rates, a change in the quantity of money demanded under fixed exchange rates, a change in domestic credit under flexible exchange rates, a change in the quantity of money demanded under flexible exchange rates.

8.4.1　A Change in Domestic Credit under Fixed Exchange Rates

Consider a country that is small, so that its economy has no effects on the price levels of foreign countries. In addition, suppose that its central bank pegs the exchange value of its currency. If the country's central bank increases domestic credit through an open market purchase of securities, then the open market purchase causes the country's money stock to rise through the multiplier process. All other things constant, the open market operation thereby causes the actual money stock to exceed the quantity of money demanded.

In this situation, households find that the quantity of money that they hold exceeds the quantity they desire to hold. Households reduce their money holdings by increasing their purchases of goods and services. Some of these additional purchases are purchases of foreign goods and services. Depending on the type of exchange rate systems, the increase in the demand for foreign goods and services will have one of two effects. Under fixed exchange rates, the additional purchases of foreign goods and services will generate a balance-of-payments deficit, with no change in the exchange value of the domestic currency. Under flexible exchange rates, the additional purchases of foreign goods and services will cause the domestic currency to depreciate, with no change in the balance of payments.

Under fixed exchange rates, the country's central bank must sell the foreign exchange reserves to meet the demand for foreign currency. As a result, foreign exchange reserves decline, while the spot exchange rate remains constant.

Let us consider the size of foreign exchange intervention that the central bank must undertake to maintain the pegged exchange value of the domestic currency. We shall denote the pegged exchange value of the domestic currency as e and the new level of domestic credit as D'. At this new level of domestic credit, the money stock exceeds the quantity of money demanded, expressed as

$$m(D' + F) > keP^* y \tag{8-35}$$

To prevent the domestic currency from depreciating, the domestic central bank must reduce the quantity of money supplied so that it equals the quantity of money demanded. To do so, the central bank must sell sufficient foreign reserves to exactly offset the increase in domestic credit, returning the money stock to its original level. At this level, households' desired quantity of money again equals the quantity of money supplied.

As discussed earlier, a decline in foreign exchange reserves is equivalent to a balance-of-payments deficit. The amount of the balance-of-payments deficit, therefore, is equal to the change in the foreign exchange reserves component of the monetary base, which is equal to the change in domestic credit brought about by the central bank's open market transaction.

We can conclude that, under fixed exchange rates, the monetary approach indicates that an increase in domestic credit generates a balance of payments deficit, while a decrease in domestic credit results in a balance of payments surplus.

8.4.2 A Change in the Quantity of Money Demanded under Fixed Exchange Rates

Let us continue our example of a small nation that pegs the exchange value of its currency. Suppose that instead of a change in domestic credit there is an increase in either the foreign price level or real income. According to the Cambridge equation that we modified by including absolute purchasing power parity, an increase in either of these two variables causes an increase in the quantity of money demanded.

In this situation, households find that their desired quantity of money falls short of their current money holdings. Households will increase their money holdings by reducing their expenditures on goods and services. As a result, households' demands for domestic and foreign goods and services decline. The decline in demand for foreign goods and services results in either a balance of payments surplus or an appreciation of the domestic currency. To maintain the pegged exchange value of the domestic currency, the central bank must buy foreign reserves.

Let us consider the size of foreign exchange intervention the central bank must undertake to maintain the pegged exchange value of the domestic currency. Let us also continue to denote the pegged exchange value of the domestic currency as e, and denote higher foreign price level or higher level real income as $(P^*y)'$. The higher foreign price level or higher level of real income causes the quantity of money demanded to exceed the quantity of money supplied, expressed as

$$m(D+F) < ke(P^*y)' \tag{8-36}$$

To prevent the domestic currency from appreciating, the domestic central bank must increase the quantity of money supplied so that it equals the quantity of money demanded. To accomplish this, the central bank buys foreign exchange reserves. The increase in foreign exchange reserves is equivalent to a balance of payments surplus, with the size of the surplus equal to the change in foreign exchange reserves.

We can conclude that a rise in either the foreign price level or domestic real income results in a balance of payments surplus. Likewise, a decline in either the foreign price level or domestic real income results in a balance of payments deficit.

8.4.3   A Change in Domestic Credit under Floating Exchange Rates

Suppose that, the domestic central bank increases domestic credit through a purchase of securities. Domestic credit and the domestic money stock rise, and the money stock exceeds the quantity of money demanded.

In this situation, households find that their money holdings exceed the quantity of money they desire. Households reduce their money holdings by increasing their expenditures on goods and services, with some of these expenditures on foreign goods and services. As households increase their expenditures on foreign goods and services, the domestic currency depreciates.

The domestic currency will continue to depreciate until the quantity of money supplied equals the quantity of money demanded. It is in this regard that the spot exchange rate is determined by the quantity of money supplied and the quantity of money demanded.

We can conclude, therefore, that under flexible exchange rates, the monetary approach indicates that an increase in domestic credit results in a depreciation of the domestic currency, while a decline in domestic credit results in an appreciation of the domestic currency.

8.4.4   A Change in the Quantity of Money Demanded under Floating Exchange Rates

If the foreign price level or domestic real income increases, then according to the Cambridge equation, the quantity of money demanded increases. As a result, the quantity of money demanded exceeds the quantity of money supplied.

In this situation, households find that their current money holdings fall short of the quantity desired. Households increase their money holdings by reducing their expenditures on domestic and foreign goods and services. The decrease in demand for foreign goods and services causes the domestic currency to appreciate. Appreciation continues until the quantity of money supplied once again equals the quantity of money demanded, so that households find that their actual money holdings match their desired money holdings.

We can conclude, therefore, that under flexible exchange rates, the monetary approach theorizes that an increase in the foreign price level or domestic real income results in an appreciation of the domestic currency. In contrast, a decline in the foreign price level or domestic real income results in a depreciation of the domestic currency.

To sum up, the monetary approach is a long-run analysis on the balance of payments adjustment. It regards the balance of payments as a monetary phenomenon and emphasizes the role of money supply and demand on the balance of payments. It maintains a deficit in the balance of payments results from the excess of domestic money supply over money demand while a surplus in the balance of payments derives from the excess of money demand over money supply. Thus, under fixed exchange rates, the disequilibrium in the balance of payments can be restored through the adjustment of money supply and money demand; while under floating exchange rates, the disequilibrium in the balance of payments can be automatically restored through changes in exchange rates.

Chapter 9

Macroeconomic Policies in Open Economy

Key Concepts and Terms

Internal Balance	内部平衡
External Balance	外部平衡
Expenditure-changing Policy	支出改变政策
Expenditure-switching Policy	支出转化政策
Fiscal Policy	财政政策
Monetary Policy	货币政策
Expansionary Policy	扩张性政策
Contractionary Policy	紧缩性政策
Tinbergen Rule	丁伯根法则
Meade Conflict	米德冲突
Mundell Assignment Rule	蒙代尔指派法则
Swan Model	斯旺模型
Mundell-Fleming Model	蒙代尔—弗莱明模型
Perfect Capital Immobility	资本完全不流动
Imperfect Capital Mobility	资本有限流动
Perfect Capital Mobility	资本完全流动
Mundell Incompatible Trinity	蒙代尔不相容三角

In this chapter, we discuss the combinations of policies and the effects of fiscal policy and monetary policy under different exchange rate systems and capital mobilities.

9.1　Internal Balance and External Balance in Open Economy

9.1.1　Internal Balance and External Balance

In an open economy, economic goals can be generally classified into internal balance and external balance. **Internal balance** means（1）full employment,（2）no inflation, or more realistically, low inflation, and（3）steady economic growth. Since steady economic growth is a goal in the long run, people care more about the first two targets. **External balance** is a status of neither the balance of payments（BP）deficits nor BP surpluses.

See Figure 9-1, the horizontal axis describes the status of internal economy. While the origin represents the internal balance, each point to the right stands for a status with inflation and the farther the point is from the origin, the more serious the inflation is. On the contrast, each point to the left stands for a status with unemployment and the farther the point is from the origin, the more serious the unemployment is. The vertical axis describes the status of external economy with the origin as the external balance. A point above the origin means a status with BP surplus while one below the origin means BP deficit. Thus the origin depicts the overall balance where an economy attains both internal balance and external

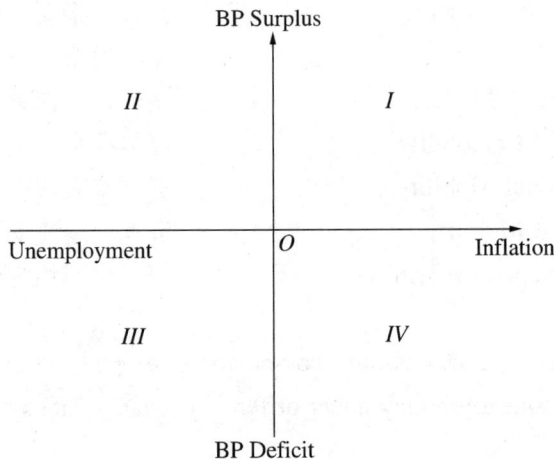

Figure 9-1　Internal Balance and External Balance

balance. Points on axes aside from the origin indicate different mixes of balance and imbalance. For example, points on the right of the horizontal axis indicate an economy in inflation internally with external balance. And points in different quadrants indicate different mixes of internal and external imbalances. For example, points in Quadrant I indicate that the economy is in inflation internally with BP surplus externally.

9.1.2　Policy Instruments

To attain the objectives of both external balance and internal balance, policy makers need to implement expenditure-changing policies and expenditure-switching policies. **Expenditure-changing policies** include fiscal policy and monetary policy, altering the level of aggregate demand for goods and services which are either produced domestically or imported. **Expenditure-switching policies** refer to exchange-rate policies, including appreciation or depreciation of the domestic currency, which shifts the direction of demand between for domestic output and for imports. Policy makers also use such direct controls as tariffs, quotas, subsidies and capital controls to selectively control particular items in the balance of payments.

When an economy is located in the disequilibrium zones of Quadrant I and III in Figure 9-1, expenditure-switching policies can restore the economy to overall balance. Suppose an economy is in Quadrant I , i. e. inflation with BP surplus. An appreciation of the domestic currency reduces the international competitiveness of its goods and leads to a fall in exports, which, on the one hand, decreases its BP surplus, and on the other hand, reduces its aggregate demand and thus output, lessening its inflation. In Figure 9-1, the currency appreciation induces movement towards the southwest, restoring both internal balance and external balance. Conversely, a currency depreciation can restore the overall balance when an economy is in Quadrant III , i. e. unemployment with BP deficit.

9.1.3　Tinbergen Rule

In an open economy, a government faces multiple policy goals. It needs to select proper policies among its tool mix to attain each goal. But one policy aiming to achieve one goal may leave another goal farther away. J. Tinbergen, the first Nobel Economics Prize winner, maintained one economic goal could be attained by at least one effective policy tool. Thus, to achieve n independent goals, we need no less than n effective policy tools.

9.1.4 Meade Conflict

Under a fixed exchange rate system, a country cannot change its exchange rate and thus loses expenditure-switching policy tools. Under this condition, the goals of internal balance and external balance may become conflicting since the government now can only resort to expenditure-changing policies.

See Figure 9-1, if an economy is located in Quadrant I, i. e. BP surplus with inflation, a contractionary expenditure-changing policy will reduce its output and income, decreasing the inflation and restoring internal balance. But reduced national income then weakens imports, enlarging its BP surplus and worsening its external imbalance. If the government uses an expansionary expenditure-changing policy, the external balance can be achieved but the internal economy will be imbalanced with more serious inflation. An economy in Quadrant III, i. e. BP deficit with unemployment, will also meet conflicts between internal balance and external balance.

Therefore, according to Tinbergen Rule, in a fixed exchange rate system where expenditure-switching policies cannot be fulfilled, we need two independent policy tools to achieve both internal balance and external balance and thus solve Meade Conflict.

9.2 Policy Mix to Achieve Both Internal Balance and External Balance

9.2.1 Mundell Assignment Rule

In the above analysis concerning Meade Conflict, we regard fiscal policy and monetary policy as the same policy tool: both of them are expenditure-changing policies. So using either fiscal policy or monetary policy to change aggregate output cannot achieve both internal balance and external balance at the same time.

Robert A. Mundell, who won the Nobel Economics Prize in 1999, pointed out that fiscal policy and monetary policy had different effects on internal economy and external economy. So even under fixed exchange rates, it is likely to utilize fiscal policy and monetary policy to achieve both internal balance and external balance.

Though fiscal policy and monetary policy may affect national income and the current account to the same extent, they have different influence on interest rates and the capital and financial account. A contractionary fiscal policy can reduce interest rates, causing capital outflows and worsening the capital and financial account. A contractionary monetary policy will increase interest rates, causing capital inflows and improving the capital and financial account. Therefore, each policy should be implemented on the goal where it has the larger influence.

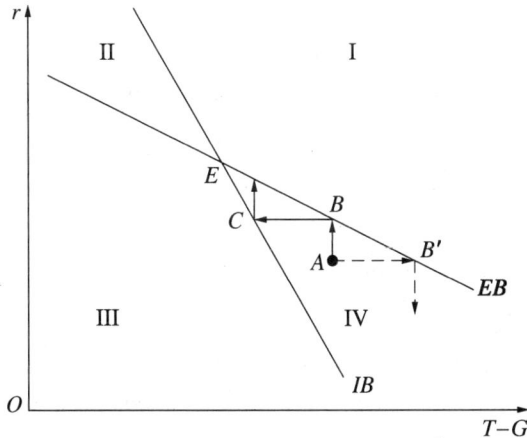

Figure 9-2   Mundell Assignment Rule

See Figure 9-2, the horizontal axis stands for fiscal surplus T-G (net tax minus government purchases) : the higher the value is, the tighter the fiscal policy is. The vertical axis stands for the interest rate r, which describes monetary policy with higher interest rate meaning tighter monetary policy. *IB* line describes the mix of fiscal and monetary policies keeping internal balance. It slopes downward for the reason that a contractionary fiscal policy (more tax T or less government purchases G) causes lower national income, and then an expansionary monetary policy (lower interest rate r) is required in order to encourage private investment and consumption and increase national income. To the right of *IB* line is unemployment as a result of tighter fiscal policy than required. On the contrary, to the left of *IB* line is inflation caused by stronger fiscal stimulus than needed. *EB* line describes the mix of fiscal and monetary policies keeping external balance. It also slopes downward since a contractionary fiscal policy reduces national income, leading to less import and improving the balance of payments, which in turn needs an expansionary monetary policy to lower interest rates and induce capital outflows and further worsen the balance of payments to restore external balance. Above the *EB* line is BP surplus which can be explained by tighter monetary policy than necessary causing higher interest rates and excess capital inflows. Below the *EB* line is BP deficit because exorbitant expansion of monetary policy leads to lower interest rates and capital outflows. Point *E* represents both internal balance and external balance.

It is worth noticing that *EB* line is flatter than *IB* line. The answer lies in the fact that monetary policy has more powerful influence on external economy than fiscal policy. While fiscal policy affects the current account, monetary policy affects the current account as well as the capital and financial account via interest rate changes. When the government implements an expansionary fiscal policy, monetary policy only needs to make a little adjustment to keep external balance.

In Figure 9-2, suppose an economy is at Point *A*, i.e. BP deficit with unemployment. Policy makers can impose a contractionary monetary policy (1) to raise interest rates, induce capital inflows and improve the capital and financial account, and (2) to reduce national income, cause less imports and improve the current account, and thus improve the balance of payments. The economy moves from *A* to *B*, where external economy is in balance but internal economy experiences even more serious unemployment. At the same time, the government can use expansionary fiscal policy to stimulate internal economy, impelling the economy to move from *B* to *C*, where external economy is in imbalance again with BP deficit. The alternant implementation of contractionary monetary policy and expansionary fiscal policy will finally propel the economy to the overall balance, Point *E*.

If policy makers now assign fiscal policy to solve external imbalance and monetary policy to solve internal imbalance, they need to use a contractionary fiscal policy to reduce national income, causing less imports and improving the current account and thus the balance of payments. The economy then moves from

A to B', where it is in external balance with internal unemployment which requires an expansionary monetary policy and the economy then diverges from the overall balance, Point E. Hence, according to Mundell Assignment Rule, monetary policy should be assigned to solve external imbalance and fiscal policy should be assigned to solve internal imbalance. Otherwise, the economy will diverge from the overall balance.

9.2.2　Swan Model

Mundell Assignment Rule solves Meade Conflict under a fixed exchange rate system by assigning fiscal policy and monetary policy effectively. Here, Swan Model aims to achieve both internal balance and external balance by combining expenditure-changing policies and expenditure-switching policies when exchange rates are allowed to change. The model ignores the international flow of capital. Hence, external balance now is equivalent to the balance of current account.

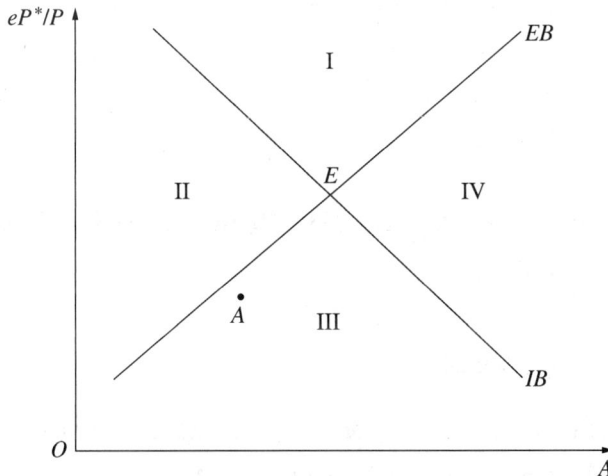

Figure 9-3　Swan Model

In Figure 9-3, the horizontal axis indicates absorption A (i.e. domestic expenditure) and the vertical axis indicates the real exchange rate eP^*/P, where e, P^* and P stand for nominal exchange rate, foreign price level and domestic price level respectively. A rise of the real exchange rate means a depreciation of the domestic currency and a drop of the real exchange rate means an appreciation of the domestic currency.

IB line shows combinations of real exchange rates and absorptions to keep internal balance. *IB* line slopes downward since a drop of the real exchange rate leads to less imports and more exports, which requires reducing absorption to keep the internal balance. To the right of *IB* line is inflation arising from excess absorption and to the left of *IB* line is unemployment as a result of insufficient absorption. *EB* line indicates combinations of real exchange rates and absorptions to keep external balance. *EB* line slopes upward because a rise of the real exchange rate leads to more exports and less imports, which requires adding absorption to induce more imports so as to keep external balance. Above *EB* line is BP surplus because over-depreciation of domestic currency brings excess export while below *EB* line is BP deficit resulting from over-appreciation of the domestic currency.

Suppose an economy lies in Quadrant Ⅲ, say, Point *A*. That is, it suffers BP deficit with unemployment. Policy makers can implement an expansionary expenditure-changing policy to deal with the internal unemployment and adopt a depreciation of the domestic currency to restore its balance of payments. The combination of expenditure-changing policies and expenditure-switching policies restores the overall balance.

9.3 Effects of Macroeconomic Policies under Fixed Exchange Rates

9.3.1 IS-LM-BP Model

Recall IS-LM model in microeconomics. In an *r-Y* coordinate plane, *IS* curve slopes downward, describing combinations of the interest rate *r* and national income *Y* when goods market is in equilibrium. *LM* curve slopes upward, describing combinations of the interest rate *r* and national income *Y* when money market is in equilibrium. An expansionary fiscal policy drives *IS* curve to shift rightward and a contractionary fiscal policy pulls *IS* curve to the left. And an expansionary monetary policy causes *LM* curve to shift rightward while a contractionary monetary policy pulls *LM* curve to the left.

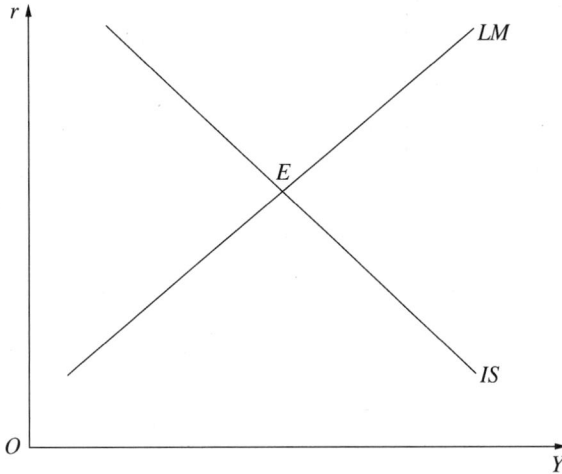

Figure 9-4   IS-LM Model

Now in an open economy, we need to add a new tool, *BP* curve, to describe combinations of the interest rate r and national income Y when the balance of payments is in equilibrium. Let us first see Figure 9-5 (b). In the figure, *BP* curve slopes upward. That is because when national income Y rises, imports will increase accordingly and worsen the current account, which requires a rise in the interest rate r to attract the inflow of international capital and improve the capital and financial account so as to keep the balance of payments in balance. To the right of *BP* curve is BP deficit because high national income brings about too more imports which worsens the current account. To the left of *BP* curve is BP surplus since low national income reduces imports, improving the current account. In this case of upward-sloping *BP* curve, capital can flow with limits or barriers by the impact of interest rates. We call it the case of **imperfect capital mobility**. If capital flows are strictly controlled and capital totally cannot flow with the change of interest rates, *BP* curve will be vertical (See Figure 9-5 (a)) and we call it the case of **perfect capital immobility**. If a slight change of domestic interest rates away from the world interest rates can cause tremendous capital flows, *BP* curve will be horizontal (See Figure 9-5 (c)) and we call it the case of **perfect capital mobility**. When we add *BP* curve into IS-LM plane, IS-LM-BP model is then formed.

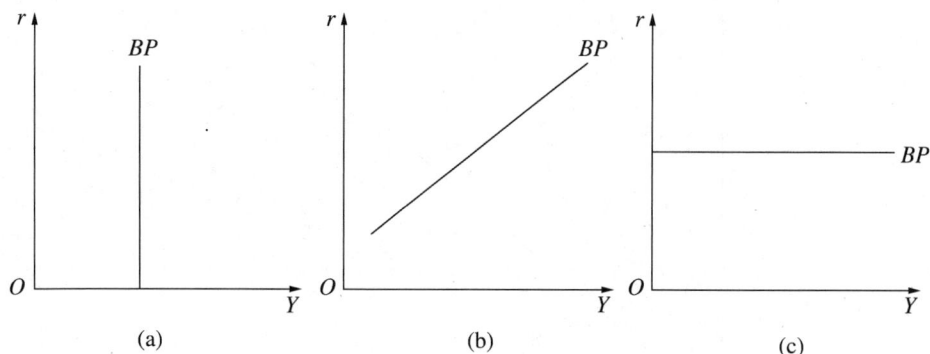

Figure 9-5   *BP* Curve

In 1960s, Robert A. Mundell and J. Marcus Fleming analyzed the effects of fiscal policy and monetary policy under different exchange rate systems and capital mobilities. Their findings are called as **Mundell-Fleming Model**. Before we go ahead, please remember the following presuppositions: (1) national output is determined by the demand side; (2) the price levels of both home country and foreign country are fixed, so real exchange rates and nominal exchange rates are changing in proportion; (3) the country in discussion is a small nation, so its interest rate r is determined by the world interest rate; and (4) there is no exchange rate expectation, so exchange rates can be adjusted without time lags.

9.3.2   Effects of Fiscal Policy under Fixed Exchange Rates

Case of Perfect Capital Immobility

In the case of perfect capital immobility, *BP* curve is vertical. See Figure 9-6, an economy has its initial equilibrium E_0. Suppose the government enacts an expansionary fiscal policy, i. e. an increase in government purchases ($G\uparrow$) or a cut in tax, which enhances aggregate demand ($AD\uparrow$), pushing *IS* curve rightward ($\overrightarrow{IS}$) to *IS'*. The economy moves to its temporary equilibrium E_1, where national income rises ($Y\uparrow$) from Y_0 to Y_1 and the interest rate is also driven up ($r\uparrow$) from r_0 to r_1 by intensive money demand resulting from more aggregate demand. The rise in national income leads to more imports ($M\uparrow$), causing *BP* deficit (BP^-) (current account deficit, CA^-) and the stress on depreciation of domestic currency ($e\uparrow$). Since capital flow is confined, the higher interest rate can not lead to any capital inflow ($\bar{K}$). In order to keep a fixed exchange rate ($e\uparrow \times$), the central bank has to sell its foreign exchange ($f\uparrow$) to meet desired foreign exchange demand and passively buy domestic currency from the market. That causes a shrink of money supply ($Ms\downarrow$) and means a contractionary monetary policy — LM curve is pulled leftward to LM' ($\overleftarrow{LM}$). The economy then moves from E_1 to E_2, where the interest rate increases ($r\uparrow$) further from r_1 to r_2 and national income falls back ($Y\downarrow$) to Y_0. The fall of national income leads to less imports and the balance of payments is then restored. The finally unchanged national income implies that private investment is crowded out by government purchases to the same quantity of the latter.

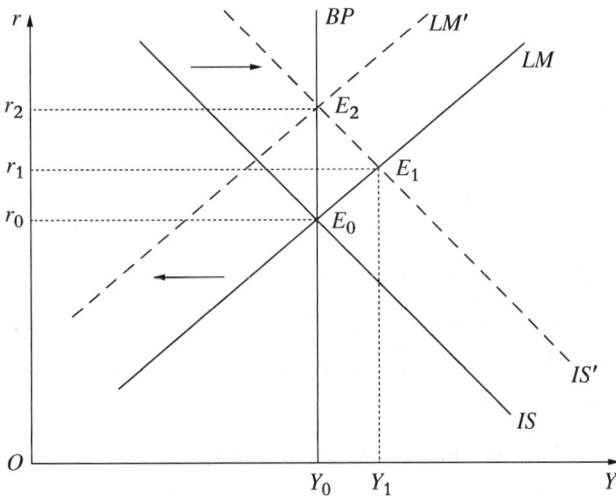

Figure 9-6 Effect of Fiscal Policy (Perfect Capital Immobility) under Fixed Exchange Rates

$$\bar{e} + \bar{K}:$$
$$G\uparrow \Rightarrow AD\uparrow \Rightarrow \overrightarrow{IS} \Rightarrow E_1: Y\uparrow(Y_1) \Rightarrow M\uparrow \Rightarrow CA^-$$
$$r\uparrow(r_1) \Rightarrow \bar{K} \Rightarrow \overline{KA}$$
$$CA^- > \overline{KA} \Rightarrow BP^- \Rightarrow e\uparrow \times \Rightarrow f\uparrow \Rightarrow Ms\downarrow \Rightarrow \overleftarrow{LM} \Rightarrow E_2: Y\downarrow(Y_0) \ ; \ r\uparrow(r_2)$$

In conclusion, fiscal policy has no effect on economy under fixed exchange rates when capital is perfectly immobile, only to find a higher interest rate.

Case of Imperfect Capital Immobility

In the case of imperfect capital immobility, *BP* curve slopes upward. The more the flow of capital is sensitive to the change of interest rates, the flatter *BP* curve slopes. Since *LM* curve also slopes upward, we need to distinguish three situations: (a) *BP* curve steeper than *LM* curve; (b) *BP* curve coinciding with *LM* curve; and (c) *BP* curve flatter than *LM* curve.

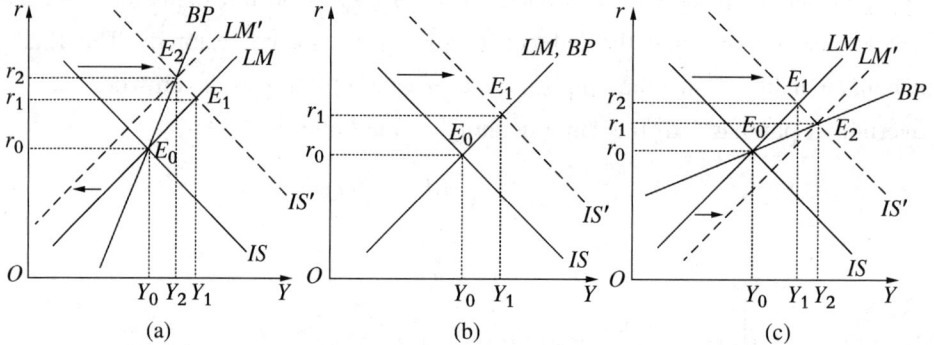

Figure 9-7   Effect of Fiscal Policy (Imperfect Capital Mobility) under Fixed Exchange Rates

When *BP* curve is steeper than *LM* curve (See Figure 9-7 (a)), it means capital flows are rather insensitive to the change of interest rates. When the government increases its government purchases, augmented aggregate demand leads to a rightward shift of *IS* curve. The economy reaches its temporary equilibrium E_1, where national income increases from Y_0 to Y_1 and the interest rate rises from r_0 to r_1. Increased national income results in more imports and then worsens the current account. Higher interest rate attracts capital to flow in and improves the capital and financial account. But the amount of capital inflow cannot compensate that of current account deficit, so the balance of payments is in deficit as a whole. That generates the stress of depreciation. So the central bank has to sell foreign exchange to keep the exchange rate fixed. The passive supply of domestic currency leads to a leftward shift of *LM* curve and the economy finds its final equilibrium in E_2. In the new equilibrium, national income falls from Y_2 to Y_1 but is still larger than Y_0; the interest rate rises further from r_1 to r_2; and the balance of payments is restored.

$\bar{e} + \hat{K}(BP > LM)$:

$G\uparrow \Rightarrow AD\uparrow \Rightarrow \overrightarrow{IS} \Rightarrow E_1 : Y\uparrow (Y_1) \Rightarrow M\uparrow \Rightarrow CA^-$

$\qquad\qquad\qquad r\uparrow (r_1) \Rightarrow K\uparrow \Rightarrow KA^+$

$CA^- > KA^+ \Rightarrow BP^- \Rightarrow e\uparrow \times \Rightarrow f\uparrow \Rightarrow Ms\downarrow \Rightarrow \overleftarrow{LM} \Rightarrow E_2 : Y\downarrow (Y_2 > Y_0)$;

$\qquad\qquad\qquad\qquad\qquad\qquad\qquad r\uparrow (r_2)$

When BP curve coincides with LM curve, it comes to Figure 9-7 (b). An expansionary fiscal policy propels IS curve to shift rightward to IS' and the economy reaches E_1, where national income adds up from Y_0 to Y_1 and the interest rate rises from r_0 to r_1. The in-flowed capital attracted by the higher interest rate exactly compensates the current account deficit which is caused by the income-induced imports. So the balance of payments is in neither deficit nor surplus. E_1 is the final equilibrium of the economy!

$\bar{e} + \hat{K}(BP = LM)$:

$G\uparrow \Rightarrow AD\uparrow \Rightarrow \overrightarrow{IS} \Rightarrow E_1 : Y\uparrow (Y_1) \Rightarrow M\uparrow \Rightarrow CA^-$

$\qquad\qquad r\uparrow (r_1) \Rightarrow K\uparrow \Rightarrow KA^+(CA^- = KA^+ \Rightarrow \overline{BP})$

When BP curve is flatter than LM curve (See Figure 9-7 (c)), it means capital flows are quite sensitive to the change of interest rates. An expansionary fiscal policy pushes IS curve rightward to IS' and the economy reaches E_1, where national income increases from Y_0 to Y_1 and the interest rate rises from r_0 to r_1. Since capital is rather sensitive to the change of interest rates, the in-flowed capital attracted by the higher interest rate can compensate more than the current account deficit which is caused by the income-induced imports. That leads to the overall surplus of the balance of payments which in turn brings the stress of appreciation. To keep a fixed exchange rate, the central bank has to buy foreign exchange in the market with domestic currency, passively expanding money supply. LM curve shifts rightward to LM' and the economy moves from E_1 to E_2, where national income increases further from Y_1 to Y_2 and the interest rate falls from r_1 to r_2 but is still higher than r_0. The balance of payments is now restored.

$$\overline{e} + \hat{K}(BP < LM):$$
$$G\uparrow \Rightarrow AD\uparrow \Rightarrow \overrightarrow{IS} \Rightarrow E_1: Y\uparrow(Y_1) \Rightarrow M\uparrow \Rightarrow CA^-$$
$$r\uparrow(r_1) \Rightarrow K\uparrow \Rightarrow KA^+$$
$$CA^- < KA^+ \Rightarrow BP^+ \Rightarrow e\downarrow \times \Rightarrow f\downarrow \Rightarrow Ms\uparrow \Rightarrow \overrightarrow{LM} \Rightarrow E_2: Y\uparrow; r\downarrow(r_2 > r_0)$$

To sum up, fiscal policy has some effect on economy under fixed exchange rates when capital is imperfectly mobile. But the extent of the effect relies on the sensibility of capital flow to the change of interest rates. The more sensible the capital flow is, the larger the effect of fiscal policy will be.

Case of Perfect Capital Mobility

In the case of perfect capital mobility, *BP* curve is horizontal (See Figure 9-8). A slight change of interest rates will cause immediate tremendous capital flows. In this case, capital flow becomes our primary concern. An expansionary fiscal policy leads to the rightward shift of *IS* curve to *IS'*. National income increases. The stress of a rise in interest rates becomes enlarged, which stirs up the inflow of capital. To keep a fixed exchange rate, the central bank has to buy foreign exchange in the market with domestic currency, passively implementing

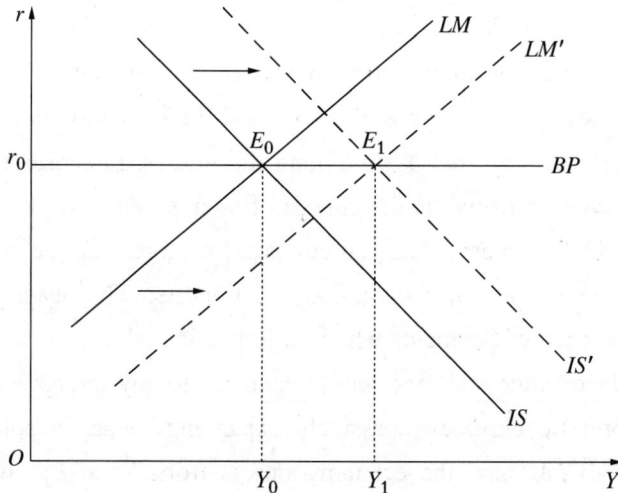

**Figure 9-8　Effect of Fiscal Policy (Perfect Capital Mobility)
under Fixed Exchange Rates**

expansionary monetary policy and pushing LM curve rightward to LM'. The economy reaches E_1, where national income increases and there is no crowding-out effect on private investment.

$\bar{e} + \tilde{K}$:

$$G \uparrow \Rightarrow AD \uparrow \Rightarrow \overrightarrow{IS} \Rightarrow Y \uparrow$$
$$r \uparrow \Rightarrow K \uparrow \Rightarrow BP^{+} \Rightarrow e \downarrow \quad \times \Rightarrow f \downarrow \Rightarrow Ms \uparrow \Rightarrow \overrightarrow{LM} \Rightarrow E_1 : Y \uparrow ;$$
$$r \downarrow (r_0)$$

In conclusion, fiscal policy has perfect effect on economy under fixed exchange rates when capital is perfectly mobile.

9.3.3   Effects of Monetary Policy under Fixed Exchange Rates

Figure 9-9 shows the effect of monetary policy in different capital mobilities under fixed exchange rates.

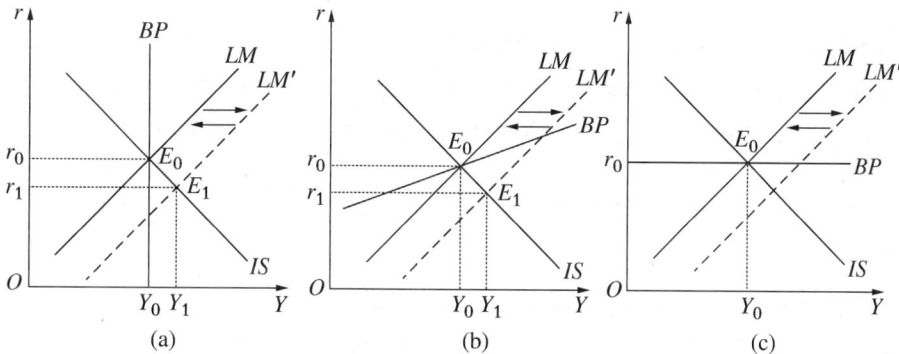

Figure 9-9   Effect of Monetary Policy under Fixed Exchange Rates

Case of Perfect Capital Immobility

When capital flows are totally insensitive to the change of interest rates, BP curve is vertical (See Figure 9-9 (a)). Suppose the central bank implements an expansionary monetary policy, i.e. an increase in money supply, which pushes LM curve rightward to LM'. The economy reaches a temporary equilibrium E_1, where national income increases and the interest rate falls. Increased national income brings more imports, which leads to a deficit of the current account and the stress of depreciation. Under fixed exchange rates, the central bank has to sell its foreign exchange in the market, causing a shrink of money supply. LM curve then shifts leftward from LM' to its previous position. The economy returns to E_0 where neither national income nor the interest rate has any changes.

$$\bar{e} + \bar{K}:$$
$$Ms \uparrow \Rightarrow \overrightarrow{LM} \Rightarrow E_1 : Y \uparrow (Y_1) \Rightarrow M \uparrow \Rightarrow CA^-$$
$$r \downarrow (r_1) \Rightarrow \bar{K} \Rightarrow \overline{KA}$$
$$CA^- > \overline{KA} \Rightarrow BP^- \Rightarrow e \uparrow \times \Rightarrow f \uparrow \Rightarrow Ms \downarrow \Rightarrow \overleftarrow{LM} \Rightarrow E_0 : Y \downarrow (Y_0); r \uparrow (r_0)$$

Case of Imperfect Capital Immobility

When capital flows are imperfectly mobile, BP curve slopes upward (See Figure 9-9 (b)). An expansionary monetary policy pushes LM curve rightward to LM'. The economy reaches E_1, where national income increases and the interest rate falls and the balance of payments is in deficit. Under fixed exchange rates, the central bank has to sell its foreign exchange in the market, leading to a shrink of money supply. LM curve then shifts leftward from LM' to its previous position. The economy returns to E_0 where there is no change in either national income or interest rates.

$$\bar{e} + \hat{K}:$$
$$Ms \uparrow \Rightarrow \overrightarrow{LM} \Rightarrow E_1 : Y \uparrow (Y_1) \Rightarrow M \uparrow \Rightarrow CA^-$$
$$r \downarrow (r_1) \Rightarrow K \downarrow \Rightarrow KA^-$$
$$CA^- + KA^- \Rightarrow BP^- \Rightarrow e \uparrow \times \Rightarrow f \uparrow \Rightarrow Ms \downarrow \Rightarrow \overleftarrow{LM} \Rightarrow E_0 : Y \downarrow (Y_0); r \uparrow (r_0)$$

Case of Perfect Capital Mobility

When capital flows are perfectly mobile, BP curve is horizontal (See Figure 9-9 (c)). An expansionary monetary policy pushes LM curve rightward to LM'. It leads to the stress of interest rate falling, which stirs up the outflow of capital. Under fixed exchange rates, the central bank has to sell foreign exchange in the market, passively taking a contractionary monetary policy. LM curve then shifts leftward from LM' to its previous position. The economy returns to E_0 where the economy has no changes.

$$\bar{e} + \tilde{K}:$$
$$Ms \uparrow \Rightarrow \overrightarrow{LM} \Rightarrow Y \uparrow$$
$$r \downarrow \Rightarrow K \downarrow \Rightarrow BP^- \Rightarrow e \uparrow \times \Rightarrow f \uparrow \Rightarrow Ms \downarrow \Rightarrow \overleftarrow{LM} \Rightarrow E_0 : Y \downarrow (Y_0);$$
$$r \uparrow (r_0)$$

To summarize, monetary policy has no effect on economy under fixed exchange rates regardless of the extent of capital mobility.

9.4   Effects of Macroeconomic Policies under Floating Exchange Rates

Under floating exchange rates, a change of exchange rates will cause shifts of *BP* curve. A depreciation of the domestic currency leads to a rightward shift of *BP* curve while an appreciation leads to a leftward shift of *BP* curve.

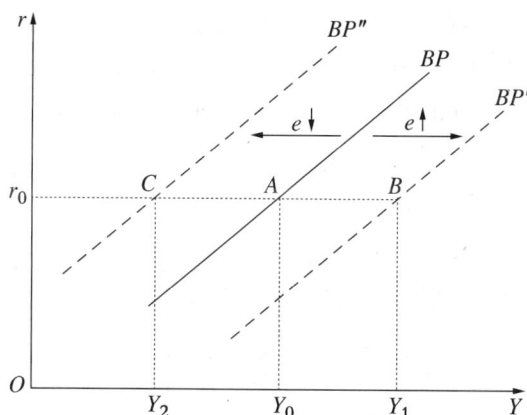

Figure 9-10   Exchange Rate Change and Shifts of *BP* Curve

See Figure 9-10, at a certain exchange rate, the mix of interest rates and national income for the external balance of an economy is shown by *BP* curve. On *BP* curve, take the interest rate r_0 for example, national income Y_0 keeps the economy in external balance. Suppose the domestic currency depreciates for some reason. The depreciation results in more exports and less imports, leading to a surplus of the balance of payments. In condition of no changes of the interest rate r_0, to digest the surplus of the balance of payments, national income needs to grow in order to encourage more imports. That is, at the interest rate r_0, the depreciation requires more national income than before to keep the external balance. At any other interest rates, the same thing happens. So the depreciation leads to a rightward shift of *BP* curve. In the same way, we educe an appreciation leads to a leftward shift of *BP* curve.

9.4.1 Effects of Fiscal Policy under Floating Exchange Rates

Under floating exchange rates, exchange rates change to market power and the central bank will not intervene.

Case of Perfect Capital Immobility

In the case of perfect capital immobility, *BP* curve is vertical (See Figure 9-11). An expansionary fiscal policy enhances aggregate demand, pushing *IS* curve rightward to *IS'*. The economy moves to E_1, where national income increases from Y_0 to Y_1 and the interest rate rises from r_0 to r_1. The enlarged imports caused by the increased national income leads to BP deficit and a depreciation of the domestic currency. The depreciation brings more exports and blocks imports, pushing *IS'* curve further to *IS"*. And *BP* curve also shifts rightward to *BP'* due to the

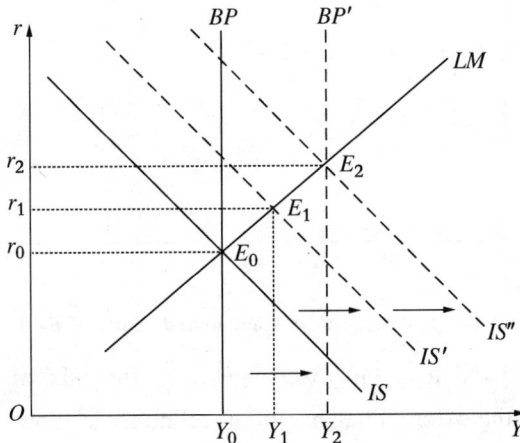

Figure 9-11   Effect of Fiscal Policy (Perfect Capital Immobility)
under Floating Exchange Rates

depreciation. The economy reaches its equilibrium at E_2, where both national income and the interest rate increase even more and an external balance comes true.

$\tilde{e} + \bar{K}$:

$G\uparrow \Rightarrow AD\uparrow \Rightarrow \overrightarrow{IS} \Rightarrow E_1: Y\uparrow (Y_1) \Rightarrow M\uparrow \Rightarrow CA^-$

$\qquad\qquad\qquad\qquad r\uparrow (r_1) \Rightarrow \bar{K} \Rightarrow \bar{KA}$

$CA^- > \overline{KA} \Rightarrow BP^- \Rightarrow e\uparrow \Rightarrow X\uparrow , M\downarrow \Rightarrow \overrightarrow{IS'}, \overrightarrow{BP} \Rightarrow E_2: Y\uparrow (Y_2); r\uparrow (r_2)$

Case of Imperfect Capital Immobility

In the case of imperfect capital immobility, we need to distinguish three situations: (a) BP curve steeper than LM curve; (b) BP curve coinciding with LM curve; and (c) BP curve flatter than LM curve.

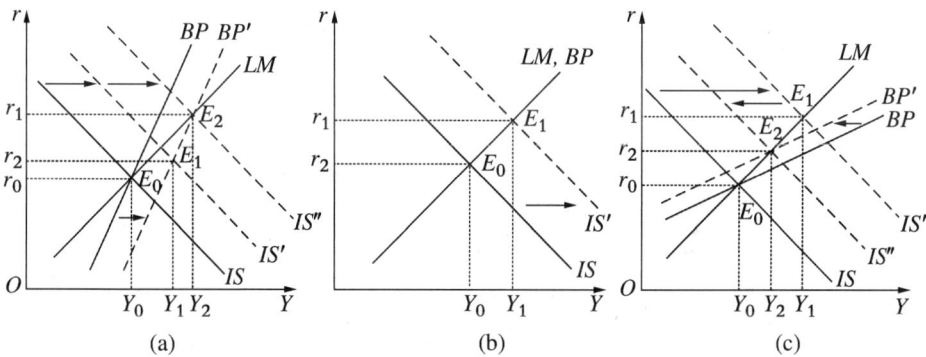

Figure 9-12   Effect of Fiscal Policy (Imperfect Capital Mobility)
under Floating Exchange Rates

The case that BP curve is steeper than LM curve is shown in Figure 9-12 (a). An expansionary fiscal policy propels IS curve rightward to IS'. The economy reaches E_1, where national income increases from Y_0 to Y_1 and the interest rate rises from r_0 to r_1. Increased national income results in more imports and then worsens the current account. Higher interest rate attracts capital to flow in and improves the capital and financial account. But the amount of capital inflow cannot compensate that of current account deficit, so the balance of payments is in deficit as a whole. That results in a depreciation of the domestic currency. The depreciation encourages exports and blocks imports, leading to the rightward shifts of IS' to IS'' and BP to BP'. The economy finds its equilibrium in E_2, where both national income and the interest rate increase even more and the external balance is restored.

$$\tilde{e} + \hat{K}(BP > LM):$$
$$G\uparrow \Rightarrow AD\uparrow \Rightarrow \overrightarrow{IS} \Rightarrow E_1: Y\uparrow(Y_1) \Rightarrow M\uparrow \Rightarrow CA^-$$
$$r\uparrow(r_1) \Rightarrow K\uparrow \Rightarrow KA^+$$
$$CA^- > KA^+ \Rightarrow BP^- \Rightarrow e\uparrow \Rightarrow X\uparrow, M\downarrow \Rightarrow \overrightarrow{IS'}, \overrightarrow{BP} \Rightarrow E_2: Y\uparrow(Y_2); r\uparrow(r_2)$$

Figure 9-12 (b) shows the case that BP curve coincides with LM curve. An expansionary fiscal policy propels IS curve to shift rightward to IS' and the economy reaches E_1, where national income increases from Y_0 to Y_1 and the interest rate rises from r_0 to r_1. The in-flowed capital attracted by the higher interest rate exactly compensates the current account deficit which is caused by income-induced imports. The balance of payments is in equilibrium.

$$\tilde{e} + \hat{K}(BP = LM):$$
$$G\uparrow \Rightarrow AD\uparrow \Rightarrow \overrightarrow{IS} \Rightarrow E_1: Y\uparrow(Y_1) \Rightarrow M\uparrow \Rightarrow CA^-$$
$$r\uparrow(r_1) \Rightarrow K\uparrow \Rightarrow KA^+(CA^- = KA^+ \Rightarrow \overline{BP})$$

The case that BP curve is flatter than LM curve is shown in Figure 9-12 (c). An expansionary fiscal policy pushes IS curve rightward to IS' and the economy reaches E_1, where national income increases from Y_0 to Y_1 and the interest rate rises from r_0 to r_1. Since capital is rather sensitive to the change of interest rates, the in-flowed capital attracted by the higher interest rate can compensate more than the current account deficit which is caused by the income-induced imports. That leads to the overall surplus of the balance of payments which in turn causes an appreciation of the domestic currency. The appreciation leads to less exports and more imports, causing the leftward shifts of IS' to IS'' and BP to BP'. The economy reaches equilibrium at E_2, where the external balance is restored and both national income and the interest rate fall but they are still higher than the initial level.

$$\tilde{e} + \hat{K}(BP < LM):$$
$$G\uparrow \Rightarrow AD\uparrow \Rightarrow \overrightarrow{IS} \Rightarrow E_1: Y\uparrow(Y_1) \Rightarrow M\uparrow \Rightarrow CA^-$$
$$r\uparrow(r_1) \Rightarrow K\uparrow \Rightarrow KA^+$$
$$CA^- < KA^+ \Rightarrow BP^+ \Rightarrow e\downarrow \Rightarrow X\downarrow, M\uparrow \Rightarrow \overleftarrow{IS'}, \overleftarrow{BP} \Rightarrow E_2: Y\downarrow(Y_2 > Y_0);$$
$$r\downarrow(r_0)$$

Case of Perfect Capital Mobility

In the case of perfect capital mobility, BP curve is horizontal (See Figure 9-13). A slight change of interest rates will cause immediate tremendous capital flow. An expansionary fiscal policy leads to the rightward shift of IS curve to IS'. National income increases. The stress of a rise in the interest rate becomes enlarged, which stirs up the inflow of capital. The capital inflows lead to a surplus of the balance of payments and an appreciation of the domestic currency. The appreciation encourages imports and reduces exports, clearing away the surplus of the balance of payments and pulling IS' leftward to its initial position. The economy returns to E_0, where there is no change in either national income or the interest rate but the government purchases crowd out exports and crowd in imports.

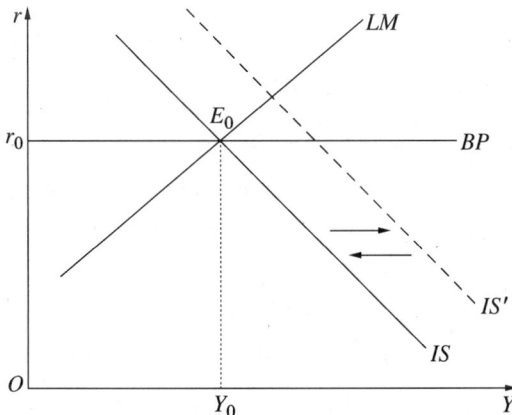

Figure 9-13   Effect of Fiscal Policy (Perfect Capital Mobility) under Floating Exchange Rates

$$\tilde{e} + \dot{K}:$$

$$G \uparrow \Rightarrow AD \uparrow \Rightarrow \overrightarrow{IS} \Rightarrow Y \uparrow$$

$$r \uparrow \Rightarrow K \uparrow \Rightarrow BP^+ \Rightarrow e \downarrow \Rightarrow X \downarrow, \ M \uparrow \Rightarrow \overleftarrow{IS} \Rightarrow E_0: Y \downarrow \ (Y_0)$$

To sum up, the effect of fiscal policy under floating exchange rates is inversely proportional to the extent of capital mobility. The less mobile capital is, the stronger effect fiscal policy has.

9.4.2　Effects of Monetary Policy under Floating Exchange Rates

Figure 9-14 shows the effect of monetary policy in different capital mobilities under floating exchange rates.

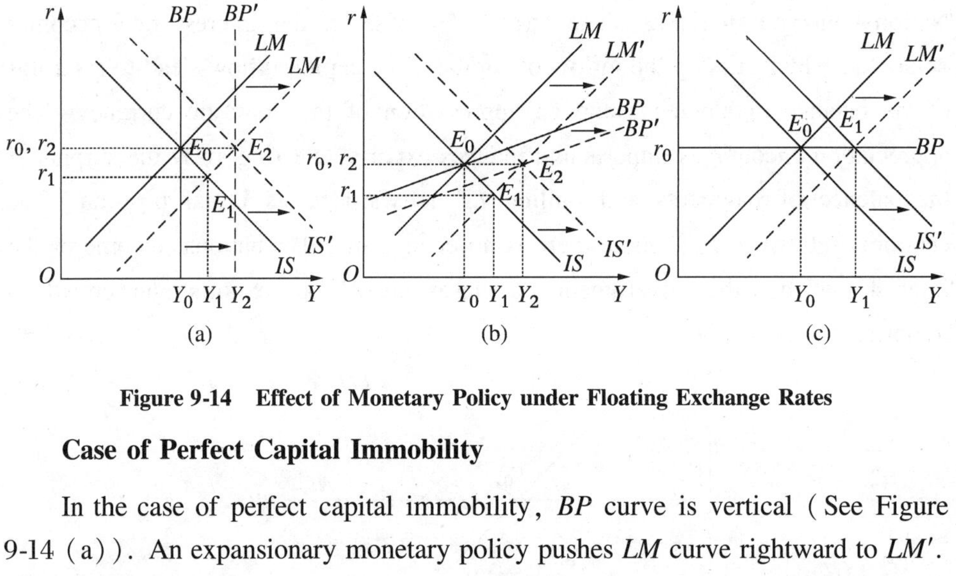

Figure 9-14　Effect of Monetary Policy under Floating Exchange Rates

Case of Perfect Capital Immobility

In the case of perfect capital immobility, BP curve is vertical (See Figure 9-14 (a)). An expansionary monetary policy pushes LM curve rightward to LM'. The economy reaches a temporary equilibrium E_1, where national income increases from Y_0 to Y_1 and the interest rate falls from r_0 to r_1. The increased national income brings more imports which in turn results in a deficit of the current account and a depreciation of the domestic currency. The depreciation encourages exports and blocks imports, leading to the rightward shifts of IS to IS' and BP to BP'. The economy reaches E_2, where national income increases further and the interest rate returns to its initial position. The external balance is restored since E_2

is on BP'.

$$
\begin{aligned}
&\tilde{e} + \overline{K}: \\
&Ms \uparrow \Rightarrow \overrightarrow{LM} \Rightarrow E_1 : Y \uparrow (Y_1) \Rightarrow M \uparrow \Rightarrow CA^- \\
&\qquad\qquad\quad r \downarrow (r_1) \Rightarrow \overline{K} \Rightarrow \overline{KA} \\
&CA^- > \overline{KA} \Rightarrow BP^- \Rightarrow e \uparrow \Rightarrow X \uparrow , M \downarrow \Rightarrow \overrightarrow{BP}, \overrightarrow{IS} \Rightarrow E_2 : Y \uparrow (Y_2); r \uparrow (r_2 = r_0)
\end{aligned}
$$

Case of Imperfect Capital Immobility

When capital flows are imperfectly mobile, BP curve slopes upward (See Figure 9-14 (b)). An expansionary monetary policy pushes LM curve rightward to LM'. The economy reaches E_1, where national income increases from Y_0 to Y_1 and the interest rate falls from r_0 to r_1. E_1 is to the right of BP curve, so the balance of payments is in deficit, bringing a depreciation of the domestic currency. The depreciation encourages exports and blocks imports, leading to the rightward shifts of IS to IS' and BP to BP'. The economy reaches E_2, where national income increases further and the balance of payments is restored.

$$
\begin{aligned}
&\tilde{e} + \hat{K}: \\
&Ms \uparrow \Rightarrow \overrightarrow{LM} \Rightarrow E_1 : Y \uparrow (Y_1) \Rightarrow M \uparrow \Rightarrow CA^- \\
&\qquad\qquad\quad r \downarrow (r_1) \Rightarrow K \downarrow \Rightarrow KA^- \\
&CA^- + KA^- \Rightarrow BP^- \Rightarrow e \uparrow \Rightarrow X \uparrow , M \downarrow \Rightarrow \overrightarrow{BP}, \overrightarrow{IS} \Rightarrow E_2 : Y \uparrow (Y_2); r \uparrow (r_2 = r_0)
\end{aligned}
$$

Case of Perfect Capital Mobility

When capital flows are perfectly mobile, BP curve is horizontal (See Figure 9-14 (c)). An expansionary monetary policy pushes LM curve rightward to LM'. It leads to the stress of interest rate falling, stirring up the outflow of capital. The capital outflow brings a depreciation of the domestic currency, which encourages exports and blocks imports. IS curve thus shifts rightward to IS'. The economy finds its equilibrium at E_1, where national income increases. The balance of payments is restored since the up-going stress of the interest rate attracts capital to flow back.

In summary, monetary policy has perfect effect on economy under floating exchange rates regardless of the extent of capital mobility.

$$\tilde{e} + \tilde{K}:$$
$$Ms \uparrow \Rightarrow \overrightarrow{LM} \Rightarrow Y \uparrow$$
$$r \downarrow \Rightarrow K \downarrow \Rightarrow BP^- \Rightarrow e \uparrow \Rightarrow X \uparrow, \ M \downarrow \Rightarrow \overrightarrow{IS} \Rightarrow E_1 : \ Y \uparrow \ (Y_1)$$

To complete Mundell-Fleming Model, we summarize the effects of fiscal and monetary policies under different exchange rate systems and capital mobilities in Table 9-1.

Table 9-1   A Summary of Mundell-Fleming Model

Exchange Rate System \ Capital Mobility		$\overline{K}$	$\hat{K}$		$\tilde{K}$
			Low Mobility	High Mobility	
$\overline{e}$	Fiscal Policy	0	+	+ +	+ +
	Monetary Policy	0	0		0
$\tilde{e}$	Fiscal Policy	+ +	+ +	+	0
	Monetary Policy	+ +	+ +		+ +

Notes:

1. $\overline{K}$, $\hat{K}$ and $\tilde{K}$ stand for perfect capital immobility, imperfect capital mobility and perfect capital mobility respectively;

2. $\overline{e}$ and $\tilde{e}$ stand for fixed exchange rate system and floating exchange rate system respectively;

3. 0, + and + + stand for no effect, some effect and large effect respectively.

9.4.3 Mundell Incompatible Trinity

From Mundell-Fleming Model, it is easy to find that with perfect capital mobility, monetary policy has no effect on internal economy under fixed exchange rates while fiscal policy has no effect under floating exchange rates. On the contrary, when capital can move freely, fiscal policy has a strong effect on the internal economy under fixed exchange rates while monetary policy has a strong effect under floating exchange rates. The reason behind is that under fixed exchange rates monetary policy becomes a tool to change foreign reserves and under floating exchange rates fiscal policy becomes a means of adjusting the trade balance. In other words, if capital can move freely, monetary policy is invalid under fixed exchange rates but effective under floating exchange rates. One country cannot have a fixed exchange rate system, free capital movement and an independent monetary policy at the same time. This is called as **Mundell Incompatible Trinity** (Shown in Figure 9-15).

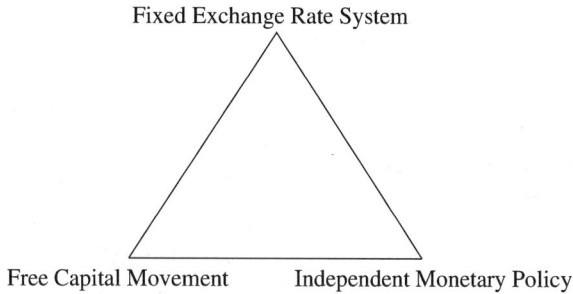

Figure 9-15   Mundell Incompatible Trinity

Chapter 10

International Transmission and Coordination of Macroeconomic Policies

Key Concepts and Terms

International Transmission	国际传导
Two-Nation Mundell-Fleming Model	两国蒙代尔—弗莱明模型
Beggar-thy-neighbor Policy	以邻为壑政策
Inflation Transmission	通货膨胀传导
Price Adjustment Mechanism	价格调整机制
Scandinavian Model	斯堪的纳维亚模型
Balance of Payments Mechanism	国际收支机制
Interest Rate Transmission Mechanism	利率传导机制
International Coordination	国际协调
International Monetary Cooperation	国际货币合作
Exchange Rate Unions	汇率联盟
Pseudo Exchange Rate Unions	名义汇率联盟
Monetary Integration	货币一体化
Monetary Unification	货币单一化
Optimum Currency Area	最优通货区

In Chapter 9, we have analyzed the effects of macroeconomic policies. But our analysis is by then based on the assumption that those policies do not spill over foreign countries. That is not the case. In an open world, economies are interdependent. One country's policies aiming to achieve domestic goals will cast their influence on foreign countries, arousing their reactions which in turn affect the home country. To have the whole picture, we need to learn the international transmission of macroeconomic policies and the way to coordinate policies between countries.

10.1   International Transmission of Macroeconomic Policies under Fixed Exchange Rates

10.1.1   Two-Nation Mundell-Fleming Model

Now, let us expand Mundell-Fleming Model to a two-nation condition. In the new model, it is assumed there are two countries in the world: Home and Foreign. Now, it is different from the previous model in two aspects. First, Home's income will have a spilling-over effect on Foreign. An increase in Home's income will lead to a rise in Home's imports, that is, Foreign's exports, bringing about an increase in Foreign's income then. But in our following analysis, we will only consider the spilling of Home over Foreign and ignore the reverse spillover from the latter for the purpose of simplicity. Second, we assume capital has perfect mobility. So any gaps between Home's interest rates and Foreign's interest rates will arouse capital flows across countries. The only result for equilibrium then should be Home's interest rate equal to that of Foreign.

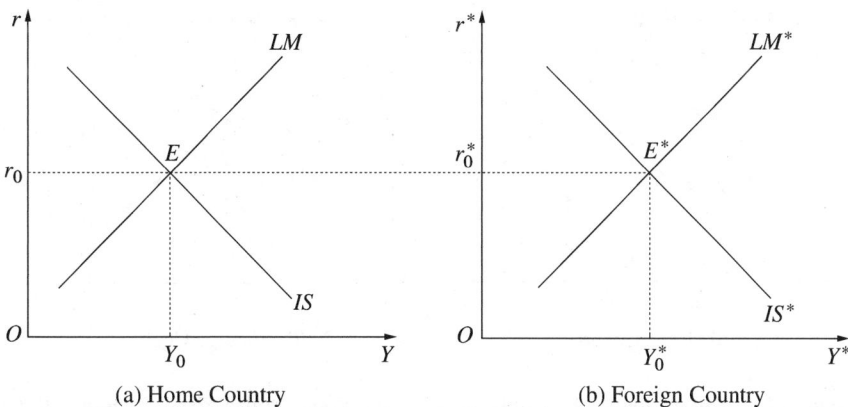

(a) Home Country   (b) Foreign Country

Figure 10-1   Two-Nation Mundell-Fleming Model

Figure 10-1 shows the overall equilibrium of two countries. Remember, variables of Foreign are labeled by a superscript asterisk*.

10.1.2 International Transmission of Fiscal Policy under Fixed Exchange Rates

See Figure 10-2 (a). Suppose Home implements an expansionary fiscal policy, causing IS curve to shift rightward to IS'. Home reaches E_1, where its income increases from Y_0 to Y_1 and its interest rate rises from r_0 to r_1. The increase of Home's income brings about more imports, i.e. more exports of Foreign.

Now Let us turn to Figure 10-2(b). More exports of Foreign push IS^* curve rightward to $IS^{*'}$ and Foreign reaches E_1^*, where its national income increases from Y_0^* to Y_1^* and the interest rate rises from r_0^* to r_1^*. But notice that the rightward shift of IS^* curve is shorter in distance than that of IS curve since the former is caused by the spilling-over effect of Home's income — only a part of Home's income can be converted to its imports, i.e. exports of Foreign. The increase of Foreign's income should be smaller than that of Home's income, causing IS^* to shift shorter in distance than IS. So it is safe to find Foreign's interest rate r_1^* is lower than Home's interest rate r_1.

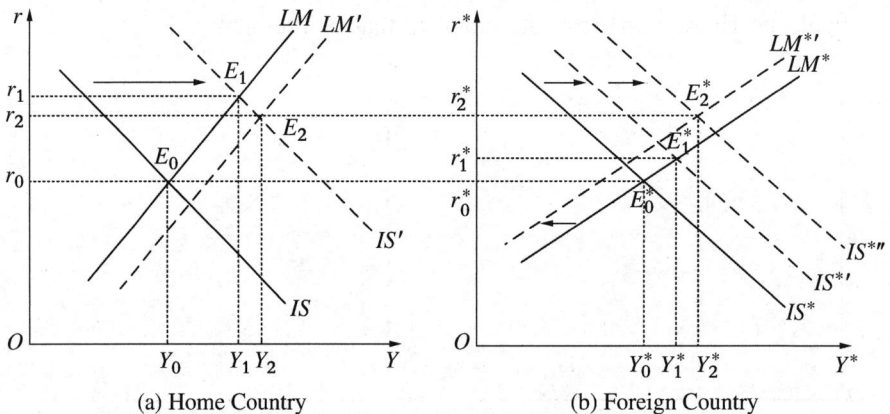

(a) Home Country   (b) Foreign Country

Figure 10-2 International Transmission of Fiscal Policy under Fixed Exchange Rates

$\bar{e} + \tilde{K}$:

$G \uparrow \Rightarrow \overrightarrow{IS} \Rightarrow E_1 : Y \uparrow (Y_1) \Rightarrow M \uparrow \Rightarrow X^* \uparrow \Rightarrow \overrightarrow{IS^*} \Rightarrow E_1^* : Y^* \uparrow (Y_1^*)$

$\qquad\qquad r \uparrow (r_1) \qquad\qquad\qquad\qquad r^* \uparrow (r_1^* < r_1)$

$r_1^* < r_1 \Rightarrow K \uparrow \Rightarrow BP^+ \Rightarrow e \downarrow \times \Rightarrow f \downarrow \Rightarrow Ms \uparrow \Rightarrow \overrightarrow{LM} \Rightarrow Y \uparrow \Rightarrow M \uparrow \Rightarrow X^* \uparrow \Rightarrow \overrightarrow{IS^*} \Rightarrow Y^* \uparrow$

$\qquad\qquad\qquad\qquad\qquad\qquad\qquad\qquad r \downarrow \qquad\qquad\qquad r^* \uparrow$

$\qquad K^* \downarrow \Rightarrow BP^{*-} \Rightarrow e^* \uparrow \times \Rightarrow f^* \uparrow \Rightarrow Ms^* \downarrow \Rightarrow \overleftarrow{LM^*} \Rightarrow Y^* \downarrow , r^* \uparrow$

$\Rightarrow E_2 : Y \uparrow (Y_2) , r \downarrow (r_2 > r_0)$

$\quad E_2^* : Y^* \uparrow (Y_2^*) , r^* \uparrow (r_2^* = r_2)$

The gap between r_1^* and r_1 causes capital to flow from Foreign to Home. Thus in Home, the balance of payments is in surplus while in Foreign it is in deficit. Home's currency meets with the stress of appreciation and Foreign's currency is subjected to the stress of depreciation. Under fixed change rates, central banks of both countries have to intervene in foreign exchange market. Foreign's central bank sells foreign exchange to the market, passively shrinking moncy supply and pulling LM^* curve leftward to $LM^{*'}$ (See Figure 10-2 (b)). Foreign's interest rate r_1^* rises further. And Home's central bank buys foreign exchange from the market, passively expanding money supply. LM curve then shifts rightward to LM' (See Figure 10-2 (a)), causing national income Y_1 to increase further and the interest rate r_1 to fall. The increased income of Home encourages more imports, i. e. exports of Foreign, indirectly pushing $IS^{*'}$ curve rightward to $IS^{*''}$ and causing Foreign's interest rate to rise. The process continues until r_2 equals to r_2^*. Home reaches E_2 and Foreign reaches E_2^*. We find both the interest rate and each country's output now are higher than before implementing the expansionary fiscal policy.

To summarize, under fixed exchange rates, an expansionary fiscal policy of Home brings about output increases of both Home and Foreign. But compared with the case of single country, the output increase of Home resulting from fiscal policy is smaller because the rise in interest rates crowds out investment. The increase of Foreign's output results from the spilling-out effect of Home's income increase but it is partly offset by the rise of interest rates.

10.1.3　International Transmission of Monetary Policy under Fixed Exchange Rates

Suppose Home adopts an expansionary monetary policy. Let us see Figure 10-3 (a). *LM* curve is propelled rightward to *LM'* and Home reaches E_1, where national income increases from Y_0 to Y_1 and the interest rate falls from r_0 to r_1. The increase of Home's income encourages its imports, i.e. Foreign's exports.

Now let us turn to Figure 10-3 (b). More exports of Foreign push IS^* curve rightward to $IS^{*'}$ and Foreign reaches E_1^*, where Foreign's output increases from Y_0^* to Y_1^* and its interest rate rises from r_0^* to r_1^*. It is obvious that Foreign's interest rate r_1^* exceeds Home's interest rate r_1.

The gap between r_1 and r_1^* drives capital to flow from Home to Foreign. Foreign then experiences a surplus of the balance of payments while Home suffers a deficit of the balance of payments. Foreign is subjected to the stress of appreciation and Home faces the stress of depreciation. Under fixed exchange rates, Foreign's central bank buys foreign exchange from the market, passively expanding money supply and pushing LM^* rightward to $LM^{*'}$ (See Figure 10-3 (b)). Foreign's income increases and its interest rate falls. Meanwhile Home's central bank sells foreign exchange to the market to keep a fixed exchange rate, passively shrinking money supply and pulling *LM'* curve leftward to *LM"* (See Figure 10-3 (a)). Home's interest rate becomes higher than r_1 and its national income falls. The decline in Home's income brings about less imports, i.e. less Foreign's exports, indirectly pulling $IS^{*'}$ curve leftward to $IS^{*'}$ (See Figure 10-3 (b)). Foreign's interest rate falls. The process continues until r_2 equals to r_2^*. Home reaches E_2 and Foreign reaches E_2^*. We find each country's output now is higher than before implementing the expansionary fiscal policy but their interest rate becomes lower as a result of more total money supply.

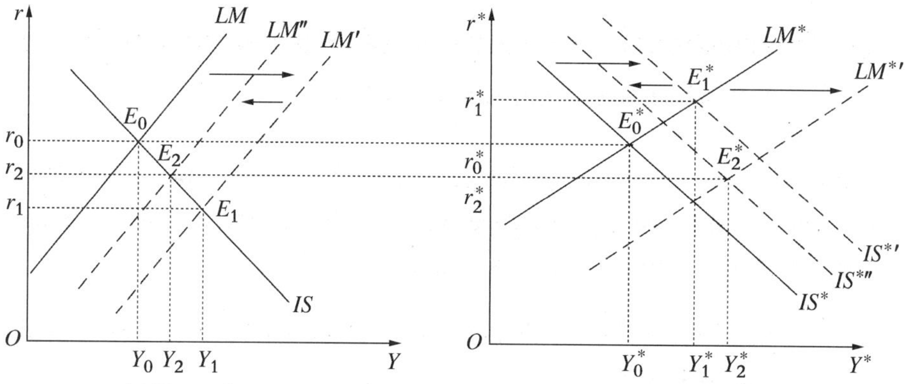

(a) Home Country   (b) Foreign Country

Figure 10-3   International Transmission of Monetary Policy under Fixed Exchange Rates

$$\bar{e} + \tilde{K}:$$

$$Ms \uparrow \Rightarrow \overrightarrow{LM} \Rightarrow E_1: \; Y \uparrow (Y_1) \Rightarrow M \uparrow \Rightarrow X^* \uparrow \Rightarrow \overrightarrow{IS^*} \Rightarrow E_1^*: \; Y^* \uparrow (Y_1^*)$$

$$r \downarrow (r_1) \qquad\qquad\qquad\qquad r^* \uparrow (r_1^* > r_1)$$

$$r_1^* > r_1 \Rightarrow K \downarrow \Rightarrow BP^- \Rightarrow e \uparrow \; \times \Rightarrow f \uparrow \; \Rightarrow Ms \downarrow \; \Rightarrow \overleftarrow{LM} \Rightarrow Y \downarrow \Rightarrow M \downarrow \Rightarrow X^* \downarrow \Rightarrow \overleftarrow{IS^*} \Rightarrow Y^* \downarrow$$

$$r \downarrow \qquad\qquad\qquad\qquad r^* \downarrow$$

$$K^* \uparrow \Rightarrow BP^{*+} \Rightarrow e^* \downarrow \; \times \Rightarrow f^* \downarrow \Rightarrow Ms^* \uparrow \Rightarrow \overrightarrow{LM^*} \Rightarrow Y^* \uparrow, \, r^* \downarrow$$

$$\Rightarrow E_2: \; Y \downarrow \; (Y_2 > Y_0), \, r \uparrow \; (r_2 < r_0)$$

$$E_2^*: \; Y^* \uparrow (Y_2^*), \, r^* \downarrow (r_2^* = r_2)$$

To sum up, under fixed exchange rates, Home's expansionary monetary policy leads to a rise in both Home's and Foreign's outputs and to a fall in the world interest rate. Compared with fiscal policy, the spilling-out effect of Home's expansionary monetary policy is larger because Foreign has to passively implement an expansionary monetary policy as a result of the midway gap between two countries' interest rates.

It is worth noticing that the above findings are based on perfect capital mobility assumption. But even if capital cannot flow totally smoothly, these conclusions will not be overthrown. An expansionary fiscal policy or monetary policy of Home still has positive spilling-over effect on Foreign. But the spilling-over effect of fiscal policy becomes stronger while that of monetary policy becomes weaker.

10.2 International Transmission of Macroeconomic Policies under Floating Exchange Rates

Different from under fixed exchange rates, a surplus or deficit of the balance of payments under floating exchange rates leads to adjustments of nominal exchange rates rather than changes of money supply.

10.2.1 International Transmission of Fiscal Policy under Floating Exchange Rates

See Figure 10-4 (a). Suppose Home implements an expansionary fiscal policy, causing IS curve to shift rightward to IS'. Home reaches E_1, where its income increases from Y_0 to Y_1 and its interest rate rises from r_0 to r_1. The increase of Home's income brings about more imports, i.e. more exports of Foreign.

Now, let us turn to Figure 10-4(b). More exports of Foreign push IS^* curve rightward to $IS^{*'}$ and Foreign reaches E_1^*, where its national income increases from Y_0^* to Y_1^* and the interest rate rises from r_0^* to r_1^*. But notice that the rightward shift of IS^* curve is shorter in distance than that of IS curve. Its reason has been explained in Section 10.1. Foreign's interest rate r_1^* is lower than Home's interest rate r_1.

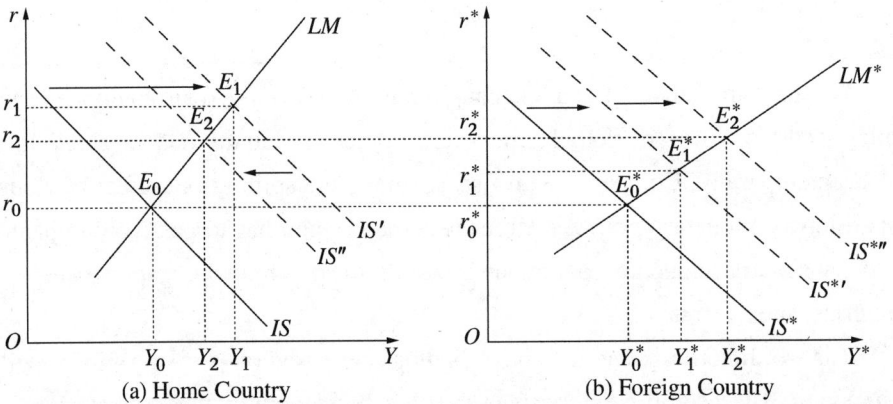

(a) Home Country   (b) Foreign Country

Figure 10-4   International Transmission of Fiscal Policy under Floating Exchange Rates

$$\tilde{e} + \tilde{K}:$$
$$G\uparrow \Rightarrow \overrightarrow{IS} \Rightarrow E_1: Y\uparrow(Y_1) \Rightarrow M\uparrow \Rightarrow X^*\uparrow \Rightarrow \overrightarrow{IS^*} \Rightarrow E_1^*: Y^*\uparrow(Y_1^*)$$
$$r\uparrow(r_1) \qquad\qquad\qquad\qquad r^*\uparrow(r_1^* < r_1)$$
$$r_1^* < r_1 \Rightarrow K\uparrow \Rightarrow BP^+ \Rightarrow e\downarrow \Rightarrow X\downarrow, M\uparrow \Rightarrow \overleftarrow{IS} \Rightarrow Y\downarrow, r\downarrow$$
$$K^*\downarrow \Rightarrow BP^{*-} \Rightarrow e^*\uparrow \Rightarrow X^*\uparrow, M^*\downarrow \Rightarrow \overrightarrow{IS^*} \Rightarrow Y^*\uparrow, r^*\uparrow$$
$$\Rightarrow E_2: Y\downarrow(Y_2 > Y_0), r\downarrow(r_2 > r_0)$$
$$E_2^*: Y^*\uparrow(Y_2^*), r^*\uparrow(r_2^* = r_2)$$

The gap between r_1^* and r_1 causes capital to flow from Foreign to Home. Thus in Home, the balance of payments is in surplus while in Foreign it is in deficit. Under floating exchanges, Home's currency appreciates and Foreign's currency depreciates. Home's currency appreciation discourages its exports and encourages its imports, pulling IS' curve leftward to IS'' (See Figure 10-4 (a)). Home's income Y_1 tends to decrease and its interest rate r_1 tends to fall. Foreign's currency depreciation stirs up its exports and blocks its imports, pushing $IS^{*'}$ curve rightward to $IS^{*''}$. Foreign's interest rate and income both become increasing further. The process continues until Home's interest rate r_2 equals to that of Foreign r_2^*. Home reaches E_2 and Foreign reaches E_2^*. We find both the interest rate and each country's output now are higher than before implementing the expansionary fiscal policy.

To summarize, under floating exchange rates, an expansionary fiscal policy of Home results in output increases of both Home and Foreign. Compared with the case of single country, the expansionary fiscal policy of Home will no longer be unable to increase output because the world interest rate is driven high and then the appreciation of Home's currency will not totally offset the expansionary effect of fiscal policy. Foreign's output increases through two channels: (1) the increase in Home's income brings about more imports of Home, i.e. exports of Foreign, causing Foreign's output to increase; (2) the higher interest rate of Home results in an appreciation of home currency and more exports of Foreign, causing Foreign's output to increase further.

10.2.2 International Transmission of Monetary Policy under Floating Exchange Rates

Suppose Home implements an expansionary monetary policy. See Figure

10-5 (a). LM curve shifts rightward to LM' and Home reaches E_1, where its national income increases from Y_0 to Y_1 and its interest rate falls from r_0 to r_1. The increase of Home's income encourages its imports, i. e. Foreign's exports.

Now let us turn to Figure 10-5 (b). More exports of Foreign push IS^* curve rightward to $IS^{*\prime}$ and it reaches E_1^*, where Foreign's output increases from Y_0^* to Y_1^* and its interest rate rises from r_0^* to r_1^*. Obviously, Foreign's interest rate r_1^* exceeds Home's interest rate r_1.

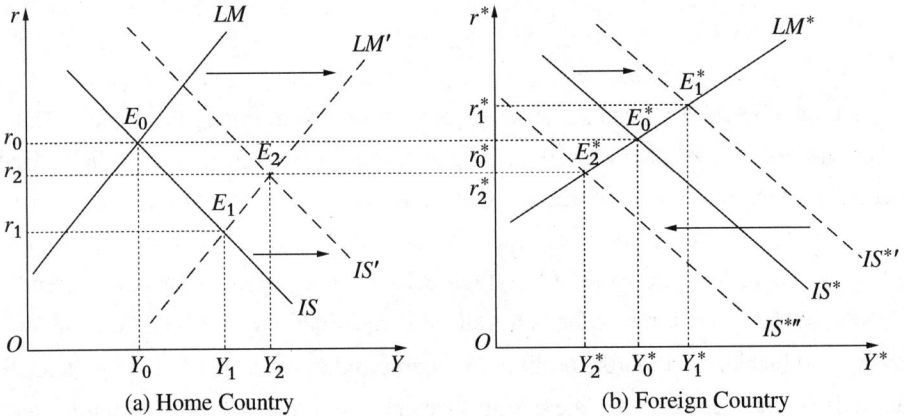

(a) Home Country (b) Foreign Country

Figure 10-5 International Transmission of Monetary Policy under Floating Exchange Rates

$\tilde{e} + \tilde{K}$:

$$Ms\uparrow \Rightarrow \overrightarrow{LM} \Rightarrow E_1: \; Y\uparrow(Y_1) \Rightarrow M\uparrow \Rightarrow X^*\uparrow \Rightarrow \overrightarrow{IS^*} \Rightarrow E_1^*: \; Y^*\uparrow(Y_1^*)$$
$$r\downarrow(r_1) \qquad\qquad\qquad r^*\uparrow(r_1^* > r_1)$$
$$r_1^* > r_1 \Rightarrow K\downarrow \Rightarrow BP^- \Rightarrow e\uparrow \Rightarrow X\uparrow, \; M\downarrow \Rightarrow \overrightarrow{IS} \Rightarrow Y\uparrow, r\uparrow$$
$$K^*\uparrow \Rightarrow BP^{*+} \Rightarrow e^*\downarrow \Rightarrow X^*\downarrow, M^*\uparrow \Rightarrow \overleftarrow{IS^*} \Rightarrow Y^*\downarrow, r^*\downarrow < r_0^*$$
$$\Rightarrow E_2: \; Y\uparrow(Y_2 > Y_0), \; r\downarrow(r_2 < r_0)$$
$$E_2^*: \; Y^*\downarrow(Y_2^* < Y_0^*), \; r^*\downarrow(r_2^* = r_2)$$

The gap between r_1 and r_1^* drives capital to flow from Home to Foreign. Foreign experiences a surplus of the balance of payments while Home suffers a deficit of the balance of payments. Home's currency depreciates and its exports increase, pushing IS curve rightward to IS' (See Figure 10-5 (a)). Home's interest rate and income both increase. Foreign's currency appreciates and its export falls, pulling $IS^{*'}$ leftward to $IS^{*''}$ (See Figure 10-5 (b)). Both the interest rate and the income of Foreign decrease. The process continues until r_2' equals to r_2^*. Home reaches E_2 and Foreign reaches E_2^*. Since the overall money supply in the world increases, the final interest rate r_2 or r_2^* is lower than the initial level r_0 or r_0^*. That determines $IS^{*''}$ curve to be located even to the left of IS^* curve and Foreign's final output Y_2^* to be even lower than its initial output Y_0^*.

To sum up, an expansionary monetary policy of Home increases its output but the effect is smaller than in the case of single country because the decrease in the world interest rate lessens Home's currency depreciation. The policy has a negative spilling-over effect on Foreign, causing Foreign's output to decrease. It is because Foreign's currency appreciation caused by the interest rate gap worsens its current account, leading to its output decrease. The decrease even exceeds the increased part generated from the added imports of Home. Hence, the increase in Home's output caused by its expansionary monetary policy is achieved partly at the expense of the decline in Foreign's output. In this sense, an expansionary monetary policy is often called as a **beggar-thy-neighbor policy.**

Before closing this section, we need again point out that the above analysis is based on perfect capital mobility. If capital is perfectly immobile, gaps between the interest rates will not cause the flow of capital, and so each country is insulated from policy shocks of other countries under floating exchange rates. We summarize the international transmission effects of fiscal and monetary policies under different exchange rate systems in Table 10-1.

Table 10-1   A Summary of International Policy Transmission

Exchange Rate System		Home Country	Foreign Country
$\bar{e}$	Fiscal Policy	+ +	+ +
	Monetary Policy	+	+ +
$\tilde{e}$	Fiscal Policy	+	+ +
	Monetary Policy	+ +	−

Notes:
1. It is on the assumption of perfect capital mobility;
2. $\bar{e}$ and $\tilde{e}$ stand for the fixed exchange rate system and the floating exchange rate system respectively;
3. + +, + and − stand for good effect, some effect and negative effect respectively.

10.3   International Transmission of Inflation

Floating exchange rates can insulate a country from the inflation of other countries. An inflation of foreign countries means their goods and services become more expensive than before, weakening their competitiveness and strengthening the competitiveness of the home country. The home country then exports more to foreign countries and imports less from foreign countries, leading to a surplus in its balance of payments. Under floating exchange rates, the home currency appreciates then. Remember the exchange rate is formulated as $e = P/P^*$, where e, P and P^* stand for exchange rate, home price level and foreign price level respectively. The fall of the exchange rate e (appreciation) offsets the rise of the foreign price level P^*. Thus the home price level P will not change. Thus, the home country is insulated from the inflation of foreign countries.

But under fixed exchange rates, inflation can transmit from one country to another through the following mechanisms.

10.3.1   Price Adjustment Mechanism of Inflation Transmission

The law of one price asserts that identical goods should cost the same in all countries if there are no transportation costs and transaction costs. Based on it, relative purchasing power parity tells us $\dot{e} = \pi - \pi^*$, where $\dot{e}$, π and π^* stand for the change percentage of exchange rates, home inflation rate and foreign inflation rate respectively. Under fixed exchange rates, if the government maintains the present exchange rate, we have $\dot{e} = 0$, so the home inflation rate should be the same to the foreign inflation rate, i.e. $\pi = \pi^*$. The reason behind is that the price differences between countries are wiped off by international commodity arbitrage. International price adjustment causes inflation rates of different countries to converge.

Scandinavian Model provides a more realistic explanation. In this model, goods are classified into tradable goods which are involved in international trade and nontradable goods which are only transacted domestically. It assumes:

(1) The country in discussion is a small nation and adopts fixed exchange rates;

(2) Prices of tradable goods are subjected to the law of one price. This deduces the equation $\dot{P}_T = \dot{P}_T^*$, where $\dot{P}_T$ and $\dot{P}_T^*$ stand for the change percentage of home and foreign tradable goods price respectively;

(3) The change percentage of wage in tradable goods sector $\dot{W}_T$ is the result of the change percentage of home tradable goods price $\dot{P}_T$ plus the growth rate of the productivity of tradable goods sector ρ : $\dot{W}_T = \dot{P}_T + \rho$. And the change percentage of wage in nontradable goods sector $\dot{W}_N$ is determined by the change percentage of home nontradable goods price $\dot{P}_N$: $\dot{W}_N = \dot{P}_N$;

(4) Labor market is perfectly competitive and labor can flow freely across tradable and nontradable sectors. Thus $\dot{W}_T = \dot{W}_N$ and from it we derive $\dot{P}_N = \dot{P}_T + \rho$.

Suppose in the home price index, the prices of tradable goods and nontradable goods account for α and $1 - \alpha$ respectively. Then home inflation is determined by the equation below:

$$\dot{P} = \alpha\dot{P}_T + (1 - \alpha)\dot{P}_N \tag{10-1}$$

Since $\dot{P}_T = \dot{P}_T^*$ and $\dot{P}_N = \dot{P}_T + \rho$, Equation 10-1 can be rearranged as:

$$\dot{P} = \dot{P}_T^* + (1 - \alpha)\rho \tag{10-2}$$

Equation 10-2 indicates the inflation of the home country results from the foreign inflation and the growth of home productivity. Thus, foreign inflation enters the home country through the price convergence of tradable goods, and vice versa.

10.3.2   Balance of Payments Mechanism of Inflation Transmission

The balance of payments mechanism refers to the transmission of inflation across countries via their balance of payments. When foreign countries experience inflation, their competitiveness becomes weaker. It causes foreign countries to export less and import more. More imports of foreign countries are equivalent to more exports of the home country and less exports of foreign countries mean less imports of the home country. Higher net exports lead to the balance of payments surplus of the home country. The home country then meets with the stress of appreciation. Under fixed exchange rates, the home central bank has the commitment to maintain fixed exchange rates and has to buy foreign exchange from the market, passively expanding its money supply. When money supply grows faster than national output, inflation occurs in the home country. Thus an initial inflation in foreign countries has been imported to the home country.

In fact, price adjustment mechanism and the balance of payments mechanism are cross functioning in inflation transmission. When foreign countries experience inflation, the price level in the home country becomes relatively lower. It causes more exports of home goods. The transaction of goods directly raises domestic prices. And the surplus of the balance of payments resulting from more exports leads to passive money supply to avoid an appreciation of the home currency, indirectly leading to the rise in domestic prices.

10.3.3   Interest Rate Transmission Mechanism

If capital is allowed to flow freely across countries in discussion, the interest rate mechanism will play more important role in inflation transmission because the foreign exchange market and the capital market adjust much faster than goods market. So even if international trade does not affect price in large scale, international capital flows will influence the balance of payments and become the major reason for the international transmission of inflation.

Suppose foreign countries experience inflation for the reason that the growth of their money supply is faster than that of their output. That lowers foreign interest rates and causes capital to flow from foreign countries to the home country. Under fixed exchange rates, the home central bank has to buy foreign exchange from the market, passively expanding its money supply. When money supply grows faster than national output, inflation occurs in the home country and thus inflation has transmitted from foreign countries to the home country.

10.4   International Policy Coordination and Monetary Cooperation

Since macroeconomic policies of one country can affect other countries and in turn re-affect the country itself, countries need to coordinate their policies to achieve their goals or attain the largest possible benefits. One tangible way is to pursue some kinds of monetary cooperation.

10.4.1   International Coordination of Macroeconomic Policies

International coordination of macroeconomic policies can be classified as follows:

- *Information Exchange.* It is the lowest level of internal policy coordination. Governments exchange their macroeconomic policy information concerning target zone, emphasis, tools and mix of policies, etc. Though governments still make decisions on an individual and separate basis, they avoid false estimation on policy regulations of other countries and thus enhance the effects of their domestic policies.

- *Crisis Management.* Governments take common policies to mitigate or tide over unexpected incidents which may bring about serious consequences toward the world economy. The management is provisional, aiming to avoid governments taking separate measures which may improve themselves but finally worsen the crisis.

- *Avoiding Conflicts over Shared Targets.* A shared target is the common target of related countries. If countries set different values to a shared target, conflicts will be inevitable. The policies taken by countries will be beggar-thy-neighbor ones. The very example is competitive devaluation of domestic currencies among countries.

- *Cooperation Intermediate Targeting.* Some variables can spill over from one country to another through economic links between countries. So it is necessary for countries to cooperate on these intermediate goals so as to avoid undesirable spilling-over effects. For example, money supply is an intermediate target needing to cooperate among countries under fixed exchange rates.

- *Partial Coordination.* Countries coordinate some but not all targets or tools concerning their domestic economy. For instance, countries coordinate their balance of payments and leave other targets alone. Or they coordinate their monetary policies, but turn their back on individual fiscal policies.

- *Full Coordination.* It is the highest but most difficult level of international policy coordination. Different countries coordinate all their policy targets and tools to obtain their maximum benefits.

International policy coordination concerns three aspects as follows:

- *Monetary Policy Coordination.* Monetary policy coordination involves coordinating the interest rates of related countries. The coordination aims at the adjustment direction of interest rates. Once a country is willing to adjust its interest rates to control economic overheat or economic recession, it needs not only to set the adjustment direction of its interest rates, but also to coordinate it with that of related countries. In a world with high flows of capital, no country can achieve its policy target smoothly when countries adjust their interest rates in an opposite direction. Actually, countries need to coordinate not only the direction but also the scope of interest rate adjustment since any interest rate gaps between countries will bring about capital flows across their boundaries. Countries also need to coordinate their growth of money supply. Some economists believe it is even better than controlling interest rates. Anyway, a successful monetary policy needs to be coordinated with those countries which have close economic relations with the home country.

- *Fiscal Policy Coordination.* In fact, the effect of monetary policy coordination depends on the coordination of fiscal policy to a great extent. If a country experiences an exorbitant fiscal expenditure, it needs the cooperation of monetary policy. This means an increase in money supply or high inflation, causing monetary policy coordination between countries unsustainable. A successful monetary policy coordination is usually accompanied by the coordination of fiscal policies.

- *Exchange Rate Policy Coordination.* In an open economy world, though a country can adopt completely floating exchange rates so that it only needs to consider its internal balance, but most countries tend to choose managed floating exchange rates so as to maintain a steady domestic economy, especially to diminish risks in foreign trade. This means a country needs to concern not only its internal balance but also its external balance. When a country suffers insufficient effective demand, it can implement the policy of currency devaluation in hope of encouraging exports and blocking imports. But when all countries take the same policy, the exchange rates between these currencies will return to the starting point.

However, because countries differ from each other in their economic development, especially the extent of their economic fluctuation, they have difficulties in coordinating their economic policies. Furthermore, difference in preference, allocation of policy coordination benefits, reluctance to abandon independent policies and other factors make countries difficult to reach consensus on policy coordination.

10.4.2   International Monetary Cooperation

As we have learned from Mundell Incompatible Trinity, a country cannot have a fixed exchange rate system, free capital movement and an independent monetary policy simultaneously. This gives rise to international monetary cooperation. The cooperation falls into the following forms:

• *Exchange Rate Union*. All the participating countries adopt fixed exchange rates which are not allowed to change and each country within the union can autonomously choose its domestic monetary policies. Apparently, capital flows need to be strictly controlled since otherwise any autonomous monetary policy of one country will bring about interest rate gaps between the participants and result in the flows of speculative capital across countries, leading to the failure of sustaining fixed exchange rates.

• *Pseudo Exchange Rate Union*. All the participating countries adopt fixed exchange rates and capital can flow freely. Participants cooperate in their monetary policies rather than integrate their monetary policies. But as we have learned, fixed exchange rates cannot be sustained for long when capital can move freely. In this sense, this union is called as "pseudo".

• *Monetary Integration*. It is also called as *currency area*. Participating countries adopt a single exchange rate, i. e. a fixed exchange rate which is not allowed to adjust. There are no controls on foreign exchange. That is, currencies can be exchanged freely among participants. Capital flows freely within the area and participating countries adopt common monetary policies.

• *Monetary Unification*. This form of international monetary cooperation consists of three factors: monetary integration, single foreign reserves and a common central bank. In this form, participants have no autonomous exchange rate policies or monetary policies which are taken over to the common central bank.

Countries participate in an international monetary cooperation to seek for such benefits as reduction of exchange rate risks, less transaction costs of currency exchange and capital flows, and economies of scale.

But participating in an international monetary cooperation also bears costs. First, participating countries lose the policy tool of exchange rates which otherwise can adjust their domestic economy. Second, participants lose the independence of their monetary policies.

When countries weigh these benefits and costs to decide whether they should join an arrangement of cooperation, the **theory of optimum currency area** (OCA) is developed. The theory is often used to judge whether or not a certain region is ready to become a currency union. The most often cited criteria include:

- *Labor mobility across the area.* This includes physical ability to travel (visas, workers' rights, etc.), lack of cultural barriers to free movement (such as different languages) and institutional arrangements (such as the ability to have superannuation transferred throughout the region).

- *Openness with capital mobility and price and wage flexibility across the area.* This is to guarantee that the market forces of supply and demand can automatically distribute money and goods to where they are needed.

- *A risk sharing system* (such as an automatic fiscal transfer mechanism to redistribute money). This usually takes the form of taxation redistribution to less developed regions of the area.

- *Similar business cycles among participating countries.* When one country experiences a boom or a recession, other countries in the union are likely to follow. This allows the shared central bank to promote growth in downturns and to contain inflation in booms.

Chapter 11

International Factor Movements and Multinational Enterprises

Key Concepts and Terms

Host Country	东道国
Ultra Antitrade	超逆贸易
Human Capital	人力资本
Brain Drain	人才流失
Offshore Assembly Provision	离岸装配条款
Risk Diversification	风险分散
Multinational Enterprises (MNEs)	跨国企业
Research and Development (R & D)	研发
Vertical Integration	垂直整合
Forward Integration	前向整合
Backward Integration	后向整合
Horizontal Integration	水平整合
Conglomerate Integration	集团整合

Some of the most dramatic changes in the world economy have been due to international flows of factors of production, including labor and capital. In the 1800s, European capital and labor (along with African and Asian labor) flowed to the United States and fostered its economic development. In the 1960s, the United States sent large amounts of investment capital to Canada and Western Europe; in the 1980s and 1990s, investment flowed from Japan to the United States. Today, workers from southern Europe find employment in northern European factories, while Mexican workers migrate to the United States. The tearing down of the Berlin Wall in 1990 triggered a massive exodus of workers from East Germany to West Germany.

The economic forces underlying international movements in factors of production are virtually identical to those underlying international flows of goods and services. Productive factors move, when they are permitted to, from countries where they are abundant (low productivity) to countries where they are scarce (high productivity). Productive factors flow in response to differences in returns (such as wages and yields on capital) as long as these are large enough to more than outweigh the cost of moving from one country to another.

This chapter is concerned with international movements of factors of production, or factor movements. Factor movements include labor migration, the transfer of capital via international borrowing and lending, and the subtle international linkages involved in the formation of multinational enterprises.

11.1   International Movement of Labor

A country in which labor is scarce can either import labor-intensive products or import labor itself. Thus, international trade in goods and services and flows of productive factors are substitutes for each other. One cannot conduct a satisfactory study of international trade without also analyzing the international mobility of labor.

Even though extensive international trade is taking place among countries of the world, it is not leading to complete factor price equalization for a number of reasons, including different technologies, imperfect competition, transportation costs, and government policies. The fact that wages do not equalize with trade leaves open the possibility that labor may have an incentive to move from one country to another.

Technically, the desire to migrate on the part of an individual depends on the expected costs and benefits of the move. Expected income differences between the two locations, and other nonpecuniary net benefits in the new location such as health facilities, educational opportunities, and greater political or religious freedom figure into the decision to migrate. Even within this more general framework, expected wage or income differences are an important factor. At the same time, the movement of labor can influence the average wage in both the old and the new locations. For both countries, the movement of labor thus has welfare implications similar to capital movements and trade in goods and services.

11.1.1 Motives for International Labor Movement

International labor migration can take place for economic as well as noneconomic reasons. Some of the international migrations that occurred in the nineteenth century and earlier were certainly motivated by the desire to escape political and religious oppression in Europe. However, most international labor migration, particularly since the end of World War II, has been motivated by the prospect of earning higher real wages and income abroad.

The decision to migrate for economic reasons can be analyzed in the same manner and with the same tools as any other investment decision. Specifically, migration, just like any type of investment, involves both costs and benefits. The costs include the expenditures for transportation and the loss of wages during time spent relocating and searching for a job in the new country. In addition, there are many other less quantifiable costs, such as the separation from relatives, friends, and familiar surroundings; the need to learn new customs and often a new language; and the risks involved in finding a job, housing, and so on in a new land. To be sure, many of these noneconomic costs are greatly reduced by the fact that migrations usually occur in waves and in chains, with many migrants moving together to areas with an already substantial number of earlier migrants from the same place of origin.

The economic benefits of international migration can be measured by the higher real wages and income that the migrant worker can earn abroad during his or her remaining working life, over and above what he or she could have earned at home. Other benefits may be greater educational and job opportunities for the migrants' children. From the excess of returns over costs, an internal rate of return for the migration decision can be estimated, just as for any other type of investment. If this rate of return is sufficiently high to also overcome the noneconomic costs associated with migration, then the worker will migrate. Of course, in the real world workers seldom, if ever, have the information to carry out this type of cost-benefit analysis explicitly. Nevertheless, they behave as if they did. This is confirmed by the fact that migrants invariably move from low-wage countries. Furthermore, younger workers migrate more readily than older workers because, among other things, they have a longer remaining working life over which to benefit from the higher wages abroad.

11.1.2   Economic Effects of Labor Movement

First, let us analyze the relation between labor movement and international trade. As we know, movement of labor can affect the composition of output and structure of trade in the countries involved. Given full employment, at constant international prices the increase in the labor force in Country B leads, according to the Rybczynski theorem, to an expansion of output of the labor-intensive good (X) and contraction in output of the capital-intensive good (Y). Assuming that Country A is the labor-abundant country, that Country B is the capital-abundant country, and that trade between the two follows the Heckscher-Ohlin pattern, the impact of the labor movement between the two can be examined. Output of the exported good in Country A declines and output of the imported good increases.

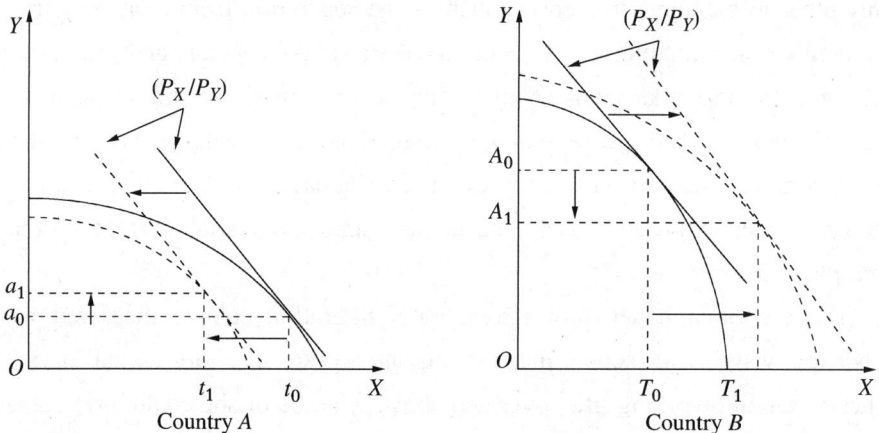

Figure 11-1   The Relation Between Labor Movement and International Trade

See Figure 11-1, the movement of labor from Country A to Country B is indicated by the outward shift of the production possibilities frontier (PPF) for Country B and the inward shift of the PPF for Country A. Assume that Country A is the labor abundant country exporting the labor-intensive good (X) and importing the capital-intensive good (Y) prior to the labor migration and that the two countries in question are small nations. The Rybczynski theorem indicates that this change in relative labor supplies will lead Country A to contract production of the labor-intensive good (X) from t_0 to t_1 and expand production of Y from a_0 to a_1. Country B, on the other hand, will expand production of X from T_0 to T_1 with the newly acquired labor and reduce the production of Y from A_0 to A_1. Both production adjustments are **ultra antitrade** in nature since factor flows have in effect substituted for trade flows.

And then, we analyze the economic effect of labor movement. Now suppose that workers are able to move between the two countries. Workers will move from the home country to the foreign country. This movement will reduce the home labor force and thus raise the real wage in the home country, while increasing the labor force and reducing the real wage in the foreign country. If there are no obstacles to labor movement, this process will continue until the marginal product of labor is the same in the two countries.

Figure 11-2 illustrates the causes and effects of international labor mobility. The horizontal axis represents the total world labor force. The workers employed in Country A are measured from the left, the workers employed in Country B from the right. The left vertical axis shows the marginal product of labor in Country A and the right vertical axis shows the marginal product of labor in Country B. Initially we assume that there are $O_A L_1$ workers in Country A and $L_1 O_B$ workers in Country B. Given this allocation, the real wage rate would be lower in Country A (Point C) than in Country B (Point B). If workers can move freely to whichever country offering higher real wage, they will move from Country A to Country B until the real wage rates are equalized. The eventual distribution of the world's labor force will be one with $O_A L_2$ workers in Country A, $L_2 O_B$ workers in Country B (Point A).

As these adjustments occur, output falls in Country A and rises in Country B. The remaining workers in Country A are better off both absolutely (due to the higher wage) and relatively, as the productivity of the other factors falls with the reduced labor supply. In Country B, the opposite takes place. With the fall in the wage rate in Country B, labor is less well-off since its wage rate has fallen. Productivity of the other factors, however, has risen with the increased use of

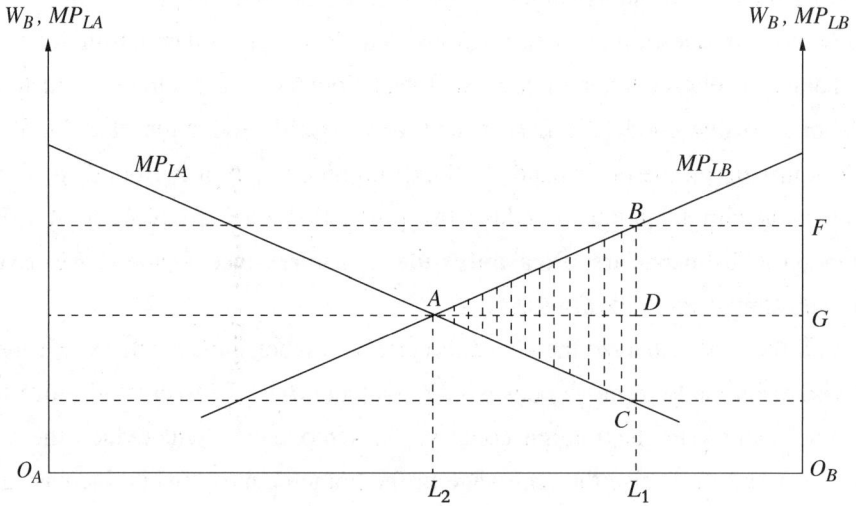

Figure 11-2　The Economic Effect of International Labor Movement

labor, so owners of these factors are better off. The other factors in Country B gain Area $ABFG$, while Country B's labor loses Area $DBFG$. The amount of income earned by the new migrants is L_1L_2AD.

What can be said about the change in overall well-being in Country A, Country B, and the world as a result of the labor movement? Given the existence of diminishing marginal productivity of labor in production, other things being equal, output in Country A falls at a slower rate than the decrease in the labor force, leading to an increase in per capita output. In Country B, output grows more slowly than the increase in the labor force, leading to a decrease in per capita output. Finally, the world as a whole gains from this migration since the fall in total output in Country A (Area ACL_1L_2) is more than offset by the increase in output in Country B (Area ABL_1L_2) by the shaded area ABC.

Three points should be noted about this redistribution of the world's labor force:

(1) It leads to a convergence of real wage rates. Real wages rise in Country A and fall in Country B.

(2) It increases the world's output as a whole. Country B's output rises by the area under its marginal product curve from L_1 to L_2, while Country A's output falls by the corresponding area under its marginal product curve. We see from the figure that Country B's gain is larger than Country A's loss, by an amount equal to the shaded area ABC in Figure 11-2.

(3) Despite this gain, some people are hurt by the change. Those who would originally have worked in Country A receive higher real wages, but those who would originally have worked in Country B receive lower real wages. As in the case of the gains from international trade, then, international labor movement, while allowing everyone to be better off in principle, leaves some groups worse off in practice.

11.1.3   Other Welfare Effects of International Labor Movement

The previous models help us understand some of the basic issues that affect the politics of labor movement. It is not surprising that labor in Country B wants restrictions against immigration because new workers lower the wage rate. On the other hand, owners of other resources such as capital favor immigration because it increases their returns. At the same time, labor in Country A favors emigration but capital owners tend to discourage the labor movement. While the simple models are useful in providing an understanding of the basic economics involved, several extensions of this analysis are important to discuss briefly.

First, new immigrants might transfer some income back to the home country. When this happens, the reduction in income (from home production) in Country A is at least partly offset by the amount of the transfer, while the increase in income resulting from the increased employment in Country B is reduced by the amount of the transfer. Assuming that the transfer is between workers in the two countries, labor income in Country A is enhanced and total income (and per capita income) available to the labor force in Country B is further reduced. In fact, a study of remittances submitted by Greek emigrants indicates that the income, employment, and capital formation benefits to Greece from these remittances are substantial, while the costs of the emigration itself to Greece are limited.

A second issue is the nature of immigration. We have assumed that the immigration is permanent, not temporary. A temporary worker is often called a guest worker. In the above analysis, all workers were assumed to be identical and new immigrants thus received the same wage-benefit package as domestic workers. This is not an unrealistic assumption because many countries do not permit employers to discriminate against permanent immigrants. A two-tier wage structure is thus not possible. However, these restrictions do not often hold for guest workers or seasonal migrants.

We need to make some observations about the nature of migrants and the implications of migrant characteristics on both countries. The assumption that workers are homogeneous is certainly not true in the real world, and the welfare implications that accompany migration can vary as a result. The labor force in each country possesses an array of labor skills ranging from the untrained or unskilled to the highly trained or skilled.

So far, we have implicitly assumed that all labor is unskilled. However, even casual observation of the real world reveals a great variety in the quality and amount of human capital (in the form of education, training, and health) embodied in different workers and labor groups. The question then arises as to the welfare effects of the migration of highly skilled workers on the countries of emigration and immigration. These welfare effects are likely to be significantly different from those arising from the migration of unskilled labor. Concern with this question has greatly increased since the 1950s and 1960s as relatively large numbers of scientists and technicians, doctors and nurses, and other highly skilled personnel have moved from developing to developed countries and from Europe to the United States. For example, of the 8.7 million people that poured into the United States from the rest of the world during the 1980s, 1.5 million were college-educated. More than 40 percent of the 200 researchers in the Communications Sciences Research wing at AT&T Bell Laboratories were foreign born, and more than 50 percent of computer science doctorates awarded by U.S. universities in the early 1990s went to foreign-born students — many of whom remained in the United States. Indeed, more and more U.S. high-immigrant scientists and engineers remain competitive in the increasingly global marketplace.

The movement of skilled labor, especially between developing and industrialized countries, is a relatively recent phenomenon. However, an increasing number of highly educated people are leaving the developing countries for the United States, Canada, and Western Europe — a movement often referred to as the **brain drain**. Higher salaries, lower taxes, greater professional and personal freedom, better laboratory conditions, and access to newer technologies, professional colleagues, and material goods and services found in these countries explain this movement of labor. In many cases, persons who have received formal training in the industrialized countries would find it difficult to readjust, at least professionally, to life in the home country.

The countries of origin of skilled migrants charge that they incur a great cost in educating and training these workers, only to see them leave and benefit the receiving countries. To be sure, many of these highly skilled workers often cannot be used effectively at home — as, for example, when a doctor only performs nursing services and engineers are used as technicians, as frequently happens in some developing countries. Nevertheless, the fact remains that the country of origin incurs the great expense of training these workers but receives little, if any, benefit in the form of emigrant remittances. It may also be that the more dynamic, more alert, and younger workers emigrate, thus reducing the stock of these qualities in the remaining labor force.

The brain drain is often encouraged by national immigration laws (as in the United States, the United Kingdom, and other developed countries) that facilitate the immigration of skilled persons but generally impose serious obstacles to the immigration of unskilled workers. This has led to demands to tax skilled emigrants at the time of exit or tax their subsequent higher earnings in the country of immigration, so that the country of origin could recoup part of the cost incurred in training them. Although these proposals seem reasonable, it should be remembered that an important element of personal freedom is involved in the ability to migrate. Thus, it might be more acceptable from the individual's point of view and more efficient from an economic point of view for the government of the receiving country to somehow compensate, through increased aid or other financial transfer to the country of origin, for the training costs of skilled immigrants, particularly if the country of origin is a developing country.

11. 2   International Movement of Capital

Labor is not the only factor that flows across international boundaries. Capital, both in financial and in physical forms, does as well. In fact, international flows of capital have become an everyday fact of life in the international economy and, because of their enormous size, they are probably much more important than labor flows in influencing rates of economic growth and the location of economic activity.

11.2.1 Data on International Movement of Capital

Now, we consider the case of the United States. Throughout the nineteenth century, it was a capital-importing country. Other countries, most notably the United Kingdom, lent a substantial proportion of the financial capital that enabled the construction of railroads, factories, and communication systems, thereby helping to propel the U.S. economy to the status of an industrial giant. Imports of European-made capital goods (in exchange for U.S. agricultural products) also helped promote the development of the U.S. industrial base.

For much of the twentieth century, the United States was a capital exporter. That is, it lent financial capital to countries throughout the world, becoming by 1980 the world's largest net creditor. Since the 1980s, this trend has reversed. The U. S. firms, citizens, and especially the U. S. government have been borrowing in record amounts from foreigners. In the process, the United States has moved from being the world's largest net creditor to being the world's largest net debtor.

We now present some data on the size and composition of U. S. capital investments in foreign countries and foreign capital investments in the United States from 1950 to 2001.

We can see from Table 11-1 that both U.S. private holdings of foreign long-term securities (stocks and bonds) and foreign private holdings of U.S. long-term securities increased very rapidly from 1950 to 2001, with the latter about 35 percent higher than the former at the end of 2001. Table 11-1 also shows the value of U.S. direct investments abroad and foreign direct investments in the United States at the end of various years. Foreign direct investments are valued at historical cost, at current or replacement cost, and at market value (i.e. using stock market prices). Figures for foreign direct investments at current cost are available only from 1976, and those at current values only from 1982. The need to supplement the historical values of foreign direct investments with those at current cost and at market value arises because most U.S. foreign direct investments account for the cumulative effects of inflation rather than foreign direct investments in the United States do, which has occurred mostly since the 1980s. Table 11-1 shows that both the stock of U.S. direct investments abroad and foreign direct investments in the United States also increased very rapidly from 1950 to 2000 and were similar in amount at the end of 2001 when measured at market value.

Table 11-2 also shows that from 1950 to 2000, the stock of U.S. direct investments in Europe grew much more rapidly than the stock of U.S. direct investments in Canada and Latin America. This was due to the rapid growth of the European Union and the United States' desire to avoid the common external tariff imposed by the EU on imports from outside the EU.

Table 11-1   U.S. Foreign Long-Term Private International Investment Position in Selected Years, 1950-2001 (billions of U.S. dollars)

Year	1950	1960	1970	1980	1990	2000
U.S. assets abroad						
Foreign securities	4.3	9.5	20.9	62.4	342.3	2,389.4
Direct investments at						
Historical cost	11.8	31.9	75.5	214.5	421.5	1,239.4
Current cost				369.2	616.7	1,515.3
Market value					731.8	2,674.2
Foreign assets in the U.S.						
U.S. assets	2.9	9.3	34.8	74.1	460.6	2,623.6
Direct investments at						
Historical cost	3.4	6.9	13.3	83.0	403.7	1,214.3
Current cost				125.9	505.3	1,374.8
Market value					539.6	2,766.0

Source: Salvatore, D., *International Economics*, eighth edition, John Wiley & Sons Inc., 2004.

Table 11-2   U.S. Direct Investments Abroad by Area in Selected Years, 1950-2001 (billions of U.S. dollars, at historical cost, at year end)

Year	Total	Canada	Europe	Latin America	Asia and Pacific	of which Japan	Others
1950	11.8	3.6	1.7	4.6	0.3	0.0	1.6
1960	31.9	11.2	7.0	8.4	1.2	0.3	4.1
1970	78.2	22.8	24.5	14.8	8.3	1.5	7.8
1980	215.6	45.0	96.5	38.9	25.3	6.2	9.9
1990	421.5	68.4	204.2	72.5	63.6	21.0	12.8
2000	1,293.4	128.8	679.5	251.9	205.3	59.4	27.9
2001	1,381.7	139.0	725.8	269.6	216.5	64.1	30.8

Source: Salvatore, D., *International Economics*, eighth edition, John Wiley & Sons Inc., 2004.

11.2.2   Motives for International Capital Movement

It should be clear that there is considerable mobility of capital across country borders in the world economy today. We cannot make a full examination of the motives for this, but brief mention can be made of possible cause. Above all, economists view the movement of capital between countries as fundamentally no different from movement between regions of a country (or between industries), because the capital is moved in response to the expectation of a higher rate of return in the new location than it earned in the old location. Economic agents seek to maximize their well-being. Although many additional reasons for capital movements have been suggested, all imply the seeking of a higher rate of return on capital over time. Now we list and comment briefly on several motives.

First, firms will invest abroad in response to large and rapidly growing markets for their products. Empirical studies have attempted to support this general hypothesis at the aggregative level by seeking a positive correlation between the gross domestic product (and its rate of growth) of a recipient country and the amount of foreign direct investment flowing into that country. Similarly, since manufacturing and services production in developed countries are catering increasingly to high-income tastes and wants, it can be hypothesized that firms in developed countries will invest overseas if the recipient country has a high per capita income. Another motive for direct investment in a country is that the foreign firm can secure access to mineral or raw material deposits located there and can then process the raw materials and sell them in finished form.

Second, tariffs and nontariff barriers in the host country also can induce an inflow of foreign direct investment (FDI). If trade restrictions make it difficult for the foreign firm to sell in the host country market, then an alternative strategy for the firm is to "get behind the tariff wall" and produce within the host country itself. A foreign firm may consider investment in a host country if there are low relative wages in the host country. Clearly, the existence of low wages because of relative labor abundance in the recipient country is an attraction when the production process is labor-intensive. In fact, the production process often can be broken up so that capital-intensive or technology-intensive production of components takes place within developed countries while labor-intensive assembly operations that use the components take place in developing countries. This division of labor is facilitated by offshore assembly provisions in the tariff schedules of developed countries.

Third, it has also suggested that firms may want to invest abroad as a means of risk diversification. Just as investors prefer to have a diversified financial portfolio instead of holding their assets in the stock of a single company, so firms may wish to distribute their real investment assets across industries or countries. If a recession or downturn occurs in one market or industry, it will be beneficial for a firm not to have all its eggs in one basket. Some of the firm's investments in other industries or countries may not experience the downturn or may at least experience it with reduced severity. For example, the basic motive for international portfolio investments is to earn higher returns abroad. Thus, residents of one country purchase bonds of another country if the returns on bonds are higher in the other country. This is the simple and straightforward outcome of yield maximization and tends to equalize returns internationally. According to the basic (two-nation) Heckscher-Ohlin model, returns on capital are originally higher in the country having the lower overall capital-labor ration. Residents of one country may also purchase stock in a corporation in another country if they expect the future profitability of the foreign corporation to be greater than that of domestic corporations. Since different individuals can have different expectations for the same stocks, it is possible that some investors in each country think that stocks in the other country are a better buy. This provides an explanation for two-way international portfolio investments.

11.2.3 Economic Effects of Capital Movement

The existence of substantial international capital movement in the real world has various implications for the output of the countries involved, for world output, and for rates of return to capital and other factors of production. Economists have employed a straightforward microeconomic apparatus to examine these effects, and this section presents this analytical approach.

In Figure 11-3, we examine a world of only two countries (Country A and Country B) with a total combined capital stock of $O_A O_B$. Of this total capital stock, $O_A A$ belongs to Country A and $O_B A$ belongs to Country B. MP_{KA} and MP_{KB} curves give the value of the marginal product of capital in Country A and Country B, respectively, for various levels of investments. Under competitive conditions, the value of the marginal product of capital represents the return, or yield, on capital. In microeconomic theory, a marginal physical product of capital schedule plots the additions to output that result from adding 1 more unit of capital to production when all other inputs are held constant. With constant prices, this schedule constitutes the demand for capital inputs derived from the demand for the product.

Assume in the initial situation (before international capital flows) that Country A invests its entire capital stock $O_A A$ domestically at a yield of $O_A C$. The total product (which can be measured by the area under the value of the marginal product curve) is thus $O_A FGA$, of which $O_A CGA$ goes to owners of capital in Country A and the remainder of CFG goes to other cooperating factors, such as labor and land. Similarly, Country B in isolation invests its entire stock $O_B A$ domestically at a yield of $O_B H$. Total product is $O_B JMA$, of which $O_B HMA$ goes to owners of capital in Country B and the remainder of HJM goes to other cooperating factors.

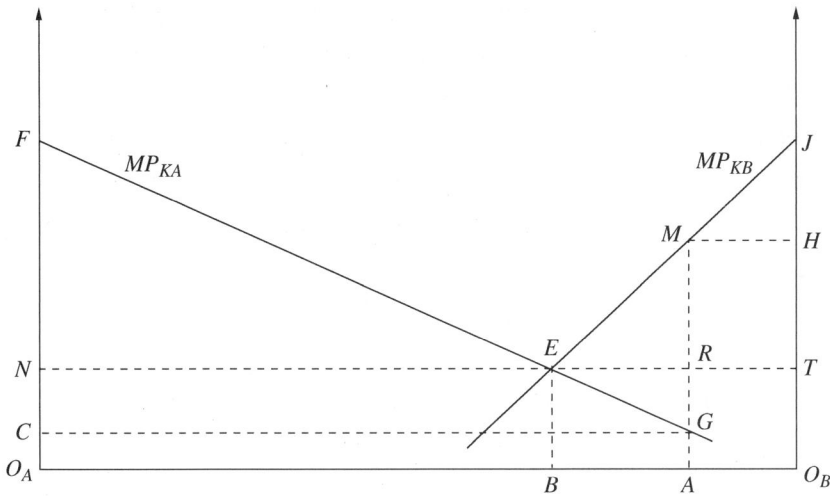

Figure 11-3   The Economic Effect of International Capital Movement

This situation will change if capital is permitted to move between countries because the rate of returns to capital in Country B exceeds that in Country A. Now, let us assume that free international capital movements are permitted. Since the returns on capital are higher in Country B ($O_B H$) than in Country A ($O_A C$), AB of capital flows from Country A to Country B so as to equalize at BE ($= O_A N$ $= O_B T$) the rate of return on capital in the two countries. Total domestic product in Country A is now $O_A FEB$, to which must be added $ABER$ as the total return on foreign investments, giving a total national income of $O_A FERA$ (with ERG greater than before foreign investments). With free international capital flows, the total return on capital in Country A increases to $O_A NRA$, while the total return on other cooperating factors decreases to NFE.

What has been the effect of capital flow AB from Country A to Country B on output in Country B? The inflow of foreign capital AB into Country B lowers the rate of returns on capital from $O_B H$ to $O_B T$. Total domestic product in Country B grows from $O_B JMA$ to $O_B JEB$. Of the increase in total product of $ABEM$, $ABER$ goes to foreign investors, so that ERM remains as the net gain in total product accruing to Country B. The total return to domestic owners of capital falls from $O_B HMA$ to $O_B TRA$, while the total return to other cooperating factors rises from HJM to TJE.

From the point of view of the world as a whole, total product increased from $O_A FGA + O_B JMA$ to $O_A FEB + O_B JEB$, or by $ERG + ERM = EGM$. Thus, international capital flows increase the efficiency in the allocation of resources internationally and increase the world output and welfare (Note that the steeper MP_{KA} and MP_{KB} curves are, the greater the total gains from international capital flows). Thus, just as free international trade in goods and services increases the efficiency of resource use in the world economy, so does the free movement of capital – and of factors of production in general. In addition, free movement of factors can equalize returns to factors in both countries, just as free international trade in the Heckscher-Ohlin model could lead to factor price equalization between the countries. In recognition of these parallel implications of trade and factor mobility for efficiency of resource use and returns to factors, economists often stress that free trade and free factor mobility are substitutes for each other.

Now, let us discuss briefly other effects on international capital movement. Assuming two factors of production, capital and labor, both fully employed before and after the capital transfer, it can be see from Figure 11-3 that the total and average return on capital increases, whereas the total and average return to labor decreases in the investing country. Thus, while the investing country as a whole gains from investing abroad, there is a redistribution of domestic income from labor to capital. Furthermore, international capital transfers also affect the balance of payments of investing and host countries. A country's balance of payments measures its total receipts from and total expenditures in the rest of the world. In the year in which the foreign investment takes place, the foreign expenditures of the investing country increase and cause a balance-of-payments deficit (an excess of expenditures abroad over foreign receipts). Of course, the counterpart to the worsening in the investing country's balance of payments is the improvement in the host country's balance of payments in the year when it receives the foreign investment. The initial capital transfer and increased expenditures abroad of the investing country are likely to be mitigated by increased exports of capital goods, spare parts, and other products of the investing country, and by the subsequent flow of profits to the investing country. Last, foreign investments, by affecting output and the volume of trade of both investing and host countries, are also likely to affect the terms of trade. However, the way the terms of trade change depends on conditions in both countries, and not much can be said without observed facts. Foreign investments may also affect the investing country's technological lead and the host country's control over its economy and ability to conduct its own independent economic policy.

11.3   Multinational Enterprises and Foreign Direct Investment Theories

One of the most significant international economic developments of the postwar period is the proliferation of **multinational enterprises** (MNEs). These are firms that own, control, or manage production facilities in several countries. Today MNEs account for about 25 percent of world output, and intrafirm trade (i. e., trade among the parent firm and its foreign affiliates) is estimated to be about one-third of total world trade in manufacturing. Some MNEs, such as General Motors and Exxon, are truly giants, with yearly sales in the tens of billions of dollars and exceeding the total national income of all but a handful of countries. Furthermore, most international direct investments today are undertaken by MNEs. In the process, the parent firm usually provides its foreign affiliates with managerial expertise, technology, parts, and a marketing organization in return for some of the affiliates' output and earnings. In this section, we discuss MNEs and foreign direct investment theories.

11.3.1   Multinational Enterprises

Although the term *enterprise* can be precisely defined, there is no universal agreement on the exact definition of a multinational enterprise. But a close look at some representative MNEs suggests that these businesses have a number of identifiable features. Operating in many host countries, MNEs often conduct research and development (R & D) activities in addition to manufacturing, mining, extraction, and business-service operations. A MNE cuts across national borders and is often directed from a company planning center that is distant from the host country. Both stock ownership and company management are typically multinational in character. A typical MNE has a high ratio of foreign sales to total sales, often 25 percent or more. Regardless of the lack of agreement as to what constitutes an MNE, there is no doubt that the multinational phenomenon is massive in size.

For the world's industrial MNEs with 2,000 sales in excess of ＄50 billion, Table 11-3 gives the home countries of parent firms, the major industries, the level of yearly sales, and the percentage of those sales made outside the home country. From the table we see that 6 (including the top 3) of these 19 MNEs have headquarters in the United States, 5 in Japan, 2 in Germany, and one each in Germany/United States, the United Kingdom, United Kingdom/Netherlands, France, Italy, and Venezuela. 7 are in motor vehicles, 6 in petroleum, 5 in electronics, and 1 in computers. Petroleos de Venezuela has the highest percentage of foreign sales (93.5), and the simple average for all the firms is 55.7 percent.

Table 11-3　The World's Largest Industrial Multinational Enterprises in 2000

Rank	Company	Home Country	Industry	Yearly Sales (billion ＄)	Percentage of Foreign Sales
1	ExxonMobil Corporation	U.S.	Petroleum	206.1	69.4
2	General Motors	U.S.	Motor vehicles	184.4	26.1
3	Ford Motor Company	U.S.	Motor vehicles	170.1	30.4
4	DaimlerChrysler	Germany/U.S.	Motor vehicles	152.4	32.0
5	Royal Dutch/ Shell Group	U.K./Netherlands	Petroleum	149.1	54.4
6	British Petroleum	U.K.	Petroleum	148.1	71.3
7	General Electric	U.S.	Electronics	129.9	38.1
8	Toyota	Japan	Motor vehicles	125.6	49.6
9	Chevron Texaco	U.S.	Petroleum	117.1	55.5
10	Total Fina Elf	France	Petroleum	105.8	78.0
11	IBM	U.S.	Computers	88.4	57.9
12	Volkswagen Group	Germany	Motor vehicles	79.6	72.6
13	Hitachi	Japan	Electronics	75.5	29.3
14	Siemens	Germany	Electronics	71.4	43.8

continued

Rank	Company	Home Country	Industry	Yearly Sales (billion $)	Percentage of Foreign Sales
15	Matsushita Electric	Japan	Electronics	68.9	49.3
16	Sony	Japan	Electronics	63.7	67.2
17	Honda Motor	Japan	Motor vehicles	57.5	72.9
18	Fiat	Italy	Motor vehicles	53.6	66.9
19	Petroleos de Venezuela	Venezuela	Petroleum	53.2	93.5

Source: Salvatore, D., *International Economics*, eighth edition, John Wiley & Sons Inc., 2004.

MNEs may diversify their operations along vertical, horizontal, and conglomerate lines within the host and source countries. **Vertical integration** often occurs when the parent MNE decides to establish foreign subsidiaries to produce intermediate goods or inputs that go into the production of the finished good. For industries such as oil refining and steel, such backward integration may include the extraction and processing of raw materials. Most manufacturers tend to extend operations backward only to the production of component parts. The major international oil companies represent a classic case of backward vertical integration on a worldwide basis. Oil production subsidiaries are located in areas such as the Middle East, whereas the refining and marketing operations occur in the industrial countries of the West. MNEs may also practice forward integration in the direction of the final consumer market. Automobile manufacturers, for example, may establish foreign subsidiaries to market the finished goods of the parent company. In practice, most vertical foreign investment is backward. MNEs often wish to integrate their operations vertically to benefit from economies of scale and international specialization.

Horizontal integration occurs when a parent company producing a commodity in the home country sets up a subsidiary to produce the identical product in the host country. These subsidiaries are independent units in productive capacity and are established to produce and market the parent company's product in overseas markets. Coca-Cola and Pepsi-Cola, for example, are bottled not only in the United States but also throughout much of the world. MNEs sometimes locate production facilities overseas to avoid stiff foreign tariff barriers, which would place their products at a competitive disadvantage. Parent companies also like to locate close to their customers because differences in national preferences may require special designs for their products.

Besides making horizontal and vertical foreign investments, MNEs may diversify into unrelated markets, in what is known as **conglomerate integration**. For example, in the 1980s, U. S. oil companies stepped up their nonenergy acquisitions in response to anticipated declines of future investment opportunities in oil and gas. ExxonMobil acquired a foreign copper-mining subsidiary in Chile, and Tenneco bought a French company producing automotive exhaust systems.

Now, we examine the reasons for the existence of MNEs and some of the problems they create for the home and host countries.

The basic reason for the existence of MNEs is the competitive advantage of a global network of production and distribution. This competitive advantage arises in part from vertical and horizontal integration with foreign affiliates. By vertical integration, most MNEs can ensure their supply of foreign raw materials and intermediate products and circumvent (with more efficient intrafirm trade) the imperfections often found in foreign markets. They can also provide better distribution and service networks. By horizontal integration through foreign affiliates, MNEs can better protect and exploit their monopoly power, adapt their products to local conditions and tastes, and ensure consistent product quality.

The competitive advantage of MNEs is also based on economies of scale in production, financing, research and development (R & D), and the gathering of market information. The large output of MNEs allows them to carry division of labor and specialization in production much further than smaller national firms. Furthermore, MNEs and their affiliates usually have greater access, at better terms, to international capital markets than do purely national firms, and this puts MNEs in a better position to finance large projects. The large enterprise invests abroad when expected profits on additional investments in its industry are higher abroad. Since the enterprise usually has a competitive advantage and knows its industry best, it does not usually consider the possibility of higher returns in every other domestic industry before it decides to invest abroad. That is, differences in expected rates of profits domestically and abroad in the particular industry are of crucial importance in a large enterprise's decision to invest abroad. MNEs are also in a much better position to control or change to their advantage the environment in which they operate than are purely national firms. For example, in determining where to set up a plant to produce a component, a MNE can and usually does "shop around" for the low-wage country that offers the most incentives in the form of tax holidays, subsidies, and other tax and trade benefits. In the final analysis, it is a combination of all or most of these factors that gives MNEs their competitive advantage vis-a-vis purely national firms and explains the proliferation and great importance of MNEs today.

While MNEs, by efficiently organizing production and distribution on a worldwide basis, can increase world output and welfare, they can also create serious problems in both home and host countries. The most controversial one of the alleged harmful effects of MNEs on the home country is the loss of domestic jobs resulting from foreign direct investments. These are likely to be unskilled and semiskilled production jobs in which the home country has a comparative disadvantage. Because labor unions are confined to individual countries, the multinational nature of these businesses permits them to escape much of the collective-bargaining influence of domestic unions. It is also pointed out that MNEs can seek out those countries where labor has minimal market power. Another possible harmful effect of MNEs on the home country can result from transfer pricing and similar practices. Using this technique, a MNE reports most of its profits in a low-tax country, even though the profits were earned in a high-tax country. For example, if corporate profit taxes are higher in the parent country than in the host country, and if the parent firm is exporting to its subsidiary in the host country, the MNE can lower its overall tax burden by underpricing its exports to its host country subsidiary, thus shifting profits from the parent to the subsidiary.

Host countries have even more serious complaints against MNEs. First and foremost is the allegation that MNEs dominate their economies. Foreign domination is felt in many different ways in host countries, including (1) the unwillingness of a local affiliate of a MNE to export to a country deemed unfriendly to the home country or the requirement to comply with a home country's law prohibiting such exports; (2) the borrowing of funds abroad to circumvent tight domestic credit conditions and the lending of funds abroad when interest rates are low at home; and (3) the effect on national tastes of large-scale advertising for products. Another alleged harmful effect of MNEs on the host country is the siphoning off of R & D funds to the home country. While this may be more efficient for the MNE and the world as a whole, it also keeps the host country technologically dependent. This is especially true and serious for developing countries. MNEs may also absorb local savings and entrepreneurial talent, thus preventing them from being used to establish domestic enterprises that might be more important for national growth and development. Most of these complaints are to some extent true, particularly in the case of developing host countries, and they have led many host countries to regulate foreign investments in order to mitigate the harmful effects and increase the possible benefits. Thus, Canada imposes higher taxes on foreign affiliates with less than 25 percent Canadian interest. India specifies the sectors in which direct foreign investments are allowed and sets rules to regulate their operation. Some developing countries allow only joint ventures and set rules for the transfer of technology and the training of domestic labor, impose limits on the use of imported inputs and the remission of profits, set environmental regulations, and so on.

11.3.2   Foreign Direct Investment Theories

When speaking of the international movement of capital, we need to distinguish two types of capital movements: foreign direct investment (FDI) and foreign portfolio investment. FDI is real investments in factories, capital goods, land, and inventories where both capital and management are involved and the investor retains control over use of the invested capital. Foreign portfolio investment is the entry of funds into a country where foreigners make purchases in the country's stock and bond markets, sometimes for speculation. FDI usually takes the form of a firm starting a subsidiary or taking control of another firm (for example, by purchasing a majority of the stock). Any purchase of 10 percent or more of the stock of a firm, however, is defined as direct investment by the U.S. government. In the international context, FDI is usually undertaken by multinational enterprises engaged in manufacturing, resource extraction, or services. FDI is now as important as portfolio investment as forms or channels of international private capital flows.

Table 11-4   FDI Flows to the U.S. in Selected Years, 1980-2001

(billions of U.S. dollars)

Year	FDI	Year	FDI
1980	12. 2	1991	25. 5
1981	23. 2	1992	15. 3
1982	10. 8	1993	26. 2
1983	8. 1	1994	45. 6
1984	15. 2	1995	57. 2
1985	23. 1	1996	79. 9
1986	39. 2	1997	69. 7
1987	40. 3	1998	215. 3
1988	72. 7	1999	275. 0
1989	71. 2	2000	335. 6
1990	65. 9	2001	132. 9

Source: Salvatore, D., *International Economics*, eighth edition, John Wiley & Sons Inc., 2004.

To carry out their worldwide operations, MNEs rely on FDI — acquisition of a controlling interest in an overseas company or facility. FDI typically occurs when (1) the parent company obtains sufficient common stock in a foreign company to assume voting control; (2) the parent company acquires or constructs new plants and equipment overseas; (3) the parent company shifts funds abroad to finance an expansion of its foreign subsidiary; or (4) earnings of the parent company's foreign subsidiary are reinvested in plant expansion.

Table 11-4 shows that the level of FDI in the United States was $ 12. 2 billion in 1980. It declined to $ 8.1 billion in 1983 (a recession year) before rising to $ 72. 7 billion in 1988. Afterward, it declined to $ 15. 3 billion in 1992 (another recession year) and then rose to the all-time high of $ 335. 6 billion in 2000, before falling to 132. 9 in 2001 (a recession year). Thus, flows of FDI to the United States seem to be cyclical, rising during periods of high growth and falling during periods of recession or slow growth.

The case for opening markets to FDI is compelling as it is for trade. More open economies enjoy higher rates of private investment, which is a major determinant of economic growth and job creation. FDI is actively courted by countries, not least because it generates spillovers such as improved management and better technology. As is true with firms that trade, firms and sectors where FDI is intense tend to have higher average labor productivity and pay higher wages. It is generally assumed that investment flows from regions of low anticipated profit to those of high anticipated profit, after allowing for risk. But corporate management may emphasize a variety of other factors when asked about their investment motives. These factors include market demand conditions, trade restrictions, investment regulations, labor costs, and transportation costs.

First, the quest for profits encourages MNEs to search for new markets and sources of demand. Some MNEs set up overseas subsidiaries to tap foreign markets that cannot be maintained adequately by export products. The location of foreign manufacturing facilities may be influenced by the fact that some parent companies find their productive capacity already sufficient to meet domestic demands. If they wish to enjoy growth rates that exceed the expansion of domestic demand, they must either export or establish foreign production facilities. Market competition may also influence a firm's decision to set up foreign facilities. Corporate strategies may be defensive in nature if they are directed at preserving market shares from actual or potential competition. The most certain method of preventing foreign competition from becoming a strong force is to acquire foreign businesses.

Second, MNEs often seek to increase profit levels through reductions in production costs. Such cost-reducing FDI may take a number of forms. The pursuit of essential raw materials may underlie a company's intent to be multinational. This is particularly true of the extractive industries and certain agricultural commodities. Production costs include factors other than material inputs, notably labor. Labor costs tend to differ among national economies. MNEs may be able to hold costs down by locating part or all of their productive facilities abroad. MNE location can also be affected by transportation costs, especially in industries where transportation costs are a high fraction of product value. When the cost of transporting raw materials used by a MNE is significantly higher than the cost of shipping its finished products to markets, the MNE will generally locate production facilities closer to its raw material sources than to its markets. Government policies may also lead to FDI. Some countries seeking to lure foreign manufacturers to set up employment-generating facilities in their countries may grant subsidies, such as preferential tax treatment or free factory buildings, to MNEs. More commonly, direct investment may be a way of circumventing import tariff barriers.

Now, we cover some of the alleged benefits and costs of a direct capital inflow to a host country. While there are also benefits and costs to the home country from capital outflow, we focus only on host country effects because they are more controversial and more widely discussed.

A wide variety of benefits may result from an inflow of FDI. Some of the potential gains are listed in Table 11-5.

Table 11-5   Potential Benefits of Foreign Direct Investment

Potential Benefits	Brief Discussions
Increased output	The provision of increased capital to work with labor and other resources can enhance the total output from the factors of production.
Increased wages	Some of the increase in wages arises as redistribution from the profits of domestic capital.
Increased employment	This impact is particularly important if the recipient country is a developing country with an excess supply of labor caused by population pressure.
Increased exports	If the foreign capital produces goods with export potential, the host country is in a position to generate scarce foreign exchange.
Increased tax revenues	If the host country is in a position to implement effective tax measures, the profits and other increased incomes flowing from the foreign investment project can provide a source of new tax revenue to be used for development projects.
Realization of scale economies	The foreign firm might enter into an industry in which scale economies can be realized because of the industry's market size and technological features.
Provision of technical and managerial skills and of new technology	The new technology can clearly enhance the recipient country's production possibilities when foreign capital brings in critical human capital skills in the form of managers and technicians.
Weakening of power of domestic monopoly	With the inflow of the direct investment, a new competitor is provided, resulting in a possible increase in output and fall in prices in the industry dominated by small number of firms.

Source: Appleyad, D., Fied, Jr. A. J., *International Economics*, fourth edition, McGraw-Hill Companies, Inc., 1992.

Some alleged disadvantages to the host country from a foreign capital inflow are listed and briefly discussed in Table 11-6.

Table 11-6   Potential Disadvantages of Foreign Direct Investment

Potential Disadvantages	Brief Discussions
Adverse impact on the host country's commodity terms of trade	This could occur if the investment goes into production of export goods and the country is a large country in the sale of its exports.
Decreased domestic saving	The allegation, in the context of a developing country, is that the inflow of foreign capital may cause the domestic government to relax its efforts to generate greater domestic saving.
Decreased domestic investment	Often the foreign firm may partly finance the direct investment by borrowing funds in the host country's capital market. This action can drive up interest rate in the host country and lead to a decline in domestic investment.
Instability in the balance of payments and the exchange rate	Once the FDI comes into the country, it usually provides foreign exchange. When profits are sent home to the country originating the investment, the home currency can depreciate in value.
Loss of control over domestic policy	A large foreign investment *sec*tor can exert enough power in a variety of ways so that the host country is no longer truly sovereign.
Increased unemployment	The foreign firm may bring its own capital-intensive techniques into the host country. However, these techniques may be inappropriate for a labor-abundant country.
Establishment of local monopoly	A large foreign firm may undercut a competitive local industry because of some particular advantage and drive domestic firms from the industry.
Inadequate attention to the development of local education and skills	Jobs at the subsidiary operations in the host country are at lower levels of skill and ability. The labor force and the managers in the host country do not acquire new skills.

Source: Appleyad, D., Fied, Jr. A. J., *International Economics*, fourth edition, McGraw-Hill Companies, Inc., 1992.

No general assessment can be made regarding whether the benefits outweigh the costs. Each country's situation and each firm's investment must be examined in light of these various considerations, and a judgment about the desirability of the investment can be clearly positive in some instances and negative in others. Developed and developing countries often try to institute policies that will improve the ratio of benefits to costs connected with a foreign capital inflow. Thus, performance requirements are frequently placed on foreign firms, such as stipulating a minimum percent of local employees, a maximum percent of profits that can be repatriated to the home country, and a minimum percent of output that must be exported to earn scarce foreign exchange. In addition, the output of the firm may be subject to domestic content requirements on inputs, or foreign firms may be banned altogether from certain key industries.

参考文献

Krugman, P. R. & Obstfeld, M., *International Economics*：*Theory and Policy*, sixth edition, Harper Collins Publishers, 2003.

Steven Husted & Michael Melvin, *International Economics*, English Version, 5th edition,高等教育出版社,2002 年。

Dominick Salvatore, *International Economics*, English Version, eighth edition,清华大学出版社,2004 年。

Dennis R. Appleyard & Alfred J. Field, Jr., *International Economics*, English Version,机械工业出版社,2001 年。

Paul A. Samuelson & William D. Nordhaus, *Economics*, English Version, eighteenth edition,机械工业出版社,2005 年。

Robert J. Carbaugh,《国际经济学》(英文版,第 10 版),中国人民大学出版社,2009 年。

Gaves, R. E 著,余淼杰译,《国际贸易与国际收支》(第 10 版),北京大学出版社,2008 年。

索耶,斯普林克著,刘春生等译,《国际经济学》(英文版,第 2 版),中国人民大学出版社,2009 年。

Giancarlo Gandolfo 著,王根蓓译,《国际贸易理论与政策》,上海财经大学出版社,2005 年。

李坤望,《国际经济学》,高等教育出版社,2005 年。

华民,《国际经济学》,复旦大学出版社,2004 年。

袁志刚、宋京,《国际经济学》,高等教育出版社,上海社会科学院出版社,2000 年。

陈长民、李丽霞,《国际经济学》,中国人民大学出版社,2004 年。

陈学彬,《金融学》,高等教育出版社,2003 年。

姜波克,《国际金融学》,高等教育出版社,1999 年。

尹翔硕,《国际贸易教程》(第三版),复旦大学出版社,2006 年。

杨培雷,《国际经济学》,上海财经大学出版社,2007 年。

黄卫平,《国际经济学》,对外经贸大学出版社,2008 年。

赫国胜、杨哲英、张日新,《新编国际经济学》,清华大学出版社,2003 年。

张帆、胡曙光、门淑莲,《国际经济学》,东北财经大学出版社,2003 年。

图书在版编目(CIP)数据

国际经济学(双语)/黄敏主编. —上海:复旦大学出版社,2011.5(2023.8重印)
(复旦卓越·21世纪国际经济与贸易专业教材新系)
ISBN 978-7-309-08054-4

Ⅰ.国… Ⅱ.黄… Ⅲ.国际经济学-双语教学-高等学校-教材-汉、英 Ⅳ.F11-0

中国版本图书馆 CIP 数据核字(2011)第 058591 号

国际经济学(双语)
黄　敏　主编
责任编辑/宋朝阳

复旦大学出版社有限公司出版发行
上海市国权路 579 号　邮编:200433
网址:fupnet@fudanpress.com　http://www.fudanpress.com
门市零售:86-21-65102580　团体订购:86-21-65104505
出版部电话:86-21-65642845
上海华业装潢印刷厂有限公司

开本 787×960　1/16　印张 17.75　字数 294 千
2023 年 8 月第 1 版第 3 次印刷
印数 5 201—6 300

ISBN 978-7-309-08054-4/F·1695
定价:53.00 元